What's Wrong with Social Policy and How to Fix It

What's Wrong with Social Policy and How to Fix It

BILL JORDAN

polity

First published in 2010 by Polity Press

Polity Press
65 Bridge Street
Cambridge CB2 1UR, UK.

Polity Press
350 Main Street
Malden, MA 02148, USA

ISBN-13: 978–0–7456–4740–1
ISBN-13: 978–0–7456–4741–8 (paperback)

A catalogue record for this book is available from the British Library.

Typeset in 10.25 on 13 pt FF Scala
by Servis Filmsetting Ltd, Stockport, Cheshire
Printed and bound by MPG Books Group, UK

The publisher has used its best endeavours to ensure that the URLs for external websites referred to in this book are correct and active at the time of going to press. However, the publisher has no responsibility for the websites and can make no guarantee that a site will remain live or that the content is or will remain appropriate.

Every effort has been made to trace all copyright holders, but if any have been inadvertently overlooked the publishers will be pleased to include any necessary credits in any subsequent reprint or edition.

For further information on Polity, visit our website: www.politybooks.com

Contents

Acknowledgements   vi
Introduction   1

1   The problem   18

2   Income, credit and redistribution   44

3   Services and well-being   75

4   Global social policy   119

5   Sustainability – communities and the
environment   154

6   Conclusions – transforming social policy   188

Notes and References   210
Bibliography   224
Index   244

Acknowledgements

I would like to take this opportunity to pay tribute to my brother, Charlie Jordan, who died suddenly in September 2009, aged 61. A tireless activist in the cause of empowerment and social justice, he didn't always have time to write down his ideas and insights; but I have benefited enormously from discussions of these with him in writing all my books, including this one. I am very glad that we did produce one book together in 2000, but our co-operation was continuous over many years.

This book was written under the pressure of a rapidly unfolding economic crisis, and I am very grateful also for conversations with Ian Gough, Mark Drakeford, Guy Standing, Sarah Jordan, Alex Allan and Rachel Nicholson in making some sense of this. My thanks are due too to Leigh Mueller for her sympathetic copy-editing of the text, and to Rachel Arnold for her speed and accuracy in typing it.

Introduction

In the wake of the world economic crash of September–
October 2008, the leaders of the G7 countries sat down to
plan a 'new global financial architecture' for a recovery. It was
assumed, of course, that these new institutions would follow
universal, transnational principles, suited to an integrated
world economy; the crash was, after all, a global phenomenon. It was hoped that these arrangements would also take
account of such developmental objectives as the Millennium
Development Goals, under which global poverty would be
explicitly targeted.

A month later, on 4 November, Barack Obama was elected
President of the United States of America. The soaring and
often poetic oratory of his campaign, and his environmentalist themes, along with his African origins, Hawaiian and
Indonesian upbringing, seemed to appeal to similar global
aspirations. Yet his policy proposals were often vague, pragmatic or even protectionist (as in his promise to defend jobs
in the US automobile industry). He seemed to have achieved
a shift in his country's political culture, and to have founded
a generational movement for activism and participation, without defining the public policy objectives which these might
pursue.

This book will address the apparent paradox of a historical moment in which universalism and globalism seem to be
the features of those forces most influential on human lives,
yet the resources available to individuals, communities and

governments to deal with these forces remain stubbornly local, particular and relative to their specific situations. Social policy is marooned within this space between these two levels of present-day reality. The challenge facing Obama and other political leaders, of global economic crisis and limited policy instruments, is essentially the same set of issues.

The question is therefore whether there can come into being a set of middle-ground institutions and organizational forms, capable of influencing global issues such as climate change, resource depletion and famine, which threaten all the apparent progress made in the final quarter of the twentieth century. The economic crash of 2008 has discredited the centre-right orthodoxies of that era – the Third Way as much as neo-liberalism and neo-conservatism – but a successor set of principles is still to emerge. As a left-liberal, and self-proclaimed apostle of change, Obama is now required to transform his oratory into policies, and lead his generation into this vacuum of the middle ground.

Indeed, the tasks of managing his administration's debt-ridden national economy, and avoiding a permanent decline in the US position of global hegemony, are themselves daunting. Meantime, in the UK, the country which most imitated the US economic model, as well as its most reliable geo-political ally, a 'fiscal stimulus' package presented to Parliament on 24 November 2008 led one commentator to the conclusion that 'welfare ministers might as well go and dig their allotments for a few years, for all the chance they have of advancing any reforms they have in mind'.[1]

This book is about the origins of the gap between global economic forces and political instruments for promoting human well-being. It will analyse the prospects for an emerging set of institutions to fill this gap. But the requirements for fixing social policy cannot be detached from the need to fix the world economy; in this sense, the situation is similar to the one in the 1930s, when a financial crash triggered a global recession, and new ways to manage credit, investment, employment, incomes, benefits and public services had simultaneously to be devised. The fix required is more of a transformation.

Part of this challenge is that the dominant Anglophone model of the decades before the crash was explicitly an *economic* model, which subjected social goals to a cost-benefit analysis, testing whether they contributed to overall gains in 'utility'. Although the countries at the heart of the European Union still clung to notions of solidarity, cohesion and reciprocity among citizens, and co-operation between the 'social partners', such considerations were increasingly embattled, in the face of competition with the new manufacturing superpowers of Asia and Latin America. Social policy, if it did not allow national economies to perform better in such competition, became a fetter on enhanced economic welfare.

In this context, 'welfare' had largely become synonymous with income; yet the best indicator of the model's collapse was that incomes and employment were now falling. The dominant approach had sacrificed other types of gain to the achievement of economic efficiency, but apparent growth turned out to be a fragile bubble. Meanwhile, other research had indicated that well-being was better correlated with equality, health, work satisfaction and positive relationships than with marginal gains in income.[2]

Through the hegemony of the Anglophone model, the domain of social policy institutions had become one in which principles such as individual sovereignty, choice and mobility between options were paramount, except in highly stigmatized residual services for poor and deviant citizens. In the redesign of middle-ground institutions required by the crisis, this meant that there was also a strong case for trying to reintroduce other forms of 'social value' as factors of human well-being – for instance, those arising from relationships of intimacy, kinship, association and community as well as participation in the facilities of common citizenship – into the development of structures, policies and practices.[3] But the severity of the economic crisis militated against such approaches, and seemed to reduce the scope for their application.

Yet some new principles were urgently required to fix (for which, read 'transform') social policy. Indeed it was essential for social policy to become part of the solution to the economic crisis, rather than being perceived as part of the problem, as it often had been by the public policy orthodoxy both before the crash, and in its immediate aftermath. As new institutions evolve to deal with the crisis, social policy should be an integral part of these.

I shall argue that the global financial system was precarious, and government regulation was weak, because the theory behind their workings – contract theory – was deficient. Indeed, contract theory was supposed to provide the missing links between analysis of the world economy and that of government activity, and it had informed the market-orientated transformation of the public sectors of all kinds of states worldwide. With the eclipse of the crudely neo-liberal Washington Consensus in the mid-1990s, this orthodoxy had, especially through the operations of the World Bank, and under the aegis of its Chief Economic Adviser, the Nobel laureate Joseph Stiglitz, come to dominate monetary and macro-economic policy.[4] This 'Post-Washington Consensus' presided over the situation in which the gap between often illusory forms of economic growth and largely ineffective instruments of national policy had widened. In the crash, contracts, which were claimed to have reached 'all the way down' into every economy and society, were revealed as mere paper promises.

The biggest question for this book is, therefore, what can replace contract theory at the heart of this middle ground linking global and other levels of human interactions? Some of the measures taken by governments in the wake of the crash, although they have the appearance of being a reversion to Keynesian principles, might instead be interpreted as desperate attempts to fix the contract model. In my view, it should be replaced, because it is beyond fixing. I shall argue that some version of cultural theory must enter into the analysis of the workings of institutions, economic and governmental as well as societal, if these deficiencies are to be remedied.

The crash

The global financial crisis of 2007–9 was a clear challenge for social policy. It clarified how public policy had lost its way, especially in the affluent Anglophone countries, since the early 1980s. It indicated where new approaches to social policy were needed, and provided an opportunity for them to gain political support.

In a global perspective, the crisis showed that the role of the USA in particular, and of the countries from which financial capital flowed into worldwide industrial growth more generally, was unsustainable. The key weakness in the whole system was that citizens in the affluent Anglophone countries were being encouraged to fund their lifestyles out of borrowing from banks and mortgage companies. This vast indebtedness was in turn enabled by loans from savers in Japan, China and the Middle East, attracted to the financial hubs of the West. With the collapse of the US sub-prime housing sector, the sophisticated system for regulating, insuring and trading all this debt was revealed to have been so much air in an old-fashioned bubble.

The pattern of borrowing by the old, rich economies from savers in the rapidly developing ones was in any case an odd one. It has been compared to 'pushing water uphill'; why should funds from countries with high rates of economic growth be lent to countries with far lower long-term growth prospects? Now it has been revealed that the returns on these loans had been misleadingly inflated by the artifice of banks and mortgage companies, and so these huge international funds were unlikely to be available on similar terms in any foreseeable future.

This whole edifice had been built on bets that housing and other asset prices would continue to rise; that countries like the UK could go on producing far less than they consumed; that China, Mexico, the Middle Eastern oil exporters and India could have ever-growing trade surpluses; and that deregulated financial markets could equilibrate all these imbalances. When the bubble burst, these bets turned into bad debts, and the systems which sustained them were revealed to be a zero-sum game, in which many players now held losing hands, while a few could walk away having won fortunes.

The relationships between governments, central banks and commercial credit suppliers were central to the contract model which had sustained this lopsided global economy. When the banking system failed, both remedial capital injections and increased sovereign debt were signals of the failure of the theory behind the model. But the governments' responses could also be interpreted as frantic efforts to restore its functioning. Rather than addressing huge trade imbalances, public spending deficits and shortfalls in tax revenues, the governments of the USA and UK were acting to oil the wheels of the global money markets, on which they still relied to smooth over these vast chasms. The alternative – to address these imbalances directly – seemed too daunting to contemplate.

As a result of the bursting of its housing bubble, the US Treasury was forced to bail out the companies which underwrote the nation's mortgage market, Freddie Mac and Fannie Mae, on 7 September 2008, and eventually to nationalize all the banks' bad mortgage debts (at a cost of $700 billion) two

weeks later. This was not primarily to stop the flow of default-
ing mortgage holders or to slow the collapse of house prices.
It was to try to restore faith in the 'asset-backed securities' on
which world financial markets had come to rely.

The US government's action, in effectively nationalizing
these huge risks, completely reversed its own principles for
economic management. Instead of relying on financial markets to steer and supply both industrial and social development
worldwide, it intervened to rescue the entire financial system.
Its fear was that the credit on which the bubble prosperity of
the USA and UK, in particular, was based would burst in a
catastrophic explosion. The result was a huge increase in the
US national debt, to be added to its already enormous balance
of payments deficit. The UK soon followed suit, borrowing
tens of billions of pounds on global money markets to pay
for nationalizing the Bradford and Bingley and Royal Bank of
Scotland, and part-nationalizing several other banks.

The significance of all this for social policy was that it
gave the lie to the claims of governments, especially in the
Anglophone countries, that global capitalism had made the
previous role of states an anachronism. Redistributive systems, government agencies, professional expertise and public
provision had all undergone fundamental modification in line
with the idea that individuals both wanted choice over traditional social issues and were required to be responsible for
themselves in the new global economy. They could achieve
this 'independence' by borrowing from banks rather than
looking to governments for benefits and services. Their welfare was allegedly best served if the scope for them to control
their own resources, and their access to collective facilities,
was maximized. The role of governments was to 'make work
pay', to regulate markets in financial products (such as pensions) and to discipline, resocialize or assist those who lacked
the skills for such autonomy.[5]

The story told by governments and central bankers in the Anglophone countries, and by international institutions like the International Monetary Fund (IMF), World Bank and World Trade Organization (WTO), was that this approach reconciled efficiency with social justice. In maximizing economic growth, it also rewarded effort and enterprise, and protected the most vulnerable. Above all, it promoted individual freedom by expanding control over resources and the range of options open to all.

The crash has revealed the other side of this story. Once the credit on which their prosperity was based was recognized as bad debt, most citizens found themselves in possession of depreciating assets (homes, pensions or shares). The financial sectors of these economies have been excessively expanded on illusory gains, and the rest of the population has had their real incomes held down to sustain the bubble. The state has enforced low-paid work as a condition of benefits payments to bolster the dominance of financial interests, not to enhance freedom and choice.

It has also revealed that poverty and exclusion are not residual problems of those who cannot adapt to the new realities. Before the crash, the rise in prices of oil, food and other commodities hit a far larger section of the population than the marginalized minorities of the previous decade. On the other hand, the very housing assets which had been appreciating over that period, and against which mainstream citizens had borrowed to pay for up-beat lifestyles, lost value dramatically. Finally, unemployment and short-time working re-appeared all over labour markets. Attention refocused on what governments could do to protect populations from common problems, and to pool resources or spread returns over the life-cycle.

In a broader perspective, globalization was recognized as exacerbating old problems of solidarity and cohesion, once the gloss had come off the decade of bubble expansion. Geographical mobility – the transnational movement of mainly advantaged, skilled and resourceful people from poorer countries to richer ones – had largely replaced the social mobility which had been enabled by welfare states. It provoked resentment and resistance among the least able and mobile of home populations. Nationalisms which had been repressed by state socialism (as in the former Soviet states and Yugoslavia), or made irrelevant by the processes of democratic inclusion in social citizenship (as in France, Italy and the UK), reasserted themselves as potent and divisive political forces.

Within societies – and again particularly the affluent Anglophone ones – where the market individualist model had been most comprehensively applied, citizens did not always make choices which were conducive to their own well-being, let alone to the common good. Abuse of alcohol and drugs, obesity and declining standards of public behaviour, along with evidence of increasing stress and anxiety, indicated a kind of malaise – 'affluenza'[6] – associated with the quest for self-realization in a competitive environment. Among disadvantaged communities, exclusion from the mainstream bred crime, disorder and deviant local solidarities, including the excesses of gun and knife conflict. All this drew governments into far more surveillance and coercion than their ideologies claimed to require – more prisons, security cameras and psychological services, more compulsory welfare-to-work measures, and more threats of further sanctions, as part of a regime trying to make citizens competent for self-responsibility.

The striking impotence of governments, in the face of both the financial crisis and these symptoms of personal and societal dysfunction, has revealed a paradox of current public policy orthodoxies. If individual access to resources and services is supposed to be the basis for welfare gains, and if the financial system supplies the key institutions for the development of the world economy, then these orthodoxies demand a detached, regulatory and contracting role for both political authorities ('the principals', in terms of economic theory) and central banks ('the planners').[7] But it is in these roles that they have most spectacularly failed. The theory supplies no fallback analysis, instruments or methodology for intervention. Yet there is also no readily available set of alternative approaches, short of a return to the discredited maxims of state socialism.

According to the dominant economic model, governments should understand the 'social' and the 'public' as nothing more than instances of 'interpersonal externalities'. This means situations where one individual can incur costs (or attain benefits) as a result of another's actions, without receiving (or paying) compensation. Such situations can be modified by means of adjustments in incentives (positive and negative), and the provision of information.[8] It applies to circumstances as varied as residents gaining the advantages of a crime-free district and citizens bearing the costs of low educational standards among school leavers. In this view, governments should legislate, regulate, contract, inspect and publish statistics with a view to the overall mitigation of unfairly distributed burdens, and the sharing of unmerited advantages.

But this approach, derived from the underlying economic theory, is a very narrow one. It leads governments to look for ways, for example, of inducing private individuals and firms to invest in educational and health enterprises, where they do not receive the full economic value of the benefits these confer on society as a whole. It also leads them to threaten state schools and hospitals which do not attain target standards with being taken over by more efficient management teams.

This assumes that, in setting targets and incentives, publishing league tables or contracting for services, governments can steer individuals into actions from which society derives benefits. But the complexity of the links between these spheres means that steering of this kind is anything but an exact science. There are all kinds of unintended consequences of these systems, such as teachers focusing on test results and helping pupils to cheat,[9] or dentists pulling out healthy teeth, or police arresting victims of assaults as well as perpetrators. Above all, in creating an economic (or business) model for schools, hospitals, care homes and prisons, policy induces a form of practice and service use which is self-interested, instrumental, calculative and strategic.

The aspects of what is 'social' in social policy which are left out of this approach concern a set of meanings and a form of value through which people conduct their relationships, whether as friends, members of groups and communities, or fellow-citizens. These both define how they want to be regarded and regard themselves, and restrain their actions in relation to each other. In leaving these factors out of the account of social policy activity, governments deny themselves much of the point, and many of the instruments, of this branch of their role.

Above all, what has not been recognized is that, in the process of turning citizens away from reliance on state benefits and services, and on collective action through trade unions, social movements and associations, and towards borrowing from banks for consumption-orientated lifestyles, governments have created a fragile and brittle *culture* of competitive individualism. Ever since the decline of welfare state politics in the 1980s, when the institutions of post-war settlements proved unable to meet the challenges of globalized capitalism and the rise of the newly industrializing giants of the East, this has been the dominant orthodoxy, and it has been remarkably successful in transforming the self-definitions and cultural standards of populations, first in the affluent Anglophone countries, and then all over the wealthy world. This has left citizens, as well as governments, with impoverished cultural resources for dealing with an economic downturn and with the failure of the contract model of government.

These shortcomings have been revealed in a dramatic way by the financial crisis. For example, in the UK, as early as the first six months of 2008, there was a 250 per cent increase in the number of applications for assistance from the charity which used to be called the Distressed Gentlefolk's Association.[10] This organization helps professional people who fall on hard times, and with the past cultural traditions of such groups, who used to save for a rainy day, it would have taken more than a brief recession to bring such a humiliating loss of face. But in the new culture of borrowing and spending, the simultaneous impact of higher fuel and food prices and higher interest rates has meant that illness or redundancy could lead to instant penury.

So the sudden collapse of both the instruments of government and the ruling assumptions on which populations based their lifestyles has caused a re-examination of the bases for social policies. Even the Deputy Governor of the Bank of England conceded that the downturn in the economy would 'lead to some difficult social issues'[11] – an admission that his institution had failed in its tasks, and that the management of 'social issues' could not be reduced to ones of regulating, contracting and informing by ministers and central bankers.

This book aims to diagnose the weaknesses of the model which has dominated the policies of governments and international organizations (such as the IMF, the World Bank and the WTO) since the mid-1980s, and to sketch the outlines of a new approach. It seeks to show that competitive individualism and the contractual approach to interdependence among populations give rise to cultures and institutions which are vulnerable to ordinary economic vicissitudes. Far from having banished instability and stagflation, as was promised by the neo-liberal and Third Way reformers from the late 1980s onwards, they have made populations less resilient in the face of unfavourable global contingencies and crises, and denied governments the means to mitigate the impact of such events.

The only way to fix this situation is through a rehabilitation of the collective perspective on well-being. This does not imply that the state should be revived as the fount of all wisdom and source of the essential quality of life. But it does mean that both policy and everyday social relations should recognize that the very experience of well-being and quality depends on meanings and standards that are collective in their origins and sustenance, as well as collective institutions and resources.

So social policy should return to a quest for those rules, organizations and structures which sustain relations of support, mutuality, community and solidarity among populations which are far more mobile and diverse than in the era of welfare states, and which take account of interdependencies within the world economy which are far broader. For example, social policy cannot afford to ignore world poverty, mass migration or the threat to the global environment.

Any new approach to social policy will also have to recognize that the contractual and individualized model of welfare, which discounts inequalities of incomes, has not banished problems of poverty, nor has it made social class irrelevant for people's life chances. What it has done is to bring about a disconnection between purchasing power and well-being. It has also caused unacceptable variations in health within populations in the same cities and countries. Redistribution, both national and international, will have to re-enter the political agenda.

But this shift will demand an answering one within populations. The most striking feature of the financial crisis is that individuals are so much less robust in the face of rising costs and falling incomes than they were during earlier downturns.

Consumerism and debt have eradicated the habits and networks on which past generations relied to tide them over hard times.

Above all, the effect of the previous thirty years of ideological conditioning and institutional steering – towards 'self-reliance' and 'independence' which were based on bank credit – has been reversed. People will start again – as they had done before the Thatcher–Reagan years – to look around for others in situations like their own, and to take collective action along with them. This will revive the kind of politics which both neo-liberalism and the Third Way strove to suppress, a politics of common interest, directed at least partly at the state, and demanding both participation and social justice.

There will also have to be a new recognition of the significance of collective factors in everyday experiences, both positive and negative. For example, instead of looking to experts, counselling or individual remedies for the main stresses and disorders of modern living, people should start to give attention to their relationships with family, friends, neighbours and fellow-citizens as sources of both value and self-control.

The orthodoxies of the past thirty years have deliberately erected institutional structures to steer populations away from collective action and political movements, and towards reliance on bank credit, consumer goods and 'personalized' services. No major shift towards the recognition of the importance of collective, cultural and social factors for quality of life and the health of democratic politics can happen without a similar long period of institutional change. After all, it was not until the post-Thatcher years of the 1990s that her full legacy of possessive individualism and opportunist capitalism was manifested in UK society. For example, the phenomenon of massive personal debt through credit cards appeared mainly under New Labour. These habits will take decades to alter, and new ones will require painstaking nurturing within new institutions.

But these changes will also be enabled by the shifts in the costs and benefits of different kinds of activities and resource uses that the crisis itself has brought about. During the boom/ bubble, it always paid to put money and effort into financial markets, stocks and shares, housing and private luxuries (both goods and services). In the new situation, this is no longer the case. Activities such as energy saving and environmental conservation are not only now advantageous for individuals and households. They are also forms of collective action which are advantageous for whole communities.

Where before it gave better returns for a regeneration project in a deprived neighbourhood to build office space for an insurance company or a management consultancy, and use the rent to supply an income for a 'community business', now there is more to be gained by constructing a renewable energy station, or a scheme for producing biofuels, or insulating buildings. Such projects can lead to both more inclusive productive activities, and more widespread share ownership among community members. Instead of re-enforcing private ownership and individual interests, they encourage participation, co-operative endeavour and income redistribution.

Even on an international scale, the shift in pay-offs among resource uses tends to benefit approaches which were shunned in the era of rapid growth. For instance, the UK Department for International Development, through its banking arm, was mandated primarily to pursue economic efficiency. It therefore invested mainly in expanding economies such as China and India. With the downturn, it now has an interest in promoting development in the poorest countries.

In order to fix social policy, these new opportunities for reallocating resources must be seen as part of a range of measures, redirecting attention from money markets, retailing and commercial services towards the physical and social infrastructure and the natural environment. But this requires us to use the opportunity to introduce new criteria of social and ecological value into cost-benefit analyses for public policy. While returns to individual enterprise and financial manipulation are low, there is a chance to demonstrate the longer-term benefits to be gained from collective action in pursuit of these forms of value.

This book does not attempt to supply quick fixes for social policy. For example, in the UK the government has little scope for redistribution so long as it is propping up ailing banks, and the population will be preoccupied with managing its debts for some time, before it can reassess its valuation of private and collective assets. There are not so much fixes for social policy as signposts for the new directions we should be taking.

Furthermore, it recognizes that there are real dangers in collective mobilizations during an economic crisis. The Great Depression of the 1930s saw totalitarianism and protectionism become the dominant political forces all over the world. By early 2009, mass action and protest in France, the UK, Greece, Russia and China were testing the nerves of both democratic and authoritarian regimes. But it seems unlikely that nationalism or statism will be the forces they were after the last global crash.

What seems more likely is that various kinds of fundamentalism and opportunism will combine elements of resistance to global market forces with harnessing its instruments to their purposes, rather as Al Qa'ida did in the hijacking of airliners to carry out its attack in New York. One more surreal manifestation of this tendency has been the actions by Somali pirates in seizing tankers and other vessels. Their justification for their ransom demands has been that it is 'their sea', yet they use electronic technology and international communications networks to conduct their business. Indeed, it has been reported that lawyers, negotiators and security staff in the City of London earned over £200 million as intermediaries in the release of hijacked vessels.[12]

This book argues that politics needs to adapt to the post-crash world to allow the expression of collective action for the benefits of interdependence, and to forestall the rise of a whole range of resistance groups and factions, both ideological and criminal. Social policy can be part of an inclusive global movement to restore faith in a politics of social justice.

I

The problem

In August 2008, even before the crash of the following months, the UK government was in disarray over how to deal with fuel price inflation and the mortgage crisis. The institutions for managing such issues as income maintenance, fuel poverty and affordable housing were failing in the face of new financial circumstances. The cabinet was split over whether to involve the public purse in the provision of housing finance, how to restimulate the building programme, and how to protect poor people from adverse winter weather. How had the reforms in the public sector since the mid-1980s reached this ignominious outcome?

Theorists of social policy have for some years recognized that governments' approaches to a nexus of issues over employment, income transfers and services were closely interlinked, and that both similarities and differences between types of 'regimes' could be identified. Up to the time of the global financial crisis, this seemed like no more than an exercise in hermeneutics – the conceptualization and modelling of the different paths followed by groups of nations in relation to welfare issues. Now it appears instead to mark an important set of divergences and convergences across the affluent states in the face of global economic integration, which have been fateful in determining the outcomes for their populations during and after the crash (imagine how different the situation of Icelanders might be if their rulers had embraced the Scandinavian welfare model rather than Viking capitalism).

For example, after a decade of struggling to catch up with its former rates of growth since absorbing the costs of re-unification, Germany's 'social model' was beginning to recover its poise, and its economy to function, when the crisis hit. As a result, the German government was willing only very tentatively to follow the line of the UK and USA, in borrowing to restimulate consumption. It specifically rejected the Brown-inspired European Union plans to cut taxes, having substantially reduced its national debt. Its household and industrial sectors were not burdened with excessive borrowing, nor was there a housing bubble. This was substantially because its social policy programme had not sought to enable individual projects of credit-based self-development, but had been derived from an old-style 'social partnership' between business, trades unions and government.

On 10 December 2008, the German Finance Minister, Peer Steinbrück, denounced Gordon Brown's cut in Value Added Tax the previous month as 'crass Keynesianism', saying that 'all this will do is raise Britain's debt to a level that will take a whole generation to work off'.[1] Two days later, the leader of the Christian Socialist Union (CSU) said that Brown had 'departed from the path of fiscal prudence'.[2] They made it clear that Germany had no intention of following these approaches, and no need to contemplate them.

So there were immediate consequences for its citizens from the long-term trajectory of Germany's institutional path. Its culturally conservative approach to social insurance, industrial investment, technological education and household thrift, derided as damaging to its competitive position, were initially claimed to have been strengths. It had become clear not only that the public finances of all nations were linked together by noxious fungal tendrils feeding off the decay of worthless 'assets' in the Anglophone countries, but also that the response of specific states to the crisis was closely related to their institutional structures, and the relationship between their economic and social policy systems. So, despite differences between the situations of individual states in each cluster, the schema developed by social policy theorists gave a rough guide to how the affluent countries faced up to the crisis. What were the defining features of these clusters?

In broad outline, the Scandinavian countries gave priority to sustaining high levels of income transfers (pensions, benefits and allowances) for the sake of maintaining equalities between the genders and classes, and across the life-cycle, and were able to sustain the political solidarities necessary to support consequent high tax rates. They also promoted generous public service provision, which in turn supplied high rates of employment, especially for women.[3]

The Continental European countries with strong Christian Democratic traditions used extensive transfers to sustain life-cycle continuities of income, and to offset the overall decline in rates of employment among men. While attempting to protect pay and conditions in skilled industrial jobs, these regimes were slow and late in expanding service employment in both public and private sectors, and hence in achieving gender equality.[4]

In the Anglophone states, far less attempt was made to protect either incomes or employment standards, or to sustain equalities through transfers. The growth of both public and private service employment allowed high levels of labour market participation, and governments claimed in the 1990s and early years of the twenty-first century that these regimes outperformed the other types in terms of growth, stability and resilience.[5]

The financial crisis put strains on all the affluent countries, but above all it cast new light on the central features of these regimes. In relation to *employment*, it revealed that the nature and structure of labour market institutions is far more important than mere participation levels. If high concentrations of financial services are constructed within a speculative bubble, as in the USA and UK, the massive earnings of the employees represent a kind of vulnerability in a crash. If many small businesses use low-paid staff to supply personal services to households whose affluence relies on credit, then these jobs are precarious and these workers exposed under conditions of deflation.

If the tax base rests heavily on incomes from the financial sector and household resources rely on bank credit, these features add to the exposure of private and public sectors to a downturn, and limit room for manoeuvre. Unemployment in the USA and UK rose more dramatically in the final months of 2008 than in the Continental EU countries. In the USA, a million jobs were lost in November–December 2008, whereas 200,000 a month had been created in the early 1990s;[6] 'flexibility' worked both ways. These weaknesses of the Anglophone regimes became obvious in the crisis.

But the Continental European regimes were not as immune from the effects of the crash as their justified criticisms of the Anglophone ones (where the financial crisis had originated) seemed to imply. Within a matter of weeks, the German economy had suffered a sharp downturn in its industrial output, as demand for high-tech goods in world markets slumped. It became clear that the effects on different welfare regimes were distinguishable more by their nature than by their extent. By May 2009, the European Commission was forecasting a decline of 4 per cent in income for the Eurozone in that year, but the same fall for the UK also (Ireland's Gross Domestic Product (GDP) was predicted to fall by 11 per cent, as the Celtic Tiger shrank into a slightly mangey leopard).

In relation to *transfers*, the importance of pensions and benefits for economic management in the Keynesian era had lain in their capacity to act 'countercyclically' – to sustain income and demand during downturns. The principle behind social insurance schemes was to use 'the magic of averages' to provide a system for protecting those made redundant in such conditions, as well as sick, disabled and retired citizens. But in the Anglophone countries, where reforms have 'targeted' benefits on the very poor, and imposed conditions designed to enforce low-paid and irregular work, no such instrument is now available. Instead, governments in the USA and UK have been forced into a massive rescue of the banks and mortgage companies in an attempt to prevent meltdown. In a second wave of measures, they then announced plans for spending on their physical infrastructures. New transfers to citizens have been made through one-off payments, not through the traditional social security or social assistance programmes (see pp. 28–9).

Finally, the role of *services*, especially in the Scandinavian countries, has been to provide a sector of employment in which governments have been able to generate social mobility, gender equality and support for families, as well as creating a space for solidaristic and mutual interactions between citizens.[7] In the USA and UK, the rapid expansion of health, educational and social care services has been accompanied by reforms to enable the fuller participation of commercial and civil society organizations. In the UK this has meant that the government has less control over recruitment, pay, training and practice than before. For instance, because of the privatization of residential care for frail older people, its only way to achieve an 'upskilling' of staff in this sector and more recruitment of UK citizens during the financial crisis was to stipulate the pay grades (over £8 per hour) at which staff from countries like India, the Philippines and Zimbabwe, who had come to fill around 50 per cent of vacancies for care assistants, could be brought into the country.[8]

In this chapter I shall consider the recent history of the

overhaul of social policy instruments in the Anglophone countries, and their influence on other types of regime, with these
issues in mind. I shall also address the sudden collapse of this
model during the crash, and how it was linked with the bursting of the bubble in the financial sector. My purpose is not to
trace these reforms back to their roots in the era of Margaret
Thatcher and Ronald Reagan, but to investigate the theories
and policies of the late 1990s onwards, during which those
controversial initiatives have been consolidated as mainstream
dogma and practice, and have shaped the structures and decisions of social policy agencies. It has been these processes
of adaptation and accommodation, followed by crash, which
have left governments so helpless to deal with the crisis.

But I shall also be examining how ordinary citizens have
come to adopt the concepts and thought styles of this new
orthodoxy, and how this too has left them struggling to cope
with a new situation. By adopting the ideas which were prop-
agated in the economic model, and turning them into an
individualistic, consumer culture, they have left themselves
exposed to the chill winds of recession and indebtedness.

A new approach?

The crash precipitated an expansion of government which
was totally unplanned. It was government by default, and
left its instigators looking for a purpose and a programme.
In the case of President George W. Bush, elected as a neo-
conservative, with a mandate for reducing the role of the state,
this was ironic. Bailing out the financial system, distributing
sums to every citizen to counteract deflation, his administration spent its final months attempting to stimulate production
and spending in exactly the ways he had earlier denounced as
being perniciously distorting.

The case of the UK was more complicated. Gordon Brown

had made his reputation as a Chancellor of the Exchequer who contracted out control of monetary policy and the regulation of the financial system to the Bank of England and the Financial Services Authority respectively. He laid down the 'golden rules' of fiscal prudence, put relations between government and its agencies on a business-like basis, and claimed that 'growth and stability' stemmed from these arm's-length arrangements, and the expertise of City traders. Bankers were fêted, honoured and given peerages; the City of London became a kind of offshore financial centre for the rich individuals and governments of the world. Brown was highly suspicious of the European Union as an economic authority, jealously guarding the UK's autonomy and global prominence in these spheres.

After appearing, as Prime Minister, to freeze when faced by the unfolding catastrophe of the first eight months of 2008, he managed (with the assistance of his Chancellor, Alastair Darling) to recover his poise, re-inventing himself as the polar opposite of all that he had been. A convert to seemingly limitless borrowing, both to prop up the financial system and to fund tax cuts and public spending, he adopted an unapologetic collectivism in the face of the crisis, putting government at the centre of plans for 'the recovery'. He also cast himself as the leader of the EU, the G7 and later the G20, in co-ordinating cuts in interest rates and expanding credit, winning praise for overriding the independent decision-making of central banks.

One interesting feature of this transformation was the new language used by Brown to describe and justify these actions. Phrases such as 'public works', coined by Keynes out of Adam Smith, were revived to capture the image of a collective authority which recognized its responsibility to manage national economic aggregates, to lead and intervene in maintaining confidence and demand. In all this the proprieties of separation of powers in public finance, and the sovereignty of individual choice in decisions over public goods, were relegated to secondary considerations.

The logic of this switch to government leadership was expressed in terms of 'restoration', which begged the question of which features of the former economic landscape were regarded as worth restoring. What the crash seemed to reveal was a set of contradictions in the previous orthodoxy which were likely to remain as glaringly obvious when the bottom of the downturn was reached. Were the nationalized banks to remain in public ownership, and how much should government seek to control their policies and practices, for instance on loans to businesses and bonuses to staff? If the trigger for the crash was the bursting of the house price bubble, at what new level should house prices stabilize? If personal debt had been excessive, and rates of savings too low, at what point should government stop encouraging consumers to spend their way out of recession, and give them incentives to save more? Should policy encourage employers to take back workers recently made redundant, or pursue its welfare-to-work programmes for groups like lone parents and disabled people? Once saving became a priority again, how could interest rates take better account of this, and for how long should older people who had saved for retirement be expected to put up with very low returns on their savings, for the sake of countering deflation?

Behind these questions loomed even larger ones about three aspects of sustainability. First, the affluent countries in general, and the Anglophone ones in particular, had become specialized in financial services, but had been using funds from oil-rich and newly industrializing countries to expand their profitable activities during the bubble years. If these funds were not going to return, except perhaps as loans for deficit finance to governments, what would replace this sector as a source for employment and growth? In the UK, with

28,000 workers in financial services expected to be laid off during the winter of 2008–9, the *Financial Times* headlined the threat 'It's Hell Down South';[9] the loss of each one of these highly paid posts was predicted to lead to an additional reduction of low-paid service jobs among those who had cleaned, cooked or minded children for them during the boom. The first impact would be felt in prosperous towns and suburbs. What new roles are available, and where will be the sources of employment growth?

Second, as the collapse of world trade hit manufacturing, making the industrial West Midlands the focus of the second wave of redundancies, what was the future for this sector? Would the decline in the value of sterling be enough to revive it, once the first shock had passed? Should measures be taken to bail out the automobile industry, as had happened in the early days of the Obama presidency in the USA? Would there really be compensatory new 'green manufacturing' jobs in renewable energy and other eco-friendly industries?

Although the crash removed some of the immediate pressures for a shift in priorities towards environmental conservation (because demand for depletable resources declined, and carbon emissions fell), policies for 'restoration' of stability and growth might squander a chance for salvation. Was the crisis to be seen as an unexpected opportunity to take a different path out of recession, on a trajectory which took account of the ecological imperatives of the new century, or was it merely an excuse to postpone these priorities till a bit later?

Third, what new rationale was to inform the design of institutions for the post-crash situation? It was immediately clear in the USA that the incoming President was required to give explicit answers to this question, while the outgoing one was offering feeble defences of the virtues of market capitalism as he packed his bags. President Obama was quite bold in denouncing the excesses of the financial sector in his first weeks in office, and in making it clear that he would reverse many of his predecessor's policies, but the shape of instititutional change was slower to emerge.

In the UK, the needs of the post-crash circumstances are again more nuanced. For example, the government decided, in November 2008, to cancel a process of competitive tendering for the contract to administer benefit payments, allowing the Post Office to retain this task. Reversing its previous appeal to the potential efficiency gains from introducing a new provider, and the greater choices which might be offered to beneficiaries, the responsible Minister argued that, in the post-crash situation, the Post Office was a 'trusted institution', offering a 'valuable social service', and that people 'looked forward to the experience' of visiting this community facility. All this justified applying non-commercial criteria to the decision about the contract.[10]

None of these issues relates directly to social policy, as traditionally conceived. The question of how much 'fiscal stimulus' to give, in order to counter potential deflation, is one of macroeconomics. The interest rate is one of monetary policy. Whether or not to revive the automobile industry is a question for industrial and employment policy. The Post Office, despite the Minister's words, is not a social service, like health care or education. But all these are crucially linked to social policy decisions and instruments.

For instance, in the UK the attempt to induce spending provoked a debate about how tax cuts were to achieve this goal. The rich and the middle class might pay off debt (desirable in itself, because of the banks' problems, but not a stimulus for production and employment), or just save more. So the most efficient policy would be to give tax cuts to low-income households. But many poor families paid no taxes. The Trades Union Congress proposed increasing unemployment benefits, to the same end. This would have reversed government policies for creating a differential between the incomes of those in employment and those outside it, to 'make work pay', and remove any incentive for idleness.

This seemed to put the spotlight onto tax credits for low-wage households, the most important Anglo-American income distribution innovation since the mid-1980s, and claimed to be at the root of the comparative success of the Anglophone social policy model.[11] It has been this instrument that has enabled on-costs (such as social insurance contributions) to be held down, and labour markets to be more 'flexible', in comparison with the unwieldy European Social Model, in which social insurance contributions are relatively high, as are minimum wages. But tax credits are not the most efficient instruments for stimulating immediate spending, because their administrative complexity and perverse effects at the margins of entitlement mean that access to higher rates is slow, haphazard and often creates injustices between households. Presumably for these reasons, this instrument was rejected by the Chancellor of the Exchequer in his measures of 24 November 2008.

So another possibility was the one adopted by the Bush administration in the USA during the summer of 2008 – simply to give all households a lump sum payment. The same method was used by the Australian government later in the year, when it distributed $A1,000 to each adult citizen. This had the disadvantage of lacking 'targeting' – another Anglophone shibboleth – but (if adopted in the UK also) it would have benefited the poor far more significantly than the better-off, and had the lowest administrative costs and fastest implementation. It would have run counter to the whole rationale of recent UK policy development, but could have been justified by the exigencies of the crisis. Indeed, it was the approach recommended by one prominent Labour politician, John Cruddas, in the period leading up to the Pre-Budget announcements on 24 November 2008.

In the event, this approach was confined to a one-off 'Christmas bonus' of £60 to pensioners. The rest of the measures consisted of fairly complex and arcane adjustments to taxes and allowances – a 2.5 per cent reduction in Value Added Tax; the conversion of a temporary increase in income tax allowances at the bottom of the scale (introduced belatedly to compensate low-income losers from a tax simplification the previous year) into a permanent one; and an increase in child tax credits. As critics pointed out, quite apart from the dubious effectiveness of these measures as stimuli for spending, they were scarcely redistributive towards the poor, since they spent most of their incomes on food and fuel, which were exempt from VAT, or charged at a lower rate.

All this illustrated how constrained the UK government had become in relation to one of the basic principles of social policy – that it should operate countercyclically. Even after casting off the shackles of 'prudence', the instruments available, and the interactions between any changes made within them, together with their effects on crucial political constituencies, severely limited the scope for action. While the media commented that the package, with its warnings of future tax increases, moved the government away from its ten-year principles, in the direction of 'Scandinavian' or 'Old Labour' approaches, what this meant was little more than that repayments of the huge increase in national debt (to over £1 trillion in 2010) would fall marginally more on the rich than they would have done before these changes.

Against this gloomy perspective might be set the fact that a very comparable financial and fiscal crisis to the one confronting Barack Obama on his accession to the presidency of the USA faced Franklin D. Roosevelt in 1932. He too lacked the means to implement change, and had to improvise in institutional design and social engineering. This was even more the case in post-war, debt-ridden Britain; yet the Labour government managed to create the welfare state.

The examples of the US and Australian payments to all their citizens illustrate that the crisis forced the Anglophone countries in particular to innovate, as well as revealing the limitations of existing social policy orthodoxies and systems. Such 'natural experiments' should also be examined for their possible advantages for future developments. If the US and Australian measures turn out to have been more successful in achieving their redistributive and stimulatory goals than the more cautious and conventional British package, their other effects and influences might be further explored.

Indeed, in the UK, the government re-enforced its coercive and conditional approach to state benefits at the same time as it was administering its 'fiscal stimulus'. On 2 December the Secretary of State for Work and Pensions welcomed an academic report which argued that *all* claimants of working age should be required to sign up to new 'action plans', committing them to steps towards employment.[12] This would apply to lone parents with children as young as one year old, rather than the current twelve years. The language used in the report – 'breaches' in the plans being punishable by 'non-financial penalties' (such as digging a pensioner's front garden), followed by benefit cuts for further defections – was exactly that of court orders of community service for criminal offenders. The following day, the Queen's Speech announced that a new government measure would 'tighten up' on fraudulent benefit claimants.

All this indicated that the UK government's conversion to fiscal deficits, increased public borrowing and bank nationalization would not, in the short term, be accompanied by a more liberal approach to benefits administration, or more universalistic instruments for redistribution. But the questions of credit supply, poverty relief and labour market participation could not be sustainably packaged in this way, as I shall show in chapter 2. Nor could the issues of morale and stigma among those outside employment be so easily ignored, as I shall argue in the next section, and in chapter 3.

The financial crisis has revealed how central the banks had become to *all* aspects of public policy in the Anglophone countries. Not only in the unseemly haste and reckless generosity of their rescue plans, but also in their post-bail-out indignation that banks were still not lending money, governments in these states showed how powerless they were to achieve their purposes without the active agency of these institutions. In the UK, the Governor of the Bank of England uttered dark threats of nationalization of the whole banking system on 25 November 2008.

One major dilemma faced by governments was the trade-off between lowering interest rates, in order to encourage borrowing and spending, and the consequent discouragement of saving. Not only were savers' incomes, especially those of older people, badly hit by lower interest rates: so also were the banks' efforts to attract savings, as their only remaining route to longer-term solvency (in the absence of borrowing from abroad). As rates fell towards zero, there was a risk of a vicious circle, as decreasing savings blocked a recovery of bank loans and credit, which in turn threatened further cuts in incomes, spending and saving.

Finally, governments which attempted fiscal packages to stimulate lending and spending faced the possibility that these would not work, because they did not affect long-term interest rates. To try to force these down, the US and UK administrations started buying up long-dated Treasury bonds through their central banks. This 'quantitative easing', akin to 'printing money', was recognized as a last resort – the kind of measure adopted, indeed, by President Mugabe in the face of Zimbabwe's complete economic collapse.

For these reasons, the UK government had little alternative to considering innovations which were even more contrary to its established principles, such as forcing nationalized and other banks to lend against their commercial judgement, or setting up credit facilities of its own. All this revived memories of debates about the nature of credit and the role of the banking system which had been put aside since the 1930s. These issues will be further analysed in chapter 2.

Services and well-being

Alongside the financial crisis, the second aspect of welfare states which had been squeezed out of the analysis of social policy decisions, and the design of public institutions, was the kind of social relations they promote. Of course, public services for health, education and the care of vulnerable people still aim to achieve the objectives which are explicit in their names. But in the Anglophone model, their functioning has been geared to cost-efficiency in the achievement of specific target outcomes, and to enabling well-informed citizens to choose their preferred facilities, professional expertise and fellow service users. They are no longer designed to promote solidarity, to enable civic spirit or to enhance the common good.

As I shall show in chapter 3, this approach diverges from the one taken by the founding theorists of 'welfare economics' (such as Pareto, Pigou and Hicks) as well as the founding political figures in the establishment of welfare states. The former readily acknowledged, as had Adam Smith and his followers, that public policy often gave priority to non-economic goals, such as military security, political loyalty, civic virtue and cultural tradition. Pareto, despite being best remembered for the principle of cost-benefit analysis which maximizes overall economic welfare in populations, gave considerable attention to the pursuit of 'non-logical' (i.e. social) sources of well-being, and the importance of 'sentiment' (i.e. loyalty, solidarity and culture) in public policy programmes.[13]

Although these welfare economists wrote little about the actual content of public services, they therefore acknowledged that political institutions served purposes other than efficiency, and that collective aspects of social life had to be safeguarded by governments. These principles were built into mid-twentieth-century public policy through the continuing influence of Idealist social philosophers (T. H. Green, Bosanquet and Bradley) and their social policy disciples (Tawney, Cole, Beveridge and Titmuss), as well as of the German Hegelian tradition.[14] The innovation of the final quarter of that century was the radical methodological individualism which excluded such factors from public policy analysis, or which translated collective entities into the preferences and habits of individuals (through concepts such as 'social capital').

The third challenge facing governments and their advisers during the present crisis is whether any space can be found for such collective considerations. The indications that such changes are needed come from the demoralization of poor people living in districts with concentrations of social problems, and from the stigma associated with the use of many public facilities and services. This evidence suggests that interactions involving these services do not simply bring expert skills to bear on specific individual resources, functionings and behaviours. They create and distribute kinds of cultural value or shame which have a profound effect on individual well-being as well as collective morale.

Many of the failures of public policy and of the practices of professionals in human services reflect this phenomenon. In chapter 3, I shall give examples of how the contract model of public service commissioning, management, inspection and accreditation is facing a crisis as failures at all levels are exposed. From the care of hospital patients to the financing of college building programmes, the marking of school pupils' statutory tests and the child protection system, the attempt to use the theory of information, incentives and contractual obligations to improve the efficiency of these services is in tatters.

Above all, the model has overlooked the need to deal in the interpersonal factors in the well-being which is supposed to be the province of these services. It has tried to turn the professions which engage with patients, pupils and families into technicians, applying systems according to defined processes, supplying electronically generated data, in pursuit of government targets. It has turned the management and regulation of these processes into exercises in statistical and financial manipulation. In all this, the feelings and experiences of service users, and the judgement and interactive skills of professionals, have been neglected. As a result, the quality of life – and often the life itself – of those who rely on services has been sacrificed to a narrow emphasis on ticking boxes and achieving organizational objectives.

In a broader context, interpersonal circuits of feelings and images are part of the processes through which every interaction produces and distributes the value that is an essential element in well-being.[15] In a professional exchange, service users receive a sense of meaning, social significance and status, whether this is the aim of the agency's staff or not. What is produced and distributed through these encounters has positive (empathy, validation, respect, inclusion, belonging) or negative (blame, stigma, shame, exclusion) value. Sometimes it has elements of both. In this way, human services either contribute to some kind of cohesion and integration in a community, or add to its fragmentation and anomie.

More generally, the contract model of service design and delivery in the UK should come under question, as the benefits of greatly increased investment in public and contracted-out services under New Labour come to be assessed. Behind the details of the reformed and enlarged facilities lie a number of assumptions about the processes by which human services contribute to welfare and well-being. Most fundamental of these is the idea that welfare is composed of units of 'utility' – the gains made by individuals as consequences of their choices of commodities and interactions.[16] Since individuals must be assumed to choose rationally, and to seek the best returns on their time, energy and material resources, these decisions form the basic building blocks of all measurements relevant for service outcomes.

Furthermore, services themselves can be meaningfully analysed in this model only by dividing them up into specific items of exchange, in which particular individuals receive a measurable unit of treatment, learning, behaviour modification, punishment or whatever. Each of these units can be costed, and the outcomes of each quantified. Hence it is possible to reach accurate conclusions about the effectiveness of specific service inputs, and give best value for taxpayers' money. Service providers – teachers, doctors, nurses, psychologists and social workers, as well as providers of social housing and environmental improvement – should be able to demonstrate their competence in relation to evidence-based criteria.[17]

The urgent question raised by several sets of data on all these facilities, and on the quality of life of whole populations, is whether these approaches to the evaluation of services capture important aspects of what they should be trying to achieve (and may be unintentionally damaging). If, as I shall argue, human well-being is more strongly influenced by relational factors (such as intimacy in partnerships, support among family and friends, teamwork and meaningful activity at work, involvement in neighbourhood and community, and political equality, trust and participation), then *social value* is at least as important as material welfare.[18]

This social value, I shall suggest, is derived from *collective* resources because, like all the products of interactions between members of human communities, it is constructed out of the elements in a set of cultural standards and practices.[19] As I shall show, even if it is convenient for some purposes in social policy to treat material assets, their distribution and consumption, in the manner of the methodological individualism of microeconomic orthodoxy, it makes no sense to treat human services in this way. And as part of how to fix social policy, it is essential to address cultural as well as institutional features.

This is increasingly recognized across a range of issues in public life. When 'comedians' taunted and harassed an elderly actor with lewd remarks about his granddaughter, more astute commentators put the BBC's lapse in broadcasting this down to the culture of producers, hired on short-term contracts. Conversely, when an Australian reservist's swift response saved many lives during the Mumbai massacre, this was attributed to the cultural standards of his military unit. The business model is not the best way to regulate the kinds of activities in which the quality of communications, relationships or character is the most important element.

Suddenly in early 2009, the idea that the cultures of many organizations in the UK were in need of change began to emerge as a theme in critical commentary. It was provoked by revelations about ministers' expenses claims, by fabricated rumours about Opposition figures in emails emanating from Number 10 Downing Street, by the enormous bonuses and pensions paid to senior staff in failed banks, by the behaviour of police during the G20 protests in London, and by the scandal of neglect in the Mid-Staffordshire and other NHS hospital trusts. If the contractual approach was supposed to regulate all these matters, it was failing. A new analysis, which could deal in issues of collective self-discipline among members of occupational and organizational communities, was required.

In chapter 3, I shall develop the idea of social value, and how it can be applied to policy and practice in the public services. When concepts such as well-being and quality of life were first mooted as potential contributors to the cost-benefit analyses on which such decisions were made, they were widely derided as 'soft' and 'subjective' compared with the hard evidence of choices in markets. But the financial crash has shown that money values, too, can be illusory, as billions of dollars were wiped off the prices of all kinds of assets. What gives value in terms of cultural standards and processes might be of more enduring worth than what commands a high price in a motor showroom, or a jewellery shop window.

Global sustainability

The third aspect of the global economy to be brought into a new focus by the crash was ecological sustainability. Whereas, before the crisis, governments cast around for ways to slow the bubble-powered train as it rushed towards climate catastrophe, after it they found reasons to postpone even the very modest measures they had put in place for restraining emissions, destructions and depletions. The traditional social policy instruments of welfare states had always been linked to growth, and were thus threatened by the prospect of ecological constraints. The global slowdown put agendas for redistribution within and between states in double jeopardy.

For the governments of affluent Anglophone countries, being forced to borrow massively from international money markets was a blow to their prestige and standing, and made it difficult to sustain their programmes of aid and paternal guidance for the developing world. They were scarcely in any position to go on delivering lectures on fiscal rectitude or prudent regulation. More importantly, they were unlikely ever again to wield the same influence over these parts of the global economy.

Already before the crash, China was becoming the most influential power in large parts of Africa, assisting with development funding, technology and expertise, without enforcing indebtedness in the way that the USA had done in the 1970s and 1980s.[20] These new relationships were based on reciprocity or complementarity; China needed raw materials to fuel its industrial growth, agricultural products to feed its population, and sometimes even land to grow these crops more efficiently. It had an interest in continuing to expand its sphere of influence in that continent, establishing a mode of development through trade and technological transfer which could, in the long term, be linked to goals of sustainability.

In Latin America, the USA now found itself competing for influence with Hugo Chávez's Venezuela: regimes with traces of his 'Bolivarian' model of socialism are now established in Ecuador, Peru and Bolivia. Brazil, too, has friendly relations with the oil-rich state, as of course does Cuba. As a consequence, the USA can no longer exercise the kinds of hegemonic power over that continent which prevailed in previous decades. In relation to social policies, South America had been the proving ground for extreme market-orientated experiments for thirty years (Chile had stakeholder pensions during the Pinochet regime, set up under the guidance of Milton Friedman, before Margaret Thatcher came to power in the UK). The financial woes of Latin America in the 1990s allowed the IMF to dictate the terms of its transfer systems and public services; now there are other possible models, provided by Venezuela and Brazil.[21]

Meanwhile, the EU member states met on 12–13 December 2008, in the wake of the crash, to discuss limits on and trades in carbon emissions. This resulted in a compromise, in which Poland and the other accession countries of Central Europe were granted licences for extra emissions in relation to their coal-powered industries, and Germany too was given greater latitude in respect of its high-tech production. But, overall, the goal was still to cut the EU's carbon footprint by 20 per cent by 2020. The debates and concessions indicated how concerned these countries were to maintain output and income during the recession, at the expense of more ambitious long-term plans to control climate change.

In the press release after the summit, the President of the European Commission claimed the moral high ground, stating that his continent had taken the world lead in relation to action on climate change, and sending the message to President-elect Obama of the USA that 'yes you can' join the movement to reduce emissions. But many at the simultaneous UN conference on the topic at Posnan, Poland, recognized a wide gulf between their aspirations for an effective global agreement and the EU plan.

Taken together with the rise of the Arab Gulf states, and the emergence of an Asian model of social and political institutions,[22] all this offered a diversity of visions and possible pathways for newly industrializing and less-developed societies, and a situation in which they could make the various powers compete with each other for influence. But the more important issue for the long term is whether the advanced economies can co-operate to steer overall global development along a path which is consistent with ecological survival and the conservation of depletable resources.

There was still a huge gap between the ambitions of the industrialized countries, in their efforts to gain competitive advantage within the global economy, and the international co-ordination required for environmental sustainability. Even this situation represented a step forward from the one five years earlier, when the USA, still easily the dominant world economic superpower, was run by a regime which denied the reality of climate change. With the shift in relative economic power to a more balanced situation, with Russia, India, Brazil and China all increasingly influential, there were some prospects for global negotiations on sustainable development during the lull in growth and the respite for the world's natural resources.

From the perspective of social policy, the crucial question was whether this hiatus offered an opportunity to rethink the possible reconciliation of human well-being with ecological conservation. Instead of attempting to justify growth in national output for the sake of larger welfare shares, public policy might promote mechanisms and practices which linked improved quality of life to sustainable projects and priorities. It might provide better incentives for participation in activities which were both positive for human well-being, and contributory to ecological diversity and nature's flourishing.

At a local level, there will – because of a changed structure of costs and advantages since the crash – be more opportunities for projects which combine elements of income redistribution, sustainable economic development and energy saving (or environmental improvement). These are already beginning to be recognized and, on a small scale, put into operation.

For example, in Settle, in the western part of the UK's Yorkshire Dales, a project using the defunct water power from the industrial revolution of 200 years ago (a mill weir) to run a small hydro-electric generator has all these features. Shares have been issued to all the members of the local community in a scheme to make renewable energy, using a water technology, the Archimedes screw, designed 2,500 years ago, to drive the turbine, selling the electricity to the grid, and distributing the profits to members of the co-operative. It even has a fish ladder to enable salmon to get upstream more easily than they could before the project was established, thus contributing to piscatorial conservation.[23] On the coast, a disused power station from the early twentieth century is also harnessing water power to generate electricity, using the Archimedes screw technology.[24]

At Machrihanish in Scotland, a golf course designer and entrepreneur has approached the authorities responsible for a Site of Special Scientific Interest for permission to develop a course on an environmentally valuable and vulnerable stretch of coast. By asking them to specify their requirements, rather than trying to impose his own on them, the designer has come up with a project which will enhance and conserve the environment, not threaten it. The course goes with the contours of the dunes, and the greens will be moved if the sand starts to encroach on them. This will be marketed as an old-style golf experience, replicating conditions of over 100 years ago, but the developers are confident that they can sell this.[25]

These examples illustrate that, in the affluent countries as well as the poor ones, there will be scope for small-scale projects which combine sustainable economic development with income redistribution. The goal of international institutions should be to establish a global context for the flourishing of such schemes, both by agreeing to co-ordinate very large-scale investment and transnational systems (for instance, using solar power in the Sahara to generate electricity for Southern Europe), and to share out the benefits of these systems more fairly between nations.

So the overall goals of national social policies could become more explicitly linked to ecological sustainability and to global social justice, rather than to striving for competitive advantage between individuals, firms and nations. The crash should not slow down these processes, but accelerate them. After all, it has been the cutting edge of capitalism – the global financial system, that has driven the relentless growth of population, resource depletion and climate change – which has been found incapable of sustaining even itself.

Conclusions

The financial crisis focuses attention back onto the economic analysis which drove the reforms of welfare states, the privatization of public organizations, the deregulation of financial markets and the integration of world production and commerce. This analysis insisted that markets were, in the most important respects, self-adjusting, and that contracts were the optimum form of relationship between agents (individuals, firms, governments) even when markets were not suitable. The crash showed that other factors were more significant than the laws of economics, even at the heart of a global system designed according to this logic.

Although the collapse was deemed to have been caused by the invention of fiendishly clever financial instruments, and to have spread throughout the banking world by sophisticated electronic technology, the central problems were actually quite simple. When the whistle was blown on the hedge fund headed by Bernard Madoff, the former chair of the Nasdaq exchange, he admitted that his $50 billion scam was nothing more than an old-fashioned Ponzi (or pyramid) scheme. Yet some of the world's most respected fund managers, such as Nicola Horlick, and many of the longest-established European banks, had either recommended or invested millions in it. The financial system was not proof against the crudest of swindles.

Of more concern for social policy was the revelation that pension funds and voluntary organizations, too, had lost large sums in this scam. Just as charities, local authorities and universities had been millions out of pocket in the collapse of the Icelandic banks, so here too the imperative to get the highest possible return on their money had led organizations which should have been maintaining quite different standards of care, caution and probity to risk members' and supporters' contributions.[26] In some ways this was more shocking; there will always be crooks and suckers in the greedy world of high finance, but the public and voluntary sector is supposed to follow a different ethic.

The transformation of collective life in the Anglophone countries has involved a shift in the ideas and images which

inform and regulate the behaviour of managers and accountants in the human services, as much as it has entailed a
change in the structures and functions of agencies, and of the
relations between them and government. At the same time as
individuals have been required to be 'independent' and 'self-
responsible' (to rely on bank credit rather than government
benefits and services), these organizations have been induced
to take on the features of their commercial counterparts. In
this way a single, totalitarian culture has come to rule over
collective thinking and behaviour, in every corner of society.
In many ways, the pervasive reach of these dominant ways of
seeing and acting in the world has been far more total than
was achieved by fascism or communism.

   Until this culture is challenged and changed, none of the
measures which I have proposed to fix social policy can come
into operation. The economic orthodoxy which has ruled
over collective life will not allow unconditional transfers, new
priorities in human services or a drive for sustainable development, under the cost-benefit calculations now governing
public policy decisions. So long as methodological individualism, utility maximization and commercial efficiency supply
the standards for political choices as well as private ones, there
can be no space for these alternative approaches.

   A year after the crash, the political debate in the UK had
shifted from failures of banks, markets and regulatory authorities to the need for cuts in public services. The crisis in public
finances caused by the bailout of the financial sector and falling tax revenues made government debt, not the collapse of the
institutional order, the focus for the forthcoming election. But
these cuts cannot fix the problems identified in this chapter.

   This is why, in the next chapter, I shall scrutinize and criticize the economic analysis which has underpinned public
policies since the late 1990s in order to diagnose what has to
be changed before social policy can be fixed.

2

Income, credit and redistribution

At the end of the previous chapter, I suggested that what is wrong with social policy is a result of the economic ideas which inform collective life, especially in the affluent Anglophone countries. In this one I shall show how the theories which constitute that orthodoxy came to embrace all aspects of social interaction, and specifically government decisions. In 2008–9, this caused the breakdown of the entire system of credit creation, having already led to the dismemberment of income redistribution systems. Then I shall go on to analyse how policy on income and its distribution could be fixed.

Social policy as we have come to know it sprang from the crash of the 1930s; the New Deal in the USA, and welfare states in the UK and Europe, were liberal democracies' alternatives to totalitarian communism and fascism. But they were themselves subverted by the new economic model, based on globalization, methodological individualism and contract theory, which brought about the crash of autumn 2008. Any attempt to fix social policy must address the nature and purposes of banking and credit, and replace that model with one which deals with income distribution in a more balanced and equitable way.

It is a large claim to suggest that the root cause of social policy's woes is the application of methodological individualism and cost-benefit analysis to every sphere of society, but no larger than the claims the protagonists of these ideas have made on their own behalf. I shall show how they expanded their analyses to embrace every kind of transaction – emotional, artistic, associational and political as well as economic – and succeeded in having their model adopted by the most powerful forces shaping affluent societies. The business approach to government was but a part of the utility-maximizing approach to life in general; as lovers, parents, neighbours, associates and citizens, people came to think and act like rational accumulators and bargain-hunters.

The foundations of the model rest on the assumption that individuals have *different* tastes and interests; without these differences neither markets nor polities would arise.[1] People benefit from trade and from collective arrangements because of their varied preferences and purposes, but contracts are the best way to secure the advantages of exchange and co-operation, because they are reliable, low-cost and leave individuals free in issues not stipulated in these agreements. The model's analyses of government, banking and trade are all derived from the same set of microeconomic principles.

So the model's monetary and fiscal theory stated as its first principle that governments should regulate central banks; and those banks (or separate regulatory bodies), the commercial suppliers of credit, according to contracts.[2] The terms of these contracts are seen as fundamental to the whole economic and social system; all other relationships stem from them. It follows that, if these contracts are properly specified, stability and growth will be guaranteed – 'there will be no more boom and bust', as Gordon Brown was fond of saying.

The model claimed that, both nationally and internationally, markets should be self-correcting, as long as these arrangements are in place. It did not matter that huge trade imbalances built up, or government deficits accumulated, because money markets would bridge these gaps. The idea that the entire global financial system might suddenly freeze over was not conceivable in the model's terms. Nor was the idea that this would happen because bankers had made disastrously irrational decisions.

Under the ruling assumptions, trading in financial products was bound to produce profits and improved efficiency worldwide, because traders would only agree deals which were mutually advantageous, and they were the best judges of the credit-worthiness of those to whom they loaned. But the whole approach relied on 'external' regulation, through authorities which were encouraged to use a 'light touch' and a 'limited touch' – 'no inspection without justification', as Gordon Brown put it in those days.

In her detailed first-hand study of the genesis of the crash, Gillian Tett, a social anthropologist, shows how the investment bankers who invented the various derivatives and insurances which turned into toxic assets evaded regulation. First, in the early 1990s, they used free-market arguments to win the opportunity to work outside the remit of much of the regulatory framework.[3] Then, having developed a 'groupthink' which used its own mathematical formulae to become impervious to outside scrutiny or challenge, they began 'playing around to garner good [credit] ratings and make end runs around the regulatory system'.[4]

In retrospect, it is easy to see that the financial sector also required 'internal' regulation through standards of prudence and responsibility. Its executives and staff had come to see the rules as obstacles to be got around, rather than principles for good practice in credit supply; they developed practices for evading or defeating these controls.[5] In the sustained low-interest conditions created by the US Federal Reserve and the Bank of England, they started to bet on risks derived from speculative trading with each other, using funds raised in international money markets. These were bets on certain winners so long as their own risky lending led to increasing house prices, but on certain losers once borrowers defaulted and prices began to fall.

All this illustrated the requirements of reliable interactions in this as in all other spheres. To sustain integrity and stability, what were needed were everyday ways of thinking and acting – in this case, a culture of soundness. External regulation through contract had led to a casino culture. This in turn penetrated every other organization; local authorities, charities, universities and pension funds had started putting the resources they derived from citizens, members and contributors into dodgy offshore banks, or fraudulent investment schemes. The standards taken from banking and credit had been put at the heart of collective life, and had corrupted its core.

The significance of the crash was therefore first and foremost that the economic way of thinking about social interactions was fatally flawed. First, many of the welfare gains of the previous two decades or more turned out to have been illusory, as house and share prices tumbled, jobs disappeared and frothy investment opportunities collapsed. Investment banking, seen as the driver of the new prosperity, now brought ruin to other sectors, as products claimed to eliminate risk brought down the pyramid of credit.

This was because such finance houses had become vehicles for raising money, mainly from Asia and the Middle East, lending it via intermediaries to debt-ridden citizens of the USA and UK, and then turning these loans back into assets, by bundling them up with other mortgage products, to be sold in exchange for more funds from the same foreign sources. In the process of creating very complex products, they also generated new forms of instability, because other organizations – corporations, pension funds – were forced to buy them to deal with the new risk environment. Then they were left with worthless assets when the bubble burst.

This was as good as acknowledged by the Chairman of Barclay's Bank, in an interview broadcast on 20 December 2008.[6] He stated that the banks would not start lending on an adequate scale again until the 'volatility' in the value of their 'assets' ceased, and that this might take eighteen months. But their 'assets' were ones acquired through speculative trading, risky lending and betting on anything, even the weather. Blaming the regulatory regime, as he went on to do, was like a fraudster blaming the police for not catching him.

In the meantime, while the banks constituted an enormous pit, down which government revenues were being poured, some new institutions were coming into existence to supply credit. The Chairman of Barclay's gave as examples of the needs to be met: funding for small business start-ups, loans to students and trainees, and mortgages for first-time buyers. He argued that all these exposed banks to risks, and that they were still in too fragile a state to take on such risky loans, because of their 'volatile assets' (for which, read gambling losses). So banks could not perform their most basic functions in the aftermath of the crash.

Innovations in the supply of credit would have to fill this void. First, they would have to fund certain costs of productive industries and services, associated with the gap between production processes and sales. As technologies have become more complex, these costs have tended to rise, along with the time lag between the beginnings of a product's development and its eventual sale. The drying-up of this form of credit is severely limiting output, employment and income.

The second kind of credit is that which goes to households to smooth over payments for major items of expenditure during the life-cycle, such as the purchase of houses and cars, or a period of study. This has been the source of the enormous profits of the financial sectors in the affluent Anglophone countries, and the source of the crisis when the bubble prices of housing burst. In a falling market, where borrowers are also at risk of unemployment and reduced earnings, there are no longer such profits to be made.

Yet there are innovations taking place in the supply of credit for all these purposes, and ones which are occurring outside the banking system. In essence, all of these take the form of collective supply of purchasing power by governments, firms or associations, to other firms, groups or individuals. Instead of banks creating money and charging borrowers for distributing it to them, these organizations share risks with their partners or members (other firms in the supply chain, organizations providing essential goods and services, employees or fellow citizens). This principle of risk-pooling is fundamental to the operation of social institutions, but does not involve seeking to profit solely from the supply of credit.

In this chapter, I shall argue that these innovations, still in their infancy, supply essential clues to how social policy can be fixed. They return to the principles which informed welfare states, but in a new situation, in which globalization and the environmental crisis make new demands on the collective actions of national and international authorities.

Regulating society: the role of credit

Why should the collapse of the US banking system have caused such a pervasive downturn in all economic activity worldwide? Why were governments desperate to rescue the banks, thus reducing their scope for other types of intervention? Why were they seemingly willing to risk taxpayers' money as recklessly as the banks had risked that of savers?

The answers to these questions lie in the extent to which governments, especially in the USA and UK, had passed over to financial institutions the role of regulating economies and societies. In effect, they had come to rely on them to correct every sort of disequilibrium, imbalance and distortion, from fiscal and trade deficits to personal indebtedness. Just as international money markets were supposed to smooth over the cracks in public finances and the balance of payments, so too banks were supposed to do the same for citizen-consumers. Credit was the key mechanism in all these interactions.

In effect, supplying or withholding credit, and the interest rates charged for various sums to different categories of borrowers, had replaced most other forms of regulation, both internationally and within societies, in the dominant theories of governance. Financial organizations were attributed with special powers of judgement, and entrusted with crucial responsibilities, in correcting imperfections in markets, and asymmetries in information.[7] Governments willingly ceded to them the authority over such issues wielded by their predecessor administrations.

In the theory on which this regime was founded, all relationships can be modelled as interactions between individuals, each of whom is seeking to maximize his or her utility (material and psychic satisfactions), but not all of whom are equally well informed about each other's desires, aversions and intentions. The potential benefits of these interactions can be maximized, and the costs of them reduced, by designing institutions which can deal with imperfections and asymmetries in information about others' motives and actions. The paradigms for these are employment and insurance contracts, where the 'principal' (the employer or insurance company) sets the terms which induce the 'agent' (employee or insured person) to behave in ways which minimize the potential conflicts of interest between them (e.g. working without direct supervision, or being careful to avoid accidents).[8]

This model has been generalized to include the whole economy and society. Everyone, from the head of the central bank to the claimant of benefits, is to be given incentives to act in ways which, taken as a whole, maximize the welfare of the whole population. The government acts as the principal, to set the terms of the 'social contract', and hence of all social relationships. It insures the whole economy, writing contracts for the central bank, which in turn does so for the commercial banks. As the former Chief Adviser to the World Bank and Nobel economics laureate, Joseph Stiglitz, writing with a colleague, expressed it: '[T]he regulator (the principal) tries to *control* or *affect* the behavior of the bank (the agent), to make the bank act *more* in accord with social objectives' (emphasis in original).[9] The key to understanding the role of banks in the model is their supply of credit, and 'the importance, and consequences, of imperfections of information': '[A] central function of banks is to determine who is likely to default, and in doing so banks determine the supply of loans . . . [F]inancial institutions . . . are critical in determining the behavior of the economy, and . . . the central features of banks and bank behavior can be understood in terms of (or derived from) an analysis of information imperfections'.[10]

So the model relies on those organizations which create credit to provide the mechanism for smoothing over the gaps between aspirations and expectations of each other in the population at large, and the wider realities of the global economy. This enormous responsibility is theirs, but undertaken with the active support of government – which can intervene through public policy – and the central bank as regulator: 'Households are often not perfectly rational. Households and firms . . . certainly don't have perfect information. There are often important differences in the information that they have access to (information asymmetries). Models based on more realistic assumptions . . . provide an additional rationale for government to intervene in the economy and additional tools for government and central banks to stabilise the economy'.[11]

This implies that, given the right regulatory framework, banks *can* be relied on to be rational, and (through the provision of credit) to steer all other agents along the pathways of optimal behavior. It explains why governments in the USA and UK were so slow to recognize the symptoms of the bubbles in house and share prices, or the dangers of the markets in derivatives, and why, once the crash had happened, they still tried to rescue the banks, and to induce them to resume their supply of credit. But by then the banks' own creditors were calling in their loans, and the banks were refusing to lend to each other.

In the light of subsequent events, this model of governance seems incredibly naive and simplistic. But it reflected the firm belief among economists, often compliantly accepted by other social scientists, that all human interactions could be analysed in terms of information, incentives and contracts. This was plausible only because every aspect of such interactions, from politics to sport and personal relationships, had been absorbed into an account of utility-maximizing exchanges among bargain-hunting individuals. For example, the Nobel Prize-winning theorist Gary Becker wrote, of the 'social capital' that is involved in non-material transactions, that his model

> retains the assumption that individuals maximize utility while extending the definition of individual preferences to include personal habits and addictions, peer pressure, parental influences on the tastes of children, and other neglected behavior. This extension of the utility-maximizing approach to include endogenous preferences is remarkably successful in satisfying a wide class of behavior, including habitual, social and political behavior.
>
> I do not believe that any alternative approach – be it founded on 'cultural', 'biological', or 'psychological' forces – comes close to providing comparable insights and explanatory power'.[12]

These claims had become circular; as the social world was redesigned to accommodate the pursuit of individual self-interest, with collective institutions made permeable for choice and mobility, the model's assumptions had come to be reflected in the human environment, and its ideas and images absorbed into popular cultures. So the position of credit-supplying organizations was consolidated at the heart of societies, and people turned to them both for resources for their daily lives, and for notions about how these lives should be led.

After the financial system in the affluent Anglophone countries collapsed, a vacuum appeared, not only in the provision of credit, but also in governance of social relations. As Becker argued, the economic model, with information, incentives and contract at its centre, had come to be the rationale for all interactions, and governments saw the banks as the means for reconciling the myriads of individual preferences and projects which made up society. Once the mechanisms of credit no longer functioned as the theory described, what might eventually take their place?

Alternative forms of credit

It may seem unduly apocalyptic to suggest that faith in bank credit was fatally damaged by the crash of autumn 2008. Money markets are necessary, in the global as well as the local economy, to share risks, and to ensure that these risks are borne by those best able to carry them. But the point was that both Wall Street and the City of London had embellished their positions at the pinnacle of global financial capitalism by what turned out to be reckless and fraudulent practices. They were attracting funds on world money markets only by unsustainably high returns, through massive exercises in smoke and mirrors. Now that these have been exposed as illusions, money from Asia (which was drawn to them as much by fears about the soundness of the banks in their own countries following their crisis of 1997–8, as by these promised returns) and from the Middle East will instead flow into investments in those regions. That was why some new basis for credit, and for all the functions which credit had come to fulfil in the affluent Anglophone countries, was needed.

To recognize what is required, it is necessary to trace the interlocking elements of the model of governance derived from the theory of information, incentives and contract. First, the model supplies a version of citizenship – the individual who takes responsibility for his or her project of self-realization by pursuing a set of goals in line with the fulfilment of preferences, potentials and personal values.[13] Part of this self-responsibility consists of 'independence', the willingness to turn to banks and insurance companies rather than state benefits (seen as stigmatizing reliance on others) for the credit required by this project, and to cover all other contingencies. The 'social contract' between the state and its citizens is therefore underpinned by bank credit as the source of 'independence'. Thus loans and credit cards became the foundations for the property-owning, consumer version of citizenship.

Second, the model constructs the economic environment as 'business friendly', in the sense that small enterprises can come into (and go out of) existence without incurring excessive costs. As compared with the countries of Continental Europe, the affluent Anglophone ones have low rates of social insurance contributions, and scanty employment security; hiring and firing is relatively cheap when redundancy payments and minimum wages are low. During the boom years, the banks provided the credit which was needed in such a risky environment; after the crash they did not, and many small businesses went to the wall.

Third, the financial sector is a large part of the economy, and takes priority in government decisions about the institutional environment. In the UK, this sector accounted for about a quarter of GDP in 2007, and provided more than a third of government revenue from taxes on capital.[14] This has meant that policies for interest rates, for the regulation of credit supply, and for the structure of the banking sector (for instance, the demutualization of the building societies in the UK) allowed the bubbles in house prices and shares to develop, leading to the crash. The banks were creating new risks through these loans, using borrowed funds, and selling them on to others, rather than lending to share risks with reliable producers.

Conversely, the low priority given to manufacturing and other productive industry has led to underinvestment, compared with (for example) Germany, and has also meant that these industrial companies, even the largest ones, were not seen as suitable for the kinds of unconditional bailouts provided by governments to banks. Wall Street executives travelled to and from their meetings with Washington officials for their rescue meetings in private jets; car industry chiefs arrived in theirs, but were required to return home on commercial flights as a condition for their assistance.

If the financial system can no longer oil the wheels of these interlocking elements in the Anglophone model of governance, by supplying the credit needed for its versions of citizenship, the business environment and the revenues for public finance, a different approach to all these issues is required. It will have to replace some aspects of each of these functions, but do so in ways which are complementary and interlocking, so as to supply a new approach to governance as well as to credit.

However, the clues to how this might be tackled lie in features of present social and economic relations, in the Anglophone countries and elsewhere in the world, which have been largely ignored by theory on information, incentives and contract. These concern ways of sharing resources and risks which do not involve the banks (and hence the creation of credit for interest and profit).

Individuals and households

The first category of such arrangements concerns those who are 'financially excluded' under the present model – who do not have a bank account, or who are debarred from borrowing because of their low status, earnings or level of material security. They include many immigrants as well as indigenous poor people in affluent countries, who are either forced to make other arrangements to meet gaps in their earnings or heavy expenditures, or to accumulate the start-up resources for petty trading or micro-enterprises. Some of these constitute 'self-exclusion', in the sense that these groups prefer not to be part of the official system of banking and credit, either because their activities are irregular, or because they are part of other systems of risk-sharing, for instance in their countries of origin, where they are sending substantial remittances.

The ways in which financial exclusion manifests itself vary between societies, because of their different institutional structures. In the European Union, the countries whose rates of this phenomenon are estimated to be lowest are the Netherlands, Luxemburg, Sweden and Denmark. Along with France and Belgium, these states have made special efforts to extend banking access to their whole resident populations.[15] By contrast, in the UK, measures to reduce the numbers of households without bank accounts (estimated as 2 million adults in 2004) have stalled; the creation of 'basic accounts' was left to the commercial banks, which were little motivated to comply.[16] Similarly, in the USA, about half the immigrant population are reckoned to have some form of financial exclusion.[17] So the countries with the largest financial sectors, which follow the contract model of governance most closely, do not include their whole populations in this fundamental source of the credit which is assumed to fund 'independence'.

These figures represent the outcomes of strategic interactions between disadvantaged minority individuals and banks. For the former, having a bank account may be a necessity, in order for their employer to transfer their wages, but they may prefer to deal in cash, for the sake of controlling their weekly spending. Some share accounts with settled friends, if they lack the documentation to open their own. Others, especially those in the informal economy, or working while claiming benefits, may prefer to stay right outside the banking system.[18] The banks in turn may refuse accounts to those who lack the stipulated documents, and also refuse credit to many on the grounds of their past histories or lack of assets. Risk assessments are increasingly made statistically, and based on such factors as ethnic origin or residential location, as well as earnings and job security.

On the other hand, of course, banks in the Anglophone countries also sought to widen their customer base by issuing credit cards and granting housing loans to 'sub-prime' customers. This gave the appearance of being willing to take on greater risk, but was actually a means of acquiring extra funds through repackaging and recycling such debts. It is just these groups which now find themselves either in unmanageable debt, or with no further access to credit, or both.

The relevant point here is that those who have been excluded from, or have excluded themselves from, mainstream commercial credit have developed a wide range of alternative systems. The most prevalent of these is kinship – the means of risk-sharing which is almost universal in developing countries, but also in Asia and South America generally.[19] The clearest examples in the UK concern immigrant workers, many of whom borrowed money from their families to come, and who send a proportion of their earnings home to relatives.[20] It is estimated that £3 billion a year are remitted in this way from the UK.[21]

Risk-sharing among kin is also prevalent among settled

populations, but in the affluent Anglophone countries this increasingly takes the form of loans by grandparents and parents to their descendants. The housing and share bubbles inflated the value of these assets, held by the older generations, but also made it harder for the youngest generation to acquire property. In addition to this, younger people now pay more to study and train, especially in the UK, so their parents are likely to bear some of these costs if they (who often had state support during their higher education) have wealth on which to draw.

Among the large sections of the populations of these countries without savings, and who are often burdened with credit card (or loan shark) debt, a series of alternative forms of credit have developed. The most formal of these are credit unions, where the principle of mutuality in savings for larger expenditures has been re-established to supply credit at a far lower cost than is available commercially to those on limited incomes. For some groups of recent immigrants, a similar approach to credit has been introduced, for instance in the *gun*, or 'gold day', among Turkish women.[22]

However, many other systems of risk-sharing in marginal disadvantaged communities are illegal or semi-legal; they fill the gap in the supply of credit by substituting forms of accumulation (drug-dealing, protection rackets, extortion, prostitution and other forms of crime) which allow some members of tight-knit groups to 'look after' others, gaining power over them, which can be converted into further criminal projects. These informal systems constitute 'economic clubs'[23] – exclusive membership associations in which participants pay their dues in illegal activities, and receive their benefits through clandestine redistribution of collective gains.

These systems can be recognized as rational, in terms of the economic model itself, where both commercial finance and the state's agencies have retreated from a district, leaving its residents largely to fend for themselves. This is what happened in the USA and UK in poor areas during the neo-liberal ascendancy of the 1980s. Once criminal gangs of various kinds took over the functions of businesses, banks and public services, it took a very long time for government inter-vention to change the configuration of loyalties and interests. To a great extent, these are still in existence, despite heavy out-lays of public funds by Third Way administrations during the following decade.

One illustration of the problem of replacing illegal systems of risk-sharing is the case of Northern Ireland. There, violent paramilitary organizations controlled poor districts through-out the Troubles of the 1980s and 1990s. The Peace Process attempted to draw the political leaders of these movements into democratic politics, while introducing formal economic and government agencies in place of the existing ones. But the evidence is that only some of these disadvantaged residents have gained in this transition; the paramilitary system of pro-duction and distribution was more inclusive than the formal one, which fails to 'look after' the most marginal members of these populations.[24]

As I shall show towards the end of this chapter, the aim of public policy should be to facilitate those aspects of alterna-tive credit provision among individuals and households which are conducive to economic efficiency and the well-being of populations, while reducing those which are predatory, anti-social and criminal. The limitations of bank credit have been revealed as contributory factors to the latter, and the economic downturn puts more people at risk of being forced to turn to inefficient or socially undesirable sources. The crash provides good reasons for trying to fix these problems in new ways.

Firms

The banking collapse has triggered a rapid rise in unem-ployment in the affluent Anglophone countries, as many businesses have gone into liquidation. Whereas the recessions of the 1970s, 1980s and early 1990s saw redundancies mainly in older industrial companies, mining and the utilities (i.e. a loss of traditional blue-collar jobs), this 'correction' is different. Because of the bursting of the house price and shares bubbles, those made redundant in the first wave were staff in financial services, real estate, construction, retailing, fast food and coffee outlets. The firms most affected included hedge funds, investment banks, estate agents and superstores. Later this spread to industrial companies, but – in comparison with previous downturns since the Second World War – the impact on services, and on suburban districts of affluent cities, was far more marked. Unemployment rose by 3.6 million in the USA in 2008,[25] and in the last quarter of that year was increasing twice as fast in the UK as in Germany and France.[26]

It can readily be recognized that most of these closures were necessary, because of the distortions caused by the bubbles. But all other companies and small businesses, in every other sector, have been affected by the crash. In order for more of the newly redundant to find work in more enduring and productive employments, credit needs to flow to these firms, and to other entrepreneurs with innovatory ideas appropriate to the new circumstances.

During the crisis, some business executives commented that the scarcity of credit had required them to make loans to some of their suppliers and customers, in order to keep the productive and marketing processes moving. This is a good example of risks being shared among those involved in exchange relationships, with the greatest risks allocated to the participant best able to bear them. One businessman commented that he had not expected to become a banker, but he saw the need for him to fulfil the role in that situation.

The economic theory of the firm gives no clear indications about how this might come about. One branch suggests that firms will contract with others in the production and distribution process unless they are unable to secure prompt compliance with the terms of such arrangements.[27] When defaults or delays occur, it will pay them to take over those with whom they formerly contracted. The advantages of such incorporations include more efficient control mechanisms, and savings of transaction costs between different stages of these processes.[28]

But banks which make loans to firms do not take them over when they default on payments; their supply of credit relies on a version of the principal–agent relationship, in which the expertise in production and distribution of the firm is valuable to the bank. So there are many circumstances in which specialized knowledge, experience, organization and reputation may justify retaining an independent identity for the producer or distributor, even if it requires financial support. For this reason, it makes good economic sense for some successful firms to act as 'bankers' for others which cannot access credit during a prolonged crisis such as the crash.

But the question then remains whether the 'recovery' should take the form of a return to the system under which businesses rely on loans from commercial banks, which make most of their money through complex international trading in futures and currencies, or establish new institutions of their own, more attuned to the needs of producers and their customers. There has been less tradition of this kind of credit organization in the Anglophone countries than in Continental Europe. In Germany, for instance, the banks have been far more closely linked, through the state, with large-scale manufacturing industry (as in Japan). In France and Italy, there is also a long tradition of regional and local credit organizations, such as 'crédit agricole'.

Furthermore, the evidence of France, Italy, Spain and several other European states suggests that these types of organizations are better suited to the facilitation of co-operatives between small producers. These have several advantages which are not fully recognized in the orthodox theory of the firm. Not only do they share risks over the economic cycle, and allow appropriate adaptation through planned investment strategy by members, using a strategy of complementarity rather than competition; they also allow the development and maintenance of cultures of quality among producers, which in turn give rise to cultures of appreciation of excellence among consumers.

The tradition in the UK is for new enterprises, especially ones which seek to introduce qualitative improvements in products, either by technological innovations or by returning to traditional resources or methods, to think in terms of 'niche markets'. The Continental European tradition is less one of competition through the capture of niches, and more one of co-operation between a variety of producers in the same field – pooling risks and credit. This can make small enterprises less vulnerable to a downturn in overall demand, and more able to afford to adapt and develop new strategies.

In the aftermath of the crash, these advantages are becoming more important. The requirements of sustainability and conservation have led to a revival of crafts and traditions, for example in the production, preparation and cooking of food. Whereas the business model derived from the Anglophone version of commercial credit gave rise to fast food outlets, the French, Italian and Spanish one has preserved many regional and local folkways, in growing, butchering, conserving and presenting food. These can now be recognized as important features of a more sustainable economy. Much the same can be said of aspects of the clothing and jewellery industries, where again co-operatives are strongly represented in Southern Europe.

So there may be a strong case, in social as well as economic terms, for reconfiguring the structures which supply credit to the business sector, so as to allow specialist organizations for funding enterprises, and enabling the sharing of risks co-operatively, to develop. This would allow the downturn to mark a change in direction in this sector, towards greater sustainability and quality, as well as greater expertise and skill among workers.

Governments

The crash has laid bare the emptiness of many claims by governments during the boom years. George W. Bush has left the US presidency with an almost unique record of failure in the economy as well as in his geo-political strategy. In the UK, Gordon Brown's revival in popularity at the end of 2008 was unable to disguise the rashness of his claims over employment creation and economic stability.

In the immediate aftermath of the crisis, governments were able to argue that their bailout of the banks was necessary to avoid the meltdown of global financial markets. But as the consequences of bankers' greed and folly unfolded, it was incumbent on governments to find new ways of supplying credit, while the banks recovered their equilibrium and resumed a less hubristic role. Assuming that Treasuries have learnt enough from the crash to recognize the inadequacies of the model of governance derived from information, incentives and contract theory, it will be time to look around for a more sustainable basis for any future expansion.

The public finances of most affluent countries, and of the USA and UK in particular, have been severely weakened by the bank bailout (see pp. 22–38). This makes it inevitable that more revenue will have to be raised through taxation for the foreseeable future. Furthermore, and equally seriously, the weakened position of the dollar and the pound means that borrowing on international money markets, to cover fiscal deficits and trade imbalances, is likely to be expensive.

However, such circumstances are not unique. For instance, national debt in the USA and the UK during the Second World War was proportionately as large as it was in early 2009, and there were no international money markets to borrow from, because of the disruptions of war. Both countries raised the funds for their war efforts from bonds, purchased out of their savings by citizens; as the richer ally, the USA also lent heavily to the UK.

In the new economic environment, in which the savings rates in the USA and UK are revealed as far too low, both governments could seek to make saving more attractive, and to service their public debts, by borrowing from their citizens. This might be more politically acceptable than raising taxes, because of the voluntary nature of such mechanisms. But – as in wartime – it would need to be justified in a frank admission of the need for popular subscription, which has arisen from government failure rather than from enemy attack. With commercial interest rates near zero, and the stock market volatile, it would be feasible to attract substantial funds into gilts if such an approach were openly adopted.

Much has rightly been made of the fact that the national debts of the UK and USA have risen very steeply in the immediate aftermath of the crash, and are continuing to rise. But the ratio of public debt to GDP in Japan is almost three times that of the UK, even after this relative deterioration in the latter's situation. While the UK is seen as at risk of losing its national credit rating (like Iceland), Japan is not – because its debt is held by its own citizens, mostly thrifty pensioners. A high savings ratio enables high government borrowing if the government's creditors are its own people.

The UK government's issue of gilts increased from £13.7 billion in 2001–2 to £58 billion in 2007–8, and £146 billion in 2008–9. By the middle of 2008, one-third of all of these bonds were owned by foreigners.[29] Since the crash, the banks' bailout and 'quantitative easing' have accelerated the sale of bonds, with hints of a reluctance of investors to take up all these that were not bought by the Bank of England (to combat deflation). A further increase in issues will drive their yield down, but is planned in order to finance future growth in government debt; the same is happening in many other affluent countries, to pay for stimulus packages.

An open admission that the US and UK commercial banks and companies had become far less attractive for world money markets might seem a step too far for governments, but authoritative voices in the financial media have already been proclaiming this in the case of the UK.[30] A more explicit attempt to harness citizens' loyalty, to invest in National Savings, would seem a sensible strategy in these circumstances.

Before and after the Second World War, Anglophone governments followed those in several Continental European countries in redefining the scope for financial risk-sharing through schemes for Social Insurance, in which the state, employers and employees contributed to funds for such contingencies as sickness, industrial and war injury, unemployment and retirement. Since then, the rationale for these systems, in terms of life-cycle income smoothing, counter-cyclical redistribution, demand maintenance and social justice, has weakened. Instead, Anglophone governments see benefits payments as parts of contracts, involving mutual rights and responsibilities, between states and individual citizens, where the latter have claims only when their own resources fail.

For example, very soon after gaining power in 1997, the UK New Labour administration set out its New Contract for Welfare, listing the respective duties of government and individuals. The emphasis was on self-responsibility through work and earnings; citizens were required to seek work and training where able to do so, to take up opportunities to be independent, to give support to their families and children, to save for retirement where possible, and not to defraud the taxpayer.[31] In return, the government committed itself to help people find work, to make work pay (e.g. through the minimum wage and tax credits), to make financial products such as private pensions secure through sound regulation, and to relieve poverty in old age where savings were inadequate. It also promised transparency in targeting those in need. Since then, New Labour has tightened up benefits administration and imposed work-search conditions (backed by sanctions) on more and more categories of lone parents, and people with disabilities and long-term illnesses.[32]

After the crash, the outcomes of these measures look disappointing. Unemployment rates are set to return to the levels of the early 1980s, with improvements in levels of child poverty also threatened. Numbers on invalidity benefits had begun to come down, but this progress too has stalled. Above all, the emphasis on targeted, means-tested benefits, given under conditions of work search, has been highly stigmatizing, and has divided the interests of claimants from those of taxpayers. Residents in districts with high levels of poverty have become excluded from the circuits of mainstream social relations, with inevitable consequences in terms of alienation and resistance. The enforcement of low-paid and insecure work has often been counterproductive. Both white outer-city estates and minority ethnic inner-city districts have developed inward-looking cultures, and sometimes taken violent action against each other, provoked by racist political groups.

As the income gains of recent years turn out to be illusory, and unemployment climbs, a new approach is obviously needed. The aim should be to discover ways of sharing risks and redistributing income which are not stigmatized, and do not trap people in low-paid work roles. In order to encourage a whole range of public, voluntary and locally organized

initiatives for environmental improvements, nature conservation and the creation of more convivial social environments,
such redistributive schemes should avoid stipulating employment or earnings levels; they should enable all kinds of paid
and unpaid activities, without penalties.

On pp. 28–30, I mentioned the action taken by the US and
Australian governments in distributing payments to their
whole populations unconditionally, as an emergency response
to the crash. Such schemes deserve to be given longer-term
trials, not to encourage spending, but to enable participation.
The goals set out above are highly consistent with the declared
aims of Barack Obama's election campaign, and indeed
his supporters constituted a volunteer social movement of
exactly the kind which would be facilitated by this approach.
An unconditional income for all would facilitate democratic
mobilization, as well as action for improved quality of life and
for environmental conservation.

A 'basic income' of this kind would provide a collective
source of credit to all citizens, to replace the existing complexi-
ties of tax allowances and income benefits. It would be highly
inclusive, and constitute a principle of fairness between all
citizens. It would be neutral in its treatment of different conceptions of the good life, since it would neither reward nor
penalize any type of activity, from sport, art and recreation to
politics and business.[33]

This principle is already operational in some aspects of
tax-benefit systems in the affluent states, such as child allowances in the European countries and the UK, and the citizen's
pension in New Zealand. It has also been introduced, at a low
level, in South Africa, Namibia and Brazil. The new approach
would simply extend this principle to all age groups.

Another variant of the same idea is a capital sum, given to
each resident at birth, or on attaining the age of majority.[34]
This form of credit is potentially useful as a training grant,

a business start-up fund, or a deposit on a flat. In the state of Alaska, each person who has been resident for over a year qualifies for a grant of around $1,000. In the UK, Child Trust Funds were established in 2004, giving each newborn £250, which parents could convert into shareholder accounts, to save for their children's maturity. Unfortunately, this ideologically driven attempt to link the principle of credit for all to popular capitalism has backfired, since the three-quarters of such grants which were converted in this way have declined in value by nearly 30 per cent (£0.5 billion) due to the fall in share prices in the crash.[35]

Overall, then, the crisis demands that governments look for ways of reinforcing existing sources of non-bank credit, in kinship, association, neighbourhood, businesses and elsewhere, but also that they themselves look for ways of collectively sharing risks through the tax-benefit system. The danger of informal credit systems, from credit unions to co-operatives and industrial or agricultural banks, is that they necessarily operate exclusively. Trust and mutuality can only be established among members, through the payment of contributions, and through frequent interactions, including representative deliberation and decision-making.[36] These processes can be costly, and they restrict these forms of credit to certain categories of people, by kinship, district, occupation, status, etc. So these 'clubs' are not optimal in terms of economic efficiency, even if they often have positive social effects.

Government action to supply credit directly to whole populations in the way described has none of these disadvantages. Local and national authorities may create new forms of credit in various ways. By the beginning of 2009, local government mortgages were planned in the UK in several large cities, as councils gained permission to lend at an interest rate of 3.93 per cent, in an attempt to fill the gap left by the collapse of the demutualized building societies.[37] This would revive schemes which were common until the 1980s. The Minister for Postal Affairs has also announced that a proposal to turn the Post Office into a national bank, offering loans and mortgages, would be urgently considered.[38]

The underlying point in all this is that money and credit are nothing more than conventions agreed by populations over media of exchange. In the Great Depression, firms issued tokens, and various cities all over the world have created their own currencies to finance municipal projects. As long as people trust these 'currencies', they have proved themselves successful in combating unemployment and deflation.[39]

One of the most successful of these experiments was in Germany in the 1920s, where the unorthodox economic theorist Silvio Gesell[40] was appointed Finance Minister for Bavaria. Several local currencies were designed to feature a kind of 'negative interest' – they lost value if they were not spent quickly – which countered underconsumption in recessions. Currencies of this kind were used to save local industries or towns during credit crises.

The theoretical debate in the 1920s and 1930s over banking and credit[41] should be re-opened in the face of the crash. It is not too fanciful to argue for experiments at every level, from 'quantitative easing' by the Bank of England to the 'Lewes pound', successfully issued by the Sussex town to its inhabitants. The reverence with which the financial services were treated in the USA and UK should become a thing of the past, as new approaches to risk-sharing are adopted.

Conclusions

In this chapter, I have shown that what's wrong with social policy, especially in the affluent Anglophone countries, can in large part be traced to the economic theory on which the prevailing model of governance is based. Because of the dominance of the USA in the workings of international financial organizations (the International Monetary Fund and World Bank) and in the World Trade Organization, these principles have driven the process of globalization in recent years, and hence powerfully influenced and constrained other governments and economic agents worldwide.

This model makes a close linkage between public policy and the supply of credit by installing banks at the centre of decisions which reconcile interests and shape projects in market economies. It allows capital markets to equilibrate the various imbalances and asymmetries which occur, both nationally and internationally, with governments and central banks providing the frameworks for these processes. Because of the key role played by these institutions in the model, the failure of US investment banks and insurance companies, triggering a series of banking collapses, set off the chain of events which was the crash of autumn 2008.

The crash revealed that banks and credit do indeed play a role in both global and national economies which is different from that of other organizations, such as manufacturing industries. But financial intermediaries were given far too much power by the model's prescriptions. In their reckless schemes for making money out of money, they held all the other parts of the economic system to ransom, or sucked organizations into buying exotic 'products' which were incomprehensibly risky. Social policy's goals will be at risk if they regain this excessive power.

Behind the model lies an analysis of social as well as economic relations in which individual preferences and projects are the basic units of all choices, public as well as private. The aim of government programmes is to minimize the costs of interdependence between such autonomous individuals, and to maximize their scope for mobility between options, over collective as well as private consumption goods and services.

As I have shown, this model of governance steers citizens towards bank credit for the funding they require to develop their life projects as self-responsible and independent citizens. This forms the foundation for the order of markets and property which is claimed to maximize overall welfare in populations. The social contract between the government and its citizens guarantees these freedoms, and casts the tax-benefits system in the residual roles of caring for those incapable of independence (and hence unworthy of credit), enforcing work obligations and guaranteeing the financial products (such as private pensions) of the commercial banking system.

The individualism that supplies the basis for this model is partially offset by an emphasis on 'responsible communities' in civil society, in which groups and associations recognize and take action on local issues.[42] In the World Bank approach to economic and human development, this is related to the 'social capital' formed through interactions in communities (see pp. 144–8), and this concept has also been applied to poor districts in affluent states, where efforts are made to regenerate the physical environment and combat deviant subcultures. Community is required to pick up the pieces when markets, property and self-responsibility fail.

Some social policy analysts have argued that variants of this 'liberal–communitarian' mix have become the only approaches to social policy on offer to voters in the affluent states.[43] Although, as I have argued, important differences in outcomes for populations and their incomes since the crash can be traced to longer traditions in welfare regimes, this convergence around individualism and limited voluntary associationalism is the orthodoxy which must now be challenged.

The crash both demonstrates the disastrous inadequacies of the model, and provides an opportunity for a new approach. Without new systems for credit, and new roles for government in the overall supply of credit, social policy cannot be fixed. If the role of credit supply is again recognized as the sharing of risk, and the allocation of the proportions of risk according to ability to bear it, rather than the opportunity for profit from the marketing of risk in various kinds of casino-style gambles, then credit can re-emerge at the heart of new institutions for effective social inclusion and justice.

This is not the first time that the function of banking and the nature of credit have been central for a paradigm shift in social policy. After the Wall Street crash of 1929, similar criticisms of the banking system were made, and radical alternatives proposed. Unconventional economists like Dennis Milner[44] and C. H. Douglas[45] proposed variants of the basic income and social credit. Their ideas drew support from socialists such as G. D. H. Cole,[46] and the future Nobel Economics Prizewinner, James Meade.[47] Even the dissident Tory Harold Macmillan[48] thought that the stock exchange should deal only in shares in new ventures, and that other investment should be carried out by government boards.

In the event, the economic theories of Keynes and the Roosevelt and Beveridge institutional innovations of the following two decades squeezed out these heterodox proposals, and gave states far greater roles in managing economies and societies without stripping the banks of their control over credit for the private sector. But they were constrained by monetary policy to act in ways which were consistent with the overall goals of public policy. It was only after the neo-liberal ascendancy of the early 1980s that financial organizations began to pose as the 'Masters of the Universe', convinced that they could create new wealth out of thin air, rather than the servants of governments attempting to protect their citizens from market risks.

All forms of human organization have elements of risk-sharing, and the crash again highlights this truism. The breakdown of trust between banking organizations has driven people to seek new sources of credit in new groupings and associations. This is true of every type of society, and every sector within them. But because the crash has been most dramatic in the affluent Anglophone countries, where the model was most developed, the changes there have been most evident.

For example, in the UK, home owners had been borrowing against the rising value of their houses during the property price boom; in the third quarter of 2007, when prices were rising fastest, £11 billion were borrowed in this way. But in the corresponding quarter of 2008, immediately after the crash, £6 billion was paid off mortgage debt, as home owners responded to the deterioration in the value of their assets. At the same time, larger firms which recognized that the boom period in which they had expanded was over, began to re-organize to isolate unprofitable parts of their enterprises, so as to conserve those staff and productive resources which could come under threat if loss-making sections dragged the whole company down.

All these quick reversals of the behaviour patterns that prevailed during the bank-induced bubble conditions show two things – first, that banks do not have the judgement and wisdom to fulfil the roles allocated to them by the model of governance that prevailed in these countries, and, second, that firms and households do respond rationally to the signals given to them by the wider economy. The way to fix public policy is not to restore banks to the positions of inflated importance given them in the pre-crash order, but to find new mechanisms for supplying the credit needed for a balanced, inclusive and fair society.

Such a society cannot consist of individuals seeking to minimize the costs of their interdependence. The concept of risk-sharing which underlies credit demands active measures to seek ways of gaining benefits from interdependence. These consist in recognizing where collective organizations, from firms and voluntary organizations to states, can enable well-being and prosperity. From this perspective, I have proposed several consolidations of existing organizational forms and practices which might improve the supply of credit for socially desirable purposes.

The most radical proposal is that governments themselves become providers of credit, in the form of universal grants and income streams, both to individuals and to local authorities and voluntary agencies for certain projects. Obviously this happens already in many initiatives, but the rationale under which funds are allocated has been distorted by the overall logic of an economic model based on the theory of information, incentives and contract.

The first step towards a radical change of approach to income redistribution has been recommended by a Conservative Party think tank in the UK, the Centre for Social Justice, in September 2009 it proposed the integration of the tax and benefit systems, with a massive simplification of the eligibility and assessment processes, collapsing fifty-one means-tested schemes into just two elements, resources and needs. The rationale given for this shift was that it would reduce the disincentives for employment, participation and inclusion facing people with low earnings potential, by reducing marginal tax rates as well as administrative complexity.[49] The longer-term implications of this important step towards a 'basic income' approach will be discussed in chapter 4.

In the next chapter, I shall analyse the distortions to the supply of services caused by this misleading model. Then, in chapter 4, I shall return to the question of how changes in public finance can help to fix the basis for social policy.

3

Services and well-being

Even before the financial crisis exposed the illusory nature of many of the welfare gains since the early 1990s, doubts about the quality of life enabled by the new prosperity had come to the fore. Economists themselves were engaged in a fierce debate about whether the well-being of individuals could be compared,[1] how social and political factors influenced the happiness of populations,[2] and which factors contributed most to quality of life.[3] Social policy analysts[4] and politicians[5] came late to this debate, but the crash has accelerated its importance.

In this chapter, I shall investigate the relationship between the transformation of affluent societies into predominantly service economies and the apparent failure of these societies to improve the well-being of their members (in terms of their own assessments of their overall satisfaction with their lives[6]).

For governments, this should indicate that something is wrong with their social policies, especially since populations of some far poorer countries,[7] with a much smaller proportion of both public and private services, do comparatively well by the same measurements.

In the aftermath of the crash, the immediate concern of governments has been to protect the incomes and employment of those most directly affected – these have included workers in financial and business services, retailing, property and some personal and household services. All these had been burgeoning sectors during the long boom and bubble years. But the crash raises the questions of how much they contributed to the quality of life of those they served, and how significant they could and should be in a 'recovery'.

These questions in themselves are problematic, because they seem to suggest that there are components of human well-being which can be specified, independently of the choices of individual human beings. Such 'objective' accounts of the good life[8] are strongly disputed by many philosophers as well as by most mainstream economists.[9]

The notion of a politically constructed good society seemed to have been dealt a fatal blow with the collapse of the Soviet Bloc in 1989; since then, the prevailing orthodoxy in public policy, as well as in social scientific theory, has favoured ideas and institutions which allowed individuals to choose between collective as well as between private goods. In this approach, a diversity of versions of the good life, and the opportunity to move at low cost between membership units sustaining them, have been the goals of social as well as economic policies.[10]

However, a number of persistent theories in social policy are now converging around an alternative approach, in which other priorities are appearing. First, however various tastes and preferences may be, people clearly share certain common human needs.[11] It may be feasible to create institutional contexts in which primary attention is paid to these preconditions for well-being,[12] without limiting diversity in damaging ways.

The most important of these concerns equality of incomes and life chances. The evidence is increasingly that this promotes the well-being of whole populations, and not just of poorer members of a society, and that it can do so without reducing desirable diversities. But this will be analysed in chapter 6.

Second, although professional human services have undoubtedly become more effective at 'delivering' targets and outcomes, and more efficient at supplying costed inputs within budgets, these improvements do not seem to capture all that is required to give them the qualities appropriate for promoting well-being. For example, a report from a prestigious research centre in the UK National Health Service found that its practices lacked compassion.[13] However difficult it might be to measure compassion, or price the units in which it is provided by practitioners, this appears to be an aspect of health care which is intrinsic to good quality.

Third, the elements of choice and easy access to a diversity of services do not capture aspects of the potential for public facilities in particular to combine together into a coherent infrastructure for a good-quality civic life. Enabling people to pick and choose at their convenience between options in these amenities misses the possibility that full participation in the public life of a city, or a whole society, might require just such an infrastructure, and sharing a set of public services might be an essential element in trust between citizens, and the maintenance of a democratic political culture.[14]

Fourth, the idea of 'community', though it is widely given lip-service in public policy worldwide, may be problematically related to the availability of public and commercial services, which supply many of the needs met by kinship, neighbourhood and association in societies with fewer such services. Even if it is in principle quite possible for services to complement and enhance informal interactions and voluntary organizations, unless this is a specific goal of public policy they may have the opposite effects. So, for example, even though the idea of 'social capital' (norms and networks of reciprocity and trustworthiness which promote both the economy's efficiency and democratic participation[15]) is very fashionable in public policy, its adherents have done little to show how a particular configuration of staffing or practices, or of relationships between services, might promote such social interactions in populations.

In fact, the dominant approach to public policy, derived from the affluent Anglophone countries, draws heavily on the economic theories of public choice and contract, uses cost-benefit analyses in the assessment of how particular proposals might contribute to overall welfare, and deploys social capital analyses to explain a residual category of factors, not adequately addressed by these practices.

For example, in the provision of certain services to marginal and deprived groups in affluent countries, or the rural districts of developing ones, voluntary agencies (Non-Government Organizations – NGOs) are favoured as the most suitable to reach out to such populations. But the model adopted by both the Anglophone governments and the World Bank[16] relies on tightly defined contracts for the provision of specified services, with detailed targets and outcomes, in order to promote the adaptation of such groups to markets and business-like government agencies. The 'social capital' which is built by such interventions is valued to the extent that marginal groups and communities are made better able to participate in those systems.[17]

In this chapter, I shall argue that, in order to fix social policy in relation to services, it is necessary to develop an approach to all these issues which recognizes that social interactions must be valued in a way of their own. To take advantage of the benefits of interdependence, this 'social value' should inform policy decisions. Only by balancing the economic value which is used to measure welfare[18] with this measurement of the key components of well-being will quality of life be sustained.[19]

I shall suggest that social interactions produce and distribute social value (both positive and negative) because the need to communicate and co-operate in groups and communities requires emotional support, interpersonal esteem (or respect) and the sense of belonging (or membership).[20] Analyses of the benefits of interdependence are incomplete without taking account of these essential elements in interactions.

The maintenance of interdependence also requires negative interactions (rejections, sanctions, exclusions), which must be counted among the costs of social life. This means that isolation, shame, stigma and conflict should be part of the analysis of the costs of policies, along with gains in overall welfare.

The means by which social value is produced and distributed are *cultures*.[21] These provide the resources through which interactions create this form of value, and also the restraints which limit approved actions and interactions. In other words, as well as enabling the benefits of interdependence, cultures supply the 'internal regulation' in families, groups, associations, organizations and political societies.

Cultures complement contractual systems of regulation (external regulation) through rules, conditions and penalties.[22] Again, policy should seek to balance internal and external methods of regulation.

Under the influence of the economic theories of public choice and contract, the dominant Anglophone model has imposed contractual systems on every formal collective unit in society. This has undermined cultures of interdependence, and hence the bases of the support, respect, loyalty and solidarity they sustained. In recent years, various scandals over corrupt, opportunistic or reckless behaviour in established organizations (such as game shows and competitions on the BBC, or spin by politicians, as well as greedy gambling by bankers) have led to calls for 'culture shifts' in these organizations. But the argument I shall present is that these fatal flaws will not be fixed unless the significance of cultures, and of the value they enable, can be properly analysed and included in the policy decision-making process.

This is particularly clear for services, since most of them intrinsically involve interactions between staff and service users, where support, esteem and the sense of belonging are at stake.[23] Services both provide an infrastructure for collective life, and enable actual communications between interdependent populations. Hence they are very important factors in the supply of cultural resources, for interpersonal, communal and political relations.

The individualistic, calculative, materialistic and instrumental nature of social relations in affluent Anglophone societies can largely be attributed to the dominance of the model derived from economic theory, and especially from the contractual approach to regulation within and between organizations. It undermines and subverts the cultures of support, care, loyalty and commitment which are intrinsic to good-quality human service provision. It also damages democratic civic culture, and squanders opportunities for public services to enhance participation and solidarity between groups.

I shall argue that public policy should find ways to promote well-being by including social value in cost-benefit assessments for new initiatives.[24] It should consider the whole context of the collective life of a society, and look for ways of enabling cultures of inclusion and justice to flourish, through the design of services.

Objective well-being and need

One possible response to the crash is that it clarifies the continued reality of vulnerabilities, insecurities and deprivations which were masked by the brittle prosperity of the bubble years. On this analysis, just as rising unemployment all over the world reveals the need for reliable income redistribution systems, so the collapse of public–private partnerships in social housing, the fall in demand for fee-paying education and the pressure on health care services of all kinds, all demonstrate the case for more encompassing, comprehensive public services.

But – even if such expansions of state provision could be

justified in terms of the fiscal stimulus and additional employment they would give – there are important questions about the longer-term rationale for these measures. Would the aim be to 'target' particular sections of the population, such as frail elderly people in need of social care, who are most obviously adversely affected by the crash in England, where their savings make them ineligible for state assistance, but give them no actual income to buy care (with interest rates near zero)? Or would governments aim to identify common interests in universal services (such as preventive health measures, public transport schemes or improvements in city infrastructures)? Or would they increase staffing ratios or modernize buildings within existing service facilities?

Under the orthodoxy which prevailed in the affluent Anglophone countries up to the crash, governments had a duty to minimize the costs of interdependence, and maximize the scope for individual choice over collective goods and services. The former principle implied that commercial firms should be involved in the supply of schools, hospitals and care facilities, social housing and infrastructure, both as financial investors and as managers. If they could fund these services more adequately from private sources than was possible through tax revenues, and if they could give better value for taxpayers' money through efficient management, this improved efficiency in the economy as a whole,[25] even where the government had to play an overall role in ensuring optimal provision of the collective service in question.

The second principle indicated that these same facilities were more beneficial to individuals (in terms of their gains in utility through the use of services) if they could group themselves with others of their choosing in residential districts, and into the memberships of specific school, hospital, care and housing service users. Because it was more efficient to allow these amenities to specialize, and to cater for particular preferences, the option to select among alternatives increased the satisfactions of most of those able to choose in these ways.[26]

But the whole idea of utility-maximization which underpinned these approaches to public policy over collective life assumed that individuals' satisfactions could not be compared with each other.[27] In the microeconomic analysis which had prevailed throughout the twentieth century, each person had a preference for one bundle of goods and services over another, but there was no way of measuring or ranking one person's satisfactions against another's. The principles outlined above not only dealt in individual preferences; they also discounted or ignored such factors as envy, shame, stigma and exclusion, and the stresses of competition for prestigious, 'positional goods', such as elite school and university places.[28]

The discovery that satisfactions themselves could be researched, and that this yielded consistent, durable results, comparable between individuals and communities, across a range of activities and experiences[29] allowed a group of economists and economic psychologists to argue that public policy *could* identify rules and interventions to achieve 'the greatest happiness of the greatest number'.[30] Instead of extending rivalry and exclusion to the public sector, this new 'science of well-being'[31] could allow governments to identify and pursue 'the common good' in fields of human interdependence.

This was because, with comparability of well-being data on individuals' *overall* satisfactions, and trade-offs between different dimensions of satisfaction,[32] these economists argued that they could 'deal with satisfactions as with other economic variables and . . . may use them in econometric analyses in almost the same way as "objective" variables'.[33] In principle, money values could be assigned to losses and gains in well-being, to calculate compensations for social costs and benefits.

Richard Layard has seized upon this opportunity to argue

for specific approaches to social policy which incorporate these methods. He claims that the phenomenon of 'stalled well-being' (the flat-lining of self-assessed overall satisfactions despite the rise in incomes in affluent countries over thirty or forty years[34]) can be attributed to three basic causes. These are: the negative effects of comparing our incomes with those of more prosperous others; adaptation to improved standards of material comfort; and the effects of our social environments and cultures.[35]

This leads him to make a whole range of social policy recommendations, including taxes to reduce rivalry-induced excessive work effort, selective reductions in performance-related incentive schemes in human services, improved education and training, better support for parenting, reduced mobility (including stronger immigration controls) and increased spending on mental health services.[36] The rationale for all of these is 'to maximize the sum of (cardinal) utilities, with additional weight being given to those whose utility is low'.[37]

Far from weakening the grip of economic analysis on public policy decisions, this 'new science' would therefore make such issues into technical ones, which, once general normative guidelines were in place (such as the weighting referred to), could be determined using statistical data. This objective approach to the common good sees cultures and beliefs as part of the problem to be overcome, rather than a potential resource for the social value which constitutes well-being.

An alternative basis for the reorientation of policies towards well-being is the one which seeks to identify the 'central capabilities' of all human beings – things that people are actually able to do, which 'have value in themselves, in making the life that includes them fully human'.[38] This rejects the idea that quality of life can be derived from individual preferences, or analysed in terms of gains in utility, in favour of a list of the features of a good life, which in turn make a good society.

This is the approach taken by Martha Nussbaum, who borrows the idea of 'capabilities' from Amartya Sen,[39] but goes further than him in insisting that public policy cannot be properly based on the 'subjective welfarism' of aggregated individual preferences. She argues that the 'basic social minimum' providing respect and dignity can be drawn from a list which includes life, bodily health, bodily integrity, imagination and thought, emotions, practical reason, affiliation, other species and control over one's political and material environment – central capabilities.[40] From these can be inferred *universal*, cross-cultural standards for quality of life, i.e. living 'as a thinking being, not just a cog in a machine, and . . . capable of being . . . with and towards others in a way which involves mutual recognition and humanity'.[41]

Nussbaum's moral and political theory is supposed to provide the basis for the value of each individual and the context of rights – ultimately of political justice. But in arguing that the 'subjective welfarism' of individual preferences cannot supply such a basis, and that her version of the good life avoids the 'Platonism' of an imposed regime for the good society[42] she also rejects the 'relativism' associated with cultural analysis. Her universal principles are taken to apply across the diverse, changing and dynamic standards and practices of cultures,[43] in which diversity itself has value, and provide 'a moral conception selected for political purposes only'.[44]

In addressing the questions posed at the start of this section, this approach would seem to offer general guidance on how to fix social policy for public services in the aftermath of the crash. Instead of pandering to individual preferences in the attempt to increase aggregate utility, or offering firms opportunities for profits through efficiency gains, governments should focus on improving the 'basic social minimum' enjoyed by all citizens, through health care, education, housing and social rights, as well as environmental improvements.

But this does not accord well with the data on people's self-assessed well-being. It is not just income that has risen dramatically in the affluent countries since the Second World War – so has the provision of welfare services of all kinds. Furthermore, there have been important gains in rights towards equality and full participation by women, gay people, disabled people, minority ethnic people and so on. Yet these gains have not been reflected in levels of subjective well-being (SWB), in either Europe or North America.[45] Indeed, gains have been far greater in poorer countries with fewer services, and the 'central capabilities' approach does not explain the high position of states like Mexico, Ghana, Bhutan and Vanuatu in league tables of SWB.[46]

My analysis of how to fix social policy draws on insights from both Layard's utilitarianism and Nussbaum's Aristotelianism. But it does not settle on either of these as a satisfactory basis for policy decisions. The idea of a return to Bentham would give far too much power to government technocrats, manipulating large databases about people's subjective preferences. Going back to Aristotle (or to Beveridge) would risk missing an opportunity to learn from the failures of policy and practices in public services since the Second World War, and to gain new insights into the nature and purposes of services for quality of life.

The nature of services

The impact of the recent economic crisis has been most extensive in services, which is why it has affected affluent societies, which have evolved into service economies, so adversely. As global manufacturing activity has shifted to China, Brazil, India and many other developing countries in Asia and Latin America, rich economies have come to trade in financial and business services, research and development technologies, professional and expert services, and also health and education services.[47] Indeed, one of the targets for the newly founded World Trade Organization in the 1990s was to reduce barriers to trade in services, and specifically in what had previously been regarded as public social services.[48]

Yet services have always been regarded as secondary features of economic life. In simple societies, 'services' are regulated purely culturally; they consist of those interactions, involving family, kinship, clan, tribe and society, in which tradition and custom indicate how individuals should show their concern, respect and honour for each other, and their sense of belonging to the group as a whole. Chiefs, priests and elders did not 'provide public services', they held feasts and ceremonies which – often through reciprocal giving of gifts – signified the ritual order of social relations.[49] Other interactions which in rich societies are carried out by firms or public agencies were performed as parts of the everyday cultural life of such communities, seen as sacred, and required by deities, by ancestors and by nature itself.[50]

There are two points of importance here. The first is that people are no less in need of recognition, affirmation and appreciation now than they were in those societies. The value we put on ourselves and others is still conveyed in a face-to-face way, through interactions in various social roles, both formal and informal. Sociologists from Durkheim[51] to Goffman[52] have pointed out how modern societies, through the processes of transformation from hunting and gathering to specialization and stratification of functions, still retained cultural systems through which to produce, communicate and distribute esteem, worth and status (as well as stigma, shame and sanction). But these ideas and images also inform the production and exchange of material goods. As Mary Douglas put it: 'Whenever consumption goods change hands, someone is communicating with someone else. Commodities define social categories. . . . We define inclusive and exclusive categories by rules about degrees of sharing and giving of commodities'.[53]

What has changed in modern societies is that it is increasingly now the individual who is regarded as sacred, not the group, the social role, or the natural order.[54] So the sense of meaning and value which is attributed to communications of ritual significance concerns identity, rights and choices; even contracts themselves are regarded as sacred.[55] The culture of celebrity takes this to extremes; it becomes part of the expectation of younger people, even those with little talent, to be regarded as special and chosen by others. Game shows on TV exploit these unachievable fantasies, even revelling in the humiliation of some of the losers.

Clearly the development of commercial services has tended to reinforce the transformation from traditional to modern cultures. First the rich, and then the middle classes, used paid services of many kinds, to bolster their sense of individual importance and achievement, as much as for their comfort and convenience. In recent years, a whole range of services previously regarded as luxuries – everything from restaurants and hotels to spas and therapies – has become available to a majority of the populations of affluent countries, and has further accentuated the individualization of value within a market-driven culture. But both the culture of self-realization and the economic sustainability of such ephemeral enterprises are brittle and fragile.

This links with the second important point about services in economic thought which is relevant to the current crisis. Ever since Adam Smith, services have been treated as less essential parts of an economy, because they cannot be re-used, saved or converted into other goods and services – they are 'consumed in the moment of their production'.[56] Surprisingly, this same feature is taken to distinguish services from commodities in modern microeconomic theory.[57] But, whereas Smith's description of service workers, from the monarch and the judiciary to 'opera singers and buffoons',[58] as 'unproductive labourers' cast them as a burden on the productive economy, today's services are seen as essential for employment, and hence prosperity. Indeed, it has been the ability of the affluent Anglophone countries to generate more jobs in the commercial services (especially 'flexible', part-time and low-paid work, taken by women and young people) that has distinguished them from Japan and the Continental European economies,[59] and had been claimed to constitute one of their main successes up to the crash.

So the issues about services confronting governments after the crash are whether the existing configuration of commercial enterprises is conducive to the best possible quality of life (does it underpin a sustainable set of social relations, and support a culture of well-being?), and whether it reflects a sustainable allocation of material resources, consistent with overall economic efficiency. These are specially important questions for the USA and UK, where the commercialization of social interactions of all kinds has been furthest developed.

The economic model examined in the previous chapter prescribed this approach to services, because of two interlocking features of its theories. On the one hand, its proponents insisted that the individual must always be the basic unit of analysis in political decisions as well as in markets. The Austrian and Chicago Schools, which led the neo-liberal revolution in public policy in the 1970s and 1980s, insisted on rejecting any form of collective entity from their model, whether this was the class theories of Marx, the organic view of societies in Idealism, or the aggregates postulated by Keynes: '[W]e are left with a purely individualistic conception of the collectivity. Collective action is viewed as the action of individuals when they choose to accomplish purposes collectively rather than individually, and the government is seen as nothing more than the set of processes, the machine, which allows such collective action to take place'.[60]

This strict methodological individualism was applied to the public sectors of welfare states, to show that autonomous individuals could (and should) choose the means of satisfying their private desires, including the systems through which they agreed to be ruled and to share certain goods and services collectively.[61]

Turning back to the theories of Knut Wicksell[62] at the end of the nineteenth century, they identified ways in which the principles of self-rule (sovereignty) and political consent could be combined, so that individuals chose which kind of membership organization to join, at what level of contribution (or tax rate), for which collective goods.

The result has been that, starting in the USA and UK, but spreading all over the world, there has developed a dominant orthodoxy on citizenship and government, which prescribes the diversification and privatization of services previously unified in the public sphere. Wherever interdependency provided cost-savings (and hence efficient supply), individuals who were assumed to be mobile between options and between districts were to be enabled to sort themselves into both organizations for the supply of services[63] (i.e. schools, hospitals, care homes, housing associations) and jurisdictions (localities, cities).[64] Efficiency gains were possible in the model because suppliers could charge the appropriate fee for services, or tax for local infrastructures, excluding those unable to pay – and leaving the worst-off in concentrations of low-quality provision for all their needs.[65]

So the public choice agenda gave governments a version of citizenship (a contract between self-responsible individuals and the institutions for maximizing their freedom to choose between such options), and the blueprint for an infrastructure of services, in which the public sector played a largely residual role. In the UK, only the National Health Service and compulsory schooling retained some features of the universalism which had been the hallmark of welfare states, but even within these every effort was made to provide scope for individuals to switch and shift between hospital trusts and self-governing schools, as the model required.

All this transformed the nature of services as well as the way they were supplied. It assumed that people had preferences for the acquisition of knowledge and skills, or the treatment of illnesses, or assistance with daily living, which were independent of any particular set of personal commitments, social bonds or political values. Their needs for the services of a teacher, a nurse or a care assistant were no different in kind from their choices of a fitness coach, a hairdresser or a financial adviser. In both kinds of issues, the expertise of the service provider was deployed to enhance the independence and self-fulfilment of the individual, either through attendance at a shared facility (modelled as a 'club'), or through one-to-one interaction.

The recent economic crisis allows this understanding of services to be questioned. Derived from the notion of independent and self-responsible individuals, pursuing their projects for self-realization through bank credit, it seriously under-estimated the extent of our interdependence as members of 'communities of fate', rather than in units or jurisdictions of choice. The financial crash demonstrated that people were bound together by their collective indebtedness; in the extreme case, Icelanders found that, as their banks collapsed, they were all in the same sinking ship. It was not a question of consenting to pay the taxes for their collective infrastructure, but of being part of a national struggle to regain collective solvency.

But equally important is the question of whether the use of

services is appropriately modelled as a visit to a spa, a beauty parlour or an accountant. As I argued in the first part of this section, services replaced the interactions through which the social order was created, sustained and modified (or negotiated) in traditional societies.[66] If they do not allow the members of modern societies to achieve the same purposes, to create, maintain and occasionally transform their collective lives, then the resources for achieving a good quality of such life will be impoverished.

The organization of services

The idea that social policy can be fixed by pumping more material and human resources into services has been dented by the economic crash. In several ways, that crisis has shown that the organization of services is part of the problem manifested in the crash. This is mainly because the root cause of the crisis, the contract model of governance, has deeply affected how services have been organized.

Confusingly, many of these scandals were coming to light in the UK at exactly the time of the crash, even though their origins pre-dated it. They were not a direct result of the shortage of credit or of government deficits, but of the application of the same economic principles which underlay the crash.

Examples from the UK illustrate this. As the crisis unfolded, it became clear that several of the enormous computerization projects, under which the government was attempting to accumulate the data to manage immigration, health care and education, had vastly overrun their budgets and their timetables,[67] and were therefore threatening the precarious public finances, just as fiscal deficits were escalating. These programmes were necessary for the contract approach to services, so that particular aspects of service requirements could be identified, contracted out and monitored, and so that these fragmented systems could in turn be co-ordinated (for instance, NHS patient records shared between the 'trusts' which supplied care).

Another instance concerned the contracting out of statutory tests (SATS) in schools, where the failure of the international company to supply the results of fourteen-year-olds led to its loss of a contract, and to the whole system being overhauled, with that set of tests abandoned.[68] Yet another showed up where the company contracted to pay grants to students in further and higher education failed to identify and pay a large proportion of them during the autumn term of 2008.[69]

A second set of scandals concerned the avoidable suffering and unnecessary deaths of patients in NHS hospitals, arising from the mismanagement of staffing and treatment resources. Although in a period of a few weeks there were instances involving children's facilities in Birmingham and old people's in Portsmouth, the most notorious of these scandals was that of the Mid-Staffordshire Hospital Trust. There it was revealed that the management, in search of the more generous funding which accompanied 'Foundation Hospital' status, had cut back the staff coverage of Accident and Emergency and some other wards to such an extent that is led to a decline in standards of care and safety which was estimated to have caused some 400 fatalities (see pp. 95–7).

A third set of problems was more directly linked to the collapse of bank credit. Under the neo-liberal regime of Margaret Thatcher, the construction and management of social housing had been entrusted to housing associations, which were to enter into partnership with commercial developers in their tasks; these arrangements were enthusiastically expanded under New Labour's regeneration, and other, initiatives. However, just when private house building projects were withering, and where the government social housing programme was most needed to provide a stimulus, these contractual arrangements put a locking brake on such developments. Resources were tied up in existing contracts which had run into trouble, and commercial partners were not willing to enter into new contracts with housing associations because of bank credit restrictions and their other financial problems during the crash.[70]

A fourth set of issues was revealed when it emerged that charities, local authorities and pension funds had lost money in the collapse of Icelandic banks.[71] Because they were encouraged or required to get the highest returns available on any funds they were holding, all these organizations had subscribed to the approach taken by the banks themselves – the risky search for quick gains, using others' resources. Because all were involved in social policy provision, either directly or under contract, this too had adverse effects on people in need of services. In the USA, charities also lost money in the Madoff affair, for the same reasons.

The origins of all these problems can be traced to the approach to the organization of services that was taken under the influence of the economic theories outlined in the previous section – methodological individualism, the sovereignty of the individual citizen-taxpayer, public choice, mobility between options, club theory and contract theory. The goal of the reforms of public sectors initiated by the neo-liberal regimes of the USA and UK in the 1980s, but pursued with renewed vigour by Third Way regimes in the following two decades, and influencing the World Bank and eventually the rest of the world, was to transform the collective infrastructure of services to meet consumer preferences.[72]

In order to achieve this, units of service of all kinds had to be identified and costed, so that suppliers – commercial, public and voluntary – could draw up business-like budgets, both to manage their own resources efficiently, and to charge each other for their activities. Second, the outcomes of each unit service had to be quantified and measured, so that targets could be set, and outcomes evaluated; this ensured 'best value', whichever type of organization provided the service.[73] Third, managers had to be in control of budgets and activities, to ensure that resources were deployed efficiently; the organization of services was to reflect managerial rather than professional or bureaucratic priorities.[74] Fourth, government was to set standards, targets and guidelines about what services were supposed to achieve, and how, and delegate performance to managers, under contracts.

Since the mid-1980s, these principles have led to the transformation, not merely of every level of the organizations supplying services, but of the cultures and practices of the staff who work in them. On the one hand, professionals and other practitioners have become answerable to managers and accountants for all their activities, in terms of externally defined targets and standards, set out in quasi-contractual terms. Notoriously, there have been many examples of perverse incentives, leading to wasteful use of resources, or of subversive compliance, where important needs have been neglected in favour of trivial ones which met contractual requirements. For example, a businessman who investigated his local hospital for a TV programme in the UK found that operating theatres were often left unused for parts of the week because of such perverse effects.[75]

On the other hand, staff have also adapted their practices to fit the model. Because contractual and managerial regulation substitute targets and checklists for professional judgement and cultures of learning, care and mutuality, staff have become adept at performing according to these externally imposed systems.[76] They have ensured that they met the targets and achieved the standards, at least on paper. In the UK, the scandal over the death of Baby P in Haringey, despite over sixty contacts with health and social services (see pp. 100–3), was reinforced by the revelation that the management had achieved a three-star rating from the government inspectors of children's services (Ofsted) during the period all this was happening.[77]

Furthermore, the theory which underpinned practice was also transformed in line with this new model of service organization. The expertise required for teaching, medicine and social work was broken up into 'competences', which could be taught, replicated and tested. The whole curriculum of education and training was redrawn, to focus on these practical performances, with underlying principles (both ethical and interactional) deployed to inform competences, rather than discussed for their wider moral, political and social implications. The whole approach to policy and practice – 'evidence-based programmes'[78] – was cast in terms of quantified analysis and outcomes, with more attention to technical, instrumental effectiveness, and less to social, relational and communicational consequences.

Examples of the failures of the contract approach

The Health Service

The application of the contractual approach to the NHS in the UK has led to a series of scandals in which the common theme has been that managers have focused on targets other than overall patient safety and well-being, for the sake of incentives offered through the government's funding system. The most notorious of these has been the case of the Mid-Staffordshire Hospital Trust, which illustrates most of the failings of the model.

Among the main recommendations of the investigation carried out in 2008 by the Healthcare Commission into the

Trust's mortality rates were that trusts should: 'identify when the quality of care provided to patients admitted as emergencies falls below acceptable standards and . . . ensure that a focus on elective work and targets is not to the detriment of emergency admissions';[79] 'ensure that a preoccupation with finances and strategic objectives does not cause insufficient focus on the quality of patients' care';[80] and 'ensure that systems for governance that appear to be persuasive on paper actually work in practice'.[81]

Since 2003, the Mid-Staffordshire Hospital Trust's mortality rates had been consistently higher than would have been expected. Between 2005 and 2008 the mortality rates in this Trust were between 27 and 45 per cent above the expected rates. This was first spotted by the Dr Foster Research Unit at Imperial College, London, in 2007, but in fact there had been patient complaints and the mobilization of an action group by bereaved families in the district long before the investigation was announced. The Commission received 99 critical responses immediately upon its announcement.[82]

The investigators found serious problems in the Accident and Emergency department of the hospitals, with too few nurses to carry out immediate assessments of the patients – some of whom waited in pain or with undressed wounds – and too few middle-grade doctors and consultants providing cover. There was pressure on staff to make rushed decisions to meet time targets, and some were not adequately trained to assess and care for those admitted as medical and surgical emergencies, or to read monitors. Poor records were kept of patients' intake of food and output of fluids.[83]

Medical emergencies were often nursed in non-specialist areas, because of a shortage of beds in the acute coronary unit, and relatives complained of lack of prompt attention to call bells and patients left in wet or soiled sheets, as well as dirty bathrooms: 'Nurses failed to conduct observations and identify that the condition of a patient was deteriorating, or they did not do anything about the results.'[84] Resuscitation arrangements were inadequate.

For surgical emergencies, there were no proper facilities for operations outside normal hours, and there was no trauma team in the Trust, and no system of priority for patients with traumatic injury for the one list for theatre at the weekend. Patients with a broken hip might therefore have to wait from Friday to Monday to have their operation. These patients were not allowed to eat or drink for many hours. There were many cases of death from deep vein blood clots, and the Trust did not have effective arrangements to deal with these, or comply with national guidance.[85]

The Commission's report was highly critical of the Trust's approach to its mortality rates, which were not sufficiently objective and robust, and to its governance and management of risk. Complaints about neglectful practice from patients and relatives were disregarded, having been classified as 'communication' or 'quality of care'. No information on clinical outcomes went to the Trust's board until after the Dr Foster unit had raised its concerns. The investigation revealed that, in a survey in 2006, only 27 per cent of staff said they would be happy to be cared for at the Trust, compared with 42 per cent nationally.[86]

In tracing the origins of this mismanagement, the report concluded that, although the board claimed its top priority was the safety of patients, the evidence suggested that its real top priority was the achievement of Foundation Hospital status, in order to gain extra funding, despite having a surplus in 2006–7: 'The trust set a target of saving £10 million, including a planned surplus of £1 million. This equated to about 8% of turnover. To achieve this, 150 posts were lost.'[87]

> It was clear from the minutes of the trust's board that it became focused on promoting itself as an organization, with considerable attention given to marketing and public relations. It lost sight of its responsibilities to deliver acceptable standards of care to all patients admitted to its facilities. It failed to pay sufficient regard to clinical leadership and to the experience and sensibilities of patients and their families.[88]

Perhaps the most damning fact for the government's system of inspection, accreditation and finance was that this business-like approach by the Trust was successful in gaining it Foundation Hospital status. At the very time that its board was letting patients die unnecessarily, its image and funding were being enhanced by this prestigious award from the authorities.

Another disturbing aspect was the failure of professionals to protest about the sufferings of patients. But here again, it seems as if the contract model encourages staff to exercise 'exit' rather than 'voice' options in the face of bad standards in their own organizations. Doctors and nurses are the largest professional groups subscribing to private health insurance schemes.

Further education colleges

Another aspect of the contract model is best illustrated by the establishment of large-scale quangos to manage the planning and financing of aspects of the public sector. The aim of these was partly to insulate these matters from political pressures, but mainly to implement the contract model of commissioning and public–private partnerships which has been the hallmark of New Labour administration. The approach has meant that these aspects can be conducted at 'arm's length' from the ministries which exercise overall supervision, and hence also at one remove from political responsibility.

The Learning and Skills Council (LSC) was established as

one of these organizations, and was reckoned to be the largest quango in Europe. In March 2009, the news broke that 144 further education colleges faced insolvency because their rebuilding programmes, given approval by the LSC, could not after all be confirmed. Of these, 80 had gone on to plan, prepare and commission the work, a requirement for final approval, and so had spent an average of £1 million each. Some had demolished buildings so as to be ready to start work the day after the final approval, another requirement.[89]

When interviewed, the Education Minister said that these approvals had all been 'in principle' only, and that the money was not now available. Subsequently, the head of the LSC resigned, but later gave a recriminatory account of the whole story to the House of Commons committee, saying that the Minister had made up recollections of meetings which had never taken place, in order to portray him as complacent and out of touch.

All this looked like part of the increasing evidence of failure among various initiatives involving private finance, which had stalled as a result of the collapse in bank credit. This had badly affected the building plans of housing associations, required to include private developers in their schemes. In spite of this fall-off, 600 Private Finance Initiative projects had already run up public indebtedness of £240 billion which would take the taxpayer forty years to repay.[90]

It was also very bad timing, since there was every prospect of an increase in recruitment for college courses through the absence of jobs for school leavers following the crash. And it came hard on the heels of a fiasco over allowances for sixteen- to eighteen-year-olds, with long delays in assessments and payments the previous autumn, when the private agency contracted for the task proved incompetent to perform it.

However, it later emerged that the LSC had in fact been scheduled to be closed down during the summer of 2009, as a result of a hasty decision made by the government in March 2008, just before the Budget. Its powers were to be passed to two new organizations, the Skills Funding Agency and the Young People's Learning Agency. Local authorities would also assume some of the LSC's functions.[91]

This major reorganization was being so hurriedly under-taken that large-scale waste would result, simply from the costs associated with vacating the LSC's premises. Only nineteen of the fifty buildings occupied by the LSC would be required by the new agencies. The leases on the other thirty-one premises involved the payment of substantial sums to terminate agreements. In the case of the LSC's office at St Albans, Hertfordshire, a building accommodating just thirty-two people will cost £12.5 million to give up, because the lease runs until 2018. The total national cost of terminating these agreements has been estimated at £42 million.

Among the LSC's staff of 3,100, 1,000 would be required to transfer to local authorities – a shift only 7 per cent of them were reported to be willing to make. The government faces strong resistance to compulsory transfers, including the pos-sibility of industrial action.[92]

Child protection

The final example concerns the attempt to manage tasks, involving the exercise of professional judgement and the negotiation of interpretations of evidence between profes-sions, by checklists of risk factors, electronic records and formal processes. The child protection system established under the model attempts to reduce the uncertainties which are notorious in a field where abusive parents aim to mislead officials, but are often themselves needy and the former victims of abuse.

The model seeks to introduce the benefits of information from research into the decision-making process, but has done so against a background of inadequate resources and problems of recruitment and retention of experienced social work staff – partly because these systems themselves have made the work stressful and hazardous for practitioners. The idea behind the model is that better information leads to safer and more efficient outcomes, but the tasks of filling in electronic forms and writing reports have overwhelmed face-to-face practice.

All this was made tragically clear from the case of Baby P in Haringey, London, when his mother, her boyfriend and another man were convicted of causing his death by repeated violence. In the media outcry which followed, shortcomings of every kind were found in the medical and police attention he received, as well as in the children's services which had been at the centre of the Victoria Climbié scandal only seven years earlier.

Baby P was well known to the child protection agencies; there had been sixty contacts in all. As well as being on the register of children at risk, and on the caseload of a social worker, there had been several inter-agency case conferences about him, three visits to hospital (one just before he died, when the doctor failed to recognize his broken back), and his mother was arrested twice (but not prosecuted).

It was not until six months after the convictions for the death of Baby P that his mother and the boyfriend stood trial over the rape of a two-year-old girl, of which he was convicted. It then emerged that senior staff in the social services department, who had always claimed that they were unaware of his presence in the flat, had in fact made a videotaped interview with the mother, in which she spoke quite openly about the relationship. This had never been reported to the police, so no checks on him were run, and this influenced the failure to prosecute her or remove the child.[93]

All this indicated a severe situation of mismanagement in all the major child protection agencies, and in relations between them. But perhaps the most disturbing revelations came after the first court case, when investigations revealed that around half the front-line social workers in Haringey were inexperienced, or subcontracted short-term by agencies, or both. Worse still, social workers from all over the country wrote to newspapers saying that similar situations existed in their authorities, that the risks to children were very high and that – even though they protested about the conditions under which they struggled daily – they were gagged from speaking out by their senior managers.[94]

Furthermore, many reported that they were hampered in any attempt to deal face-to-face with families and children by a new computerized assessment and recording system, which had cost £30 million to install nationally. The tasks associated with child protection cases were reckoned to take an average of 100 hours per child (including 10 hours for an initial assessment and 48 hours for a core assessment) on forms alone, and to occupy some 70 per cent of workers' time. A research report by academics at York University criticized the new system for 'obscuring the family context', and said that the level of detail demanded by ticking boxes 'sacrificed the clarity that is needed to make documentation useful'.[95]

But finally, and most damningly of all, it was also revealed that Haringey had been given a three-star ('good') rating by the inspectorate, Ofsted, at the very time of Baby P's suffering and death. In a hasty re-inspection in the wake of the first trial, it was re-assessed as 'unsatisfactory', and faults at every level of its organization were diagnosed. This led to the obvious conclusion that the paper exercises used by Ofsted could easily be fudged or falsified by the management of the local authority. Indeed Wes Cuell, the Acting NSPCC Director, later commented that there was no correlation between the star ratings and the actual death rates of children from abuse, and that 'performance data in children's services are unreliable and in some cases inaccurate'.[96]

Indeed, the Baby P case raised national concerns (yet again) about the priority given to child protection, and the effectiveness of the approaches used at every level of the system. Despite a huge increase in spending on services since the Maria Caldwell case in the early 1970s, death rates from abuse had not been reduced. The chair of the House of Commons Committee on Children, Schools and Families, Barry Sheerman, accused the Chief Inspector of Schools of complacency when she gave evidence to the Committee showing that three children a week had died in the previous year, far higher than earlier estimates.[97] Among the new measures introduced was a 'hotline' for whistleblowers, concerned about risks and standards in their authorities.

The child protection system was really a testbed for many of the ideas about data collection and information management at the heart of the contract model. It had been overhauled after the report on the death of Victoria Climbié, and indeed Haringey, where that tragedy occurred, was a kind of symbol of the new order. The case therefore signalled the failures of the model in this area of human services.

Services, relationships and cultures

For services to make the best possible contribution to the quality of life of populations, they need to enable positive social relations. As I have argued in this chapter, this means that they must promote interactions which give rise to social value – intimacy in close relationships, friendships, kinship, neighbourliness, association, community spirit and democratic participation.[98] The current organization of services in the USA and UK, with its emphasis on procedural effectiveness, economic efficiency and managed objectives, externally regulated in line with a contractual approach, does not even attempt to address people's broader needs for affirmation, or society's for an inclusive culture of belonging. In the emphasis given to individual choice and diversity of options, policy reinforces the dominant culture of market consumerism and personal self-realization.

The founding figures of welfare economics and public finance recognized that government and its agencies, as well as churches and voluntary organizations, often had to offset the operation of markets and business efficiency, and sometimes even that of rational, prudent political economy, for the sake of moral, social and broader political goals. In this they were following Adam Smith,[99] who recognized cases – for instance, of national security – where such considerations had to be overruled. Pareto, whose principles are still applied to assessments of overall utility through cost-benefit analyses, considered that 'social utility' demanded attention to traditions and beliefs: 'The art of government lies in finding ways to take advantage of . . . sentiments, not wasting one's energies in futile efforts to destroy them – the sole effect of which is simply to strengthen them . . . Legislation can be made to work in practice only by influencing interests and sentiments'.[100]

A. C. Pigou, whose work on welfare economics was a strong influence on Beveridge, thought that 'economic welfare', derived from aggregate individual utility and measured in money, was only part of the overall well-being of society. 'Non-economic welfare' should take precedence in many political decisions, and 'economic science' was ill suited to addressing such issues: '[T]he effects of economic causes are certain to be partially dependent on non-economic circumstances, in such wise that the same cause will produce somewhat different effects according to the general character of, say, the political or religious conditions that prevail'.[101]

The idea that economic welfare and efficiency must always

be accountable to social and political standards prevailed in democratic political life until the upsurge of public choice theory in the 1960s and 1970s. The shift to a contractual model has left public policy on services without a moral and social compass, and unable to address issues of quality of life through institutional design or specific programmes.

Because there are no such principles to guide service provision, there can be no attempt to influence how social value is generated and distributed in social interactions. Because services are organized to maximize choices between options and ease of exit, they are not designed to foster loyalty or solidarity, or enduring forms of sharing.

Because they are regulated externally through contracts and targets, they are not organized in line with the practices that foster well-being through support, respect and belonging, nor do they generate internal cultures conducive to the well-being of their staff. Because staff do not feel properly valued, affirmed and enabled, and are not supported in the exercise of empathy or professional judgement, they in turn are less able to offer service users the cultural resources for a better quality of life.

It became a cliché during the period of scandals in UK public services in early 2009, given as examples in the previous section, to call for a 'change of culture' in the agencies under scrutiny. But this apparently vague term means something quite specific. It implies that, instead of trying to regulate the actions of staff, their interactions with citizens, and the citizens themselves, in line with the methods derived from theories of information, incentives and contracts, the government should recognize the need for standards and practices which work through direct processes of communication between all these people.

Cultures rely on the sense that such interactants make of their social world, and allow them to negotiate about how standards and expectations apply to particular situations. They make people accountable to each other in terms of the standards of empathy, respect and sense of membership that they hold to be due to one from another, and they create social value, as well as distributing it according to these standards. Unlike computerized data-gathering or ticking boxes, or the formalized methods of inspection and management favoured by the contract model, they require judgement and experience, as well as skills in interpersonal transactions

Social relations and well-being: the role of services

In order to fix social policy on services, so that they can better contribute to quality of life, it will be necessary to set them the overall goal of improving social relations. This entails adopting an institutional framework which is conducive to well-being, rather than one which is focused solely on how specific expertise or assistance, 'delivered' in 'packages' to individuals, in carefully measured and costed units, can increase what Pigou called their 'economic welfare' (utility), or improve their productivity and functioning as self-realizing, 'independent' agents.

An example which illustrates the change required is the finding, in a comparison of the well-being of children and young people in the twenty-five European Union member states, using available official statistics from government sources, that UK children were placed twenty-first, above only those of the three Baltic recent accession countries and Slovakia. Whereas the Scandinavian countries and the Netherlands were at the top of the league table, and the Mediterranean countries (including Slovenia, Malta and Cyprus) did surprisingly well in relation to their national incomes per head, the UK came at or near the bottom for relationships with parents and peers, and for risky behaviour, scores which offset its respectable performance on educational attainment.[102]

A later study, conducted under the auspices of the United Nations' children's organization, UNICEF, found that, among the affluent OECD countries of the world, the USA and UK were in the bottom two places for children's well-being.[103] What these countries had in common was a public policy environment in which competition and material success, along with earning and consumption, were given priority over stable and supportive relationships, equality, solidarity and social participation. In these ways, services accentuated features of the wider cultures of these countries which already moulded children's thinking and activities, and their experiences of the adult world.

This study gave rise to an eighteen-month inquiry into experiences of childhood in the UK, by a panel of experts chaired by Richard Layard, whose report was published in spring 2009. Confirming the findings of the previous research, the report blamed 'excessive individualism' – 'the belief that the prime duty of the individual is to make the most of her life, rather than to contribute to the good of others'.[104] They argued for parents and professionals in children's services always to ask themselves: 'What would we do if our aim was a world based on love?'[105] A good childhood demanded priority for relationships of respect and security.

But much the same conclusions can be drawn from the research evidence on the sources of adult well-being, which found that health, work satisfaction, close relationships, friendship networks and wider social participation were all more important for self-assessed well-being than the final third of people's incomes.[106] This would suggest that developing better communications with adults and peers, group interactions and play activities could all be important in preparing children for roles in which positive feelings, self-esteem, greater security, more reliable character and a stronger sense of belonging could lead to a higher quality of life, through better social relationships. At present, their experiences and aspirations, and the social environment in which they are raised, leave UK children vulnerable to disappointment and distress. The percentages of children experiencing behavioural and emotional difficulties doubled between 1974 and 1999.[107]

In my analysis of the bases for well-being, this reflects the lack of social value accruing to children in the UK through their daily lives. By social value, I mean the emotional closeness, affection, respect and sense of belonging they get through their interactions with all the others they encounter. This had a limited amount to do with the 'parenting skills' which are regarded as crucial by the UK government, or the educational standards set by the managers of their schools. It has much more to do with the cultural resources through which they communicate and act in their families and neighbourhoods, at school and in the wider public sphere. These cultural ideas, images and standards both enable and restrain the interactions within which social value is created (or destroyed by various kinds of rejection, stigma, cruelty, violence, isolation and exclusion).

Instead of reinforcing a market-driven public culture of materialism and celebrity, of rapid shifts between fluid membership groups with permeable boundaries, and hence of insecurity and potential marginality, services for children should seek to offset these features. They should promote ideas, images and experiences of reliable loyalty and concern, of commitment, of equality, and of persevering participation. If all service organizations, from toddler groups and nursery schools to colleges and universities, were to reflect such practices and standards in their cultures, staffing and organization, children and young people would be better equipped for the adult world, which in turn would provide a social environment more conducive to well-being.

This alternative approach could be fed by insights and perspectives from feminist theory and research on social relations and social policy. Feminists have long argued that the undervaluation of emotions, informal mutuality and communal life have stemmed from the subordination of women at the birth of capitalist modernity, and the relegation of their activities in caring for children, disabled and old people from the business of production and politics.[108] The social contract theories of that period, inscribing contractual relationships at the heart of modern societies, presented women and their roles as outside the worlds of property, trade, law, rights and justice, in a sphere of passion, disorder and volatility, subversive of good order,[109] and needing to be subject to men's reason and judgement.

In principle, therefore, the revaluation of these aspects of social relations, through the empowerment of women, should lead to improvements in the quality of life, and increased well-being. The rejection of individualistic rights-based, formal conceptions of the bases for growth in welfare (as gains in aggregate utility), and the adoption of nurture and support, along with active participation in community and democratic politics, should achieve these changes. The recognition of the value of women's unpaid activities, and of its characteristic 'ethic of care',[110] could make a major contribution to this shift in policy priorities.

However, as we have seen, although women have been rapidly drawn into the formal economy, and especially the service economy, under the neo-liberal and Third Way regimes of the 1980s and 1990s in the affluent Anglophone countries, the terms of this incorporation have been masculinist ones. Above all, the dominance of market and contractual principles, and of external regulation, managerialism and targets for practitioners, has meant that women have been required to perform in ways at odds with the standards and practices of the ethic of care. Indeed, as women have been promoted to managerial roles, they have become the bearers of the contract culture, and the enforcers of performance targets and the checklist approach to service 'delivery'.[111]

This outcome is not inevitable; other countries have included women into citizenship on terms far more suited to their ethics and cultures, and with better results. In the Scandinavian countries, women have participated in high proportions in labour markets, mainly in service roles, for longer than in the Anglophone countries. These countries have generously resourced public social services, and their ethos is universal, inclusive and supportive, especially of families and children. Accordingly, they have among the highest rates of self-assessed well-being, for adults and children, in the world.

This shows that services can provide the overall framework for a high quality of life, as well as specific contributions to health and well-being, and that women can play key roles in achieving these outcomes. In order to fix social policy, the contract approach to services should be replaced by one which allows an ethic of care and inclusion, and a culture of solidarity and support, to flourish.

Trust, participation and well-being

Just as research has identified personal and communal relations as very significant factors in well-being, so too it has pointed to active participation and democratic involvement in public life as important elements.[112] Here again, the dominant influences on public policy emanating from the USA and UK work against participation in groups and communities, even though this is a sub-theme of many policy documents. Because the primary goal is to create market-like options, for 'independent' individuals to choose between business-like schools, hospitals, care facilities and social housing, performing to specific targets under contractual conditions, often with private finance, or in partnerships with commercial suppliers, public and voluntary organizations are primarily responding to consumer-like demand. The idea that they should also engage with groups of service users,[113] or parents, or whole communities, inevitably takes second place.

In the UK, the concept of well-being has been incorporated into public policy rhetoric, especially in relation to the care of adults with disabilities and chronic illnesses, without definition. It stands for a combination of service 'delivery' for the sake of 'independence' and choice (for instance, contract carers for practical support with daily living needs), but also for 'service user involvement' in shared facilities.[114] These lofty goals are proclaimed without any recognition of the tension between the 'personalization agenda', which aims at allowing each eligible individual to assemble a 'package' of support, paid for out of an allocated budget, and the maintenance of relationships, networks and communities through regular interactions within a shared culture.[115] Research indicates that service users and carers are well aware of these tensions, especially when the requirement to individualize budgets is used as a reason to close down collective facilities, such as workshops and day centres.[116]

In the creation of cultures of mutuality, respect and sharing, issues of trust and participation are intertwined. Political and economic theorists are agreed that trust in specific others, sufficient to get the full benefits of interdependence, and the full social value of positive interactions, depends on reliable information.[117] This is time-consuming and demands communication and the effort to understand and co-operate. For these reasons, arrangements which require this kind of 'personalized trust' are regarded as 'second best' in terms of economic efficiency (i.e. overall maximization of utility).[118]

The combination of markets and an order of enforceable legal rights (of property and persons) is generally cheaper, in terms of transaction costs, leaving informal co-operation and sharing as a residual category of relations, for those who cannot afford commercial service contracts, or whose needs are too overwhelming or unpredictable.

This implies that informal care, and the types of interdependence which exist in groups and communities more generally, are at best supplementary or fallback arrangements. The ideal, even for people with serious disabilities, is to be able to work, earn and pay for services – hence the emphasis on getting disabled people of working age off benefits, and into employment, announced by the UK government just before the crash.[119] Individualized budgets try to mimic the situation of those with 'their own' money, by allowing them to employ carers, or purchase other facilities. The role of family carers, though given much rhetorical praise, is regarded with ambivalence in this model. For example, parents of young people with learning disabilities are often regarded as overprotective of their offspring, denying them the independence to make their own lives.[120]

Yet there is clear evidence that services can and do promote trust through participation and involvement, and that this creates cultures conducive to well-being. Market relations may be efficient, and contracts convenient (in terms of minimizing the costs of negotiation and surveillance), but this overlooks the value gained from a collective environment which is convivial, polite and friendly.[121]

Furthermore, once we recognize that much of the social value which produces high quality of life can only be sustained through the 'internal regulation' of cultures, within associations, organizations and districts, the time and energy given to this looks a good investment. For instance, staff in services and service users in schools, day and residential centres and therapeutic clinics can create better cultures for learning, support or treatment if they participate together and trust each other. Bowles and Gintis point out that

> Communities can sometimes do what governments and markets fail to do because their members, but not outsiders, have crucial information about others' behaviours, capacities and needs. . . . This insider information is most frequently used in multilateral rather than centralised ways, taking the form of a raised eyebrow, a kind word, an admonishment, gossip, or ridicule, all of which may have particular salience when conveyed by a neighbour or a workmate whom one is accustomed to call one of 'us' rather than them.[122]

They go on to point out that information-intensive team production is increasingly replacing assembly lines and other technologies more readily regulated externally, through contract or enforcement, and that 'difficult-to-measure services' increasingly make up the main components of advanced economies which previously dealt in kilowatts of power and tons of steel; accordingly, internal regulation and group sharing of risks through qualitative, cultural processes is increasingly appropriate.[123]

Yet the tendency in the governance of public human services in the affluent Anglophone countries is quite the opposite. The contract model relies on managerialist methods to maintain surveillance over practitioners, relying on electronic information technology. Staff, including highly skilled and experienced professionals, are required to complete computerized records, often in the form of checklists and spreadsheets. That this can be counterproductive was illustrated in the aftermath of the Baby P scandal in the UK. Social workers, who had had contacts with the family, were said to be spending more than half their working time filling in electronic records systems and providing data for management.[124]

Even though the voluntary sector in these services has been

more reluctant to introduce these methods, it has inevitably been affected by their requirements when organizations rely on funding from government contracts. Under these arrangements, staff are usually required to meet target outcomes, through costed inputs of services, and to provide evidence of effectiveness and efficiency. As a result, the organization and culture of charities and community groups in the UK, for example, are increasingly like that of public bodies, and they adopt the discourses of the contract approach into their work, along with its ethos and methods. Instead of representing a distinctive contribution to the development of services, using new methods, identifying new needs and introducing a critical voice to public debates, these organizations are being absorbed into the dominant machine, through contractual regulation.[125]

All this indicates the totalitarian reach of the economic ideas and methods derived from methodological individualism, public choice and contract theories. Their style of governance and administration breaks down the networks, norms and cultural resources of service staff, as well as service users, to enable both a consumerist menu for the public, and a managerialist approach to provision. Alternatively, of course, services can be given in very authoritative, formal and legalistic ways, under threat of sanctions, as in the administration of social assistance benefits and through workfare and welfare-to-work schemes, or some aspects of child protection work, where the distinctions between social support and criminal justice intervention become blurred.[126]

In order to try to fix these features, which are so damaging to the well-being of staff and service users, it will be necessary to draw on the reserves of active, participatory and self-regulating groups and communities, which survive largely in spite of the organizational transformations carried out by neo-liberal and Third Way governments. The collective life of such groupings has largely gone underground, or functioned outside or alongside the official agencies which reflect the dominant model. To fix policy on services, it is unlikely that a top-down set of measures will suffice; new approaches need to seek out and enable the expression of these alternative views and approaches, and build on their cultural resources (see pp. 206–9).

In this endeavour, the time and effort required for communication, shared information and, hence, the trust achieved through face-to-face interactions should be seen as well spent. Social value can be generated by these processes, even though they also potentially involve conflict and frustration. Participation, discussion and critical evaluation, involving a pooling of ideas and methods between staff and service users, should become the main means of maintaining standards, not an optional extra.

Two mechanisms would help to reverse the dominant trends since the early 1980s. Service managers and staff could be made accountable to service users, rather than to taxpayers and accountants, across a far wider range of activities and facilities. And grants to voluntary organizations and community groups could be deployed, in place of many of the restrictive contracts under which they have been tied to government policy goals.

Conclusions

The emergence of service economies in the affluent countries should have been an opportunity to improve the quality of life of their populations. Instead, under regimes reflecting the economic model of the USA and UK, well-being has not risen in line with increased income. I have argued that this is because services have largely reinforced the over-individualized, market-driven forces that make life stressful and people feel vulnerable, insecure or marginal.

Many of these features can be recognized in the dominant view of *time* in affluent countries. Just as capitalist production aims constantly to increase the productivity of time,[127] so ordinary people too perceive constraints of time as the determining factor in their decisions, in leisure, recreation and family life as well as at work. Economizing on time motivates styles of eating,[128] communicating and experiencing home life. Despite the fact that the price of services has constantly tended to rise, relative to that of manufactured commodities,[129] people have done less 'self-provisioning' and, especially since the 1980s, behaved as if the only scarce resource was the time available to them to achieve their ends,[130] consuming 'fast food', substituting counselling for friendship, taking part in 'speed-dating' and using mobile phones rather than meeting others. Hence services in particular come to be priced in terms of the time required to use them.

Making social interaction accountable to the calculus of time-productivity is clearly a powerful transformative influence on social relations. It constantly makes people count the costs of interdependence, and obscures its benefits. Above all, it hides the social value of relationships and communications within cultures in which the gains are intrinsic to the shared activities undertaken. This includes participation in many kinds of association and community projects, and indeed in democratic politics itself.

Services have been adapted to supply the infrastructure to support the lifestyle in which individuals constantly seek to realize themselves through 'projects of self'[131] – the development of credit-based consumption of goods and services, in order to fulfil one's personal identity and potential. Public policy has pursued a long-term trajectory, starting in the USA and UK, to adapt the infrastructure for such projects, and to ensure that services are appropriate for that ethos. The contract model of governance has been the means to that end.

But these processes, which erode cultures conducive to social value, and hence well-being, in service organizations and in society, can be halted and then reversed. The transformation of collective life has not been universal, and – outside the Anglophone countries – there are centres of resistance to it. For instance, the Scandinavian countries still devote far larger proportions of national resources to public services than do other countries of comparable income levels. The ethos promoted by these services, and within them, is intended to influence wider social relations, and to affect the whole political culture. It is no coincidence that the participation, commitment and solidarity generated within and through these services give rise to the highest levels of well-being,[132] and of trust between citizens,[133] in the world.

The big question raised by this chapter is how economic efficiency can be combined with improvements in well-being through public policy programmes, and through the design of institutions. Because of the dominance of the contract model of governance, and of the individualistic culture in collective life, I have emphasized the part played by economic theory in what's wrong with social policy. But I have probably not yet given a fully convincing account of an alternative.

For a model of how a very different approach might work, we need (I would argue) to turn to another sphere, where high finance, dynamic marketing and committed voluntary effort combine together to allow both profitable enterprise and cultures of well-being. Music and sport[134] are examples of activities which have all these features, because they are able to engage millions of people who value aspects of them enough to put time and energy into communities of appreciation and enjoyment. The collective life of music and sport transcends time constraints, because they are seen as intrinsically valuable by participants and spectators/audiences. They provide opportunities for entrepreneurial activity and prospects for profit, but the value of the activities and experiences themselves is always (in the last resort) paramount.

I shall return to the examples of music and sport in later chapters, because they seem to offer models of how services might combine highly paid and voluntary effort, and individual excellence with group and community endeavour. They also create cultural resources which span genders, faiths, ethnicities and nations; they are truly global in their reach.

In the next chapter, I shall analyse why social policy has been threatened by globalization, why the crash brings dangers of policies which are protectionist or xenophobic, and how social policy might be made more reconcilable with the forces for globalization.

4

Global social policy

The economic crash has drawn attention to the perils which have come with the integration of the world economy. The greed and dishonesty of bankers and financial market traders, mainly using instruments pioneered in Wall Street and the City of London, have brought about dramatic falls, first in stock markets and in the profits of financial service companies, and then in global output, income and employment.

Whatever the benefits bestowed by globalization during the boom years, the crash has reminded the whole world that economic interdependence without adequate institutions for sharing risks is a very fragile set of arrangements. Gordon Brown acknowledged, at the World Economic Forum on 30 January 2009, that what he had thought of as spreading risks worldwide turned out to be spreading contagion.[1]

Apart from poor and marginal people all over the world, the most obvious losers from the crisis have been national governments. Under the influence of the contract model of governance promoted by the USA, and by the international organizations (the IMF, World Bank and WTO), most of them had sold off their assets, and handed many of their powers to central banks, commercial companies or various 'arms'-length' regulatory bodies, during the years leading up to the crash.

For the traditional role of social policy, in protecting the citizens of nation states from the vagaries of world markets, redistributing income over the life-cycle and in favour of the most vulnerable, supplying basic education for all and pooling risks of illness and disability, all this has been damaging. During the years since affluent societies consolidated welfare states (in the 1960s), many of the equalities of rights and life chances, as well as overall standards of literacy and physical health, have been eroded.

In the developing world, some countries which had come close to the standards of developed ones in these respects (such as Sri Lanka and Argentina) have slipped back. Although new models of social policy development have come into being in Asia and parts of Latin America, almost the whole continent of Africa has experienced regimes of continual instability and insecurity for populations.[2]

Although it would be misleading to characterize the effects of globalization as a 'race to the bottom' in social protection,[3] the crash has exposed the weakening of national governments in the face of enormous, impersonal economic forces. As I argued in the introduction and chapter 1, monetary theory encouraged states to rely on international financial markets to iron out such features as budget and trade deficits over time. The failure of the whole global system of credit showed that economic tides which governments imagined they had harnessed to their purposes could easily engulf them, and leave them mastless and rudderless in a tempest-torn sea.

Indeed, so successful have these forces been in turning the world into 'one big market'[4] that national boundaries have become largely irrelevant, feeble barriers against international movements of money, technology and people, and (in the theory behind integration) minor distortions of the drive towards global efficiency. The crash merely illustrated their ineffectiveness; the agents who conjured up the bubble, unleashing the storm of its collapse, were both more powerful than governments, and operating largely in a zone beyond their ken.

Yet it has been governments that have had to try to rebuild national economies from the wreckage left by the crash, and the former 'masters of the universe' have been keen enough to accept the bailouts offered them. Overstretched as they have been, governments have ultimately had to bear the risks run by banks and hedge funds with their citizens' savings. They have also had to try to conserve the skills and work cultures of those citizens for the sake of future development, through expanded education and training during the rise in unemployment.

In this chapter, I shall analyse the systems of interdependence which have come into being through the period of global economic integration, to see how they contributed to the crash, how they influenced the institutions of national government, and what might be done to achieve reliable forms of transnational social policy systems. The attempt to reconstruct national control over capital flows, trade and production is at best futile, and likely to be counterproductive. But to establish effective institutions for international social justice and human development is an enormous challenge, at a time when the poorest people in the world are the main victims of the crash.

The processes of globalization which have taken place since the early 1980s have not lacked a theory of government to underpin them. The counterpart to public choice theory has been that of 'fiscal federalism'.[5] In this analysis, which again rests on methodological individualism, collective authority is created by mobile economic agents (people and firms), choosing to do things collectively on various scales, from the construction of new cities and the confederation of groups of nations to the creation of academies or medical insurance schemes. These 'clubs' and jurisdictions overlap, and the choice of size and unit, and whether it is functional or territorial, is made according to criteria of economic efficiency. Inevitably nation states have a residual role in this theory, as the historical legacy of a pre-global age. They pick up those functions which, for one reason or another, it is not optimal to run through larger territorial or smaller specialist units.

I shall argue that the crash has revealed the weaknesses of this approach, and the incomplete or misleading assumptions on which it is based. But the challenge of the crash is to find an alternative basis for public finance, which can mobilize people into convincing and sustainable forms of collective authority, which are capable of commanding loyalty and solidarity. These will not necessarily be welfare states of the old kind, since they no longer reflect the interdependences of an integrated world economy, nor do they represent a convincing version of global social justice.

The most obvious weakness of fiscal federalist theory is that it fails to account for those collective units and political movements which have nothing much to do with economic efficiency, and indeed which often come into being to resist the imposition of systems of authority derived from economic principles. In reaction against globalization and the contract model, all over the world the politics of faiths, blood and soil has re-emerged in various forms, to oppose the march of big money, big business, the rationalization of administrative boundaries or the destruction of natural environments.

This could be seen as a manifestation of Karl Polanyi's 'second movement'[6] – the attempt to defend various kinds of social arrangements for the creation and conservation of human value against the destructive power of capitalism and markets. As in the past, such diverse protests, movements and policies have no coherent logic or common theme, are frequently backward-looking and traditional, and are only sporadically successful, through an often chance combination of oddly matched forces. Although the attempt to restrain and direct the forces of economic integration relies on capturing and steering some of these forms of resistance, it requires a progressive and forward-looking dynamic of its own.

During the boom which led up to the crash, the most prominent of these movements was the Islamist one. Although the activities of Al Qa'ida, first in Afghanistan and then in Iraq and the cities of the West, were defined in terms of power politics, and often selected iconic targets, symbolic of economic globalization, other groups combined social provision with militant action. For instance, both Hisbollah in the Lebanon and Hamas in the Gaza Strip started out as organizations to assist poor and needy populations, and to give them better representation in resistance politics. Since the crash, resistance to globalization has spread throughout the world, and includes workers' rebellions and protests to protect their employment, or to gain access to jobs taken by internal migrants or foreign labour.

So in every region of the world there are groups and movements fighting rearguard actions on behalf of beleaguered communities, or asserting the claims of ethnicities or local loyalties, against the 'rationalization' of collective life. In the economic analysis of such actions, they either embody the attempt of fading interest groups to cling on to property and power, or the misguided efforts of those who relied on outmoded methods for survival to defend these against a future which offers them far better long-term prospects.

In only one respect does the dominant approach to collective authority recognize a positive contribution by traditional, communal social relations. It does acknowledge that there are circumstances in which very marginal populations are excluded from markets, and from the circuits of business-like government policies and agencies.[7] They may therefore need to be linked into these systems, to gain the benefits of globalization.

The key concept in the dominant model's analysis of these

issues is 'social capital'.[8] This is the pseudo-economic term for the social bonds between people through which they accomplish purposes collectively, experience their lives together and negotiate their identities and roles. Within the model deployed by the World Bank,[9] social capital is both what marginal communities have as the basis for their disadvantaged existence, allowing them to eke out a living on the fringes of the world economy, and what they need (in a different form) to enable them to join the mainstream. Indeed, social capital is the 'glue' which allows all collective units to function, and in this sense it is necessary for the efficient running of democratic political institutions,[10] so social capital can and should be complementary to the principles of fiscal federalism and public choice, supplying both the overall emulsion in which collective organizations perform smoothly, and the specific bonding between individuals to give such arrangements a desirable degree of stability.

I shall argue that this approach is inadequate and misleading. To install system of collective authority appropriate for a global economy, able to capture the benefits of new interdependences, and achieve a measure of justice between diverse populations worldwide, we require a much better way of understanding the collective life of societies than social capital theory can provide. Indeed, the social capital approach is part of what is wrong with social policy, and what needs to be fixed.

Interdependency in the global economy

One of the most damaging features of the crash has been the revelation that economic interdependences, previously seen as benign, dragged prudent and successful economies down with rashly indebted ones. What the integration of capital markets and the new global division of labour had achieved was a complementarity between the export-led growth of the new manufacturing giants (China, India, Brazil, etc.), and the financial hubs of the USA, UK and Europe, also involving Russia and the Gulf states as suppliers of fossil fuels.

But this in turn rested on the high savings ratios of Chinese, Japanese and other Asian citizens, and of Germans in Europe, along with the sovereign wealth funds of the oil-rich countries, which funded the budget and trade deficits of many affluent states – above all, the USA. The loss of paper assets (estimated value $2.8 trillion) in mortgage-backed securities and corporate bonds by financial institutions worldwide[11] caused falls in share prices which were worse in the Far East and Russia than in the countries where these toxic innovations had been generated. The Hang Seng and Nikkei indexes lost over 40 per cent of their value in 2008, as did the German DAX30, while the Shanghai composite index fell 65 per cent, and the Russian RTS index 72 per cent.[12]

The significance of this for social policy was that it signalled that global risks needed to be shared in more reliable ways. The thrifty populations of Asia had effectively loaned their savings to the US government and banks, so that American citizens could pay for the manufactured goods they were producing. These savings had been gambled away by bets on the US sub-prime housing market. The UK mirrored all this, on a smaller scale.

In Europe, the German and French governments at first saw the failure of Lehman Brothers and Northern Rock as symptoms of the weaknesses of the Anglo-Saxon model, from which they were largely insulated. But their financial institutions' exposure to these risks, and the consequences for their economies, became evident in the later autumn of 2008. The German economy, the largest and most stable in the EU, was forecast to shrink by 2.2 per cent in 2009, and the biting sarcasm of its Finance Minister's comments on the Keynesian response by the UK government to the crash has had to be renounced. In mid-January 2009, a new fiscal stimulus package, comprising road and rail investment, incentives to buy cars, tax cuts and a 100–euro grant for every child was unveiled, in the face of the sudden sharp fall in German exports.[13]

Another example of the perils of interdependence has been the Gas War between Russia and the Ukraine, leading to whole countries in Central and Eastern Europe losing their gas suppliers in January 2009. Because the distribution pipeline to Central and Western Europe runs through the Ukraine, the Russian government was able to use its majority shareholding in Gazprom, the supplier, to exert political pressure on that government, accusing it of siphoning off part of the allocation to other countries, and failing to pay for what it had consumed. Here, Russia, which had suffered disproportionately from the downturn in oil and gas prices which followed the crash, was using Europe's dependence on its reserves to try to exploit its market power.

Above all, of course, the developing countries, which depended for their share of the benefits of globalization on the exports of agricultural products, minerals and semi-manufactures, were hardest hit by the crash. Commodity prices, which had been rising during the bubble years, suddenly plummeted. But food prices for their home populations, driven up by climate change and fuel costs, did not fall so quickly. As a result, the world's poorest suffered most.

In all of this, international financial institutions (the IMF and World Bank, and their subsidiary agencies) were conspicuous by their invisibility. They drove through the massive restructurings from 1980 onwards, under the neo-liberal Washington Consensus (1980–95). These were based on the deregulation of capital markets, seeing the adequacy of the capital holdings of banks as the only important variable, and encouraging them to innovate, using new technologies. In this model, the tasks were to keep governments out of the financial system, to minimize regulation, and to encourage the rapid integration of global money markets through new technology (electronic trading, credit cards, etc.).[14] The claim was that this provided greater efficiency, and a larger supply of credit.

From the perspective of the late 1990s, all this was seen as placing too much trust in market mechanisms alone, and as having had many bad consequences, especially for the developing economies, and for the post-communist states of the former Soviet Bloc.[15] In the Asian bank crises of 1997–8, the IMF's policies were seen to have contributed to speculative lending. Having capital adequacy as the only standard applying to banks' loans meant that they had an incentive to go for the riskiest assets with the highest potential returns. In this way, the banking system in Thailand, for instance, was brought to ruin, having previously been sound enough.[16]

In the Russian crisis, a greater role was played by the failure of new institutions to supply a reliable framework of law and property rights, leading to corruption, fraud and the theft of state assets.[17] A speculative boom was the outcome of a process in which a few oligarchs became extremely wealthy.

In general terms, then, financial market liberalization exposed developing countries to external shocks. As one commentator put it: 'The movement towards financial (and capital) market deregulation – focusing on capital adequacy standards – is now recognised to have played a central role in the financial instability which has characterised so much of the developing world for the past quarter of a century'.[18]

This led to major debates, and a reformulation of the theory behind the workings of the IMF and World Bank.[19] The new Post-Washington Consensus which emerged at the end of the century gave much more emphasis to the importance of *institutions*, and a larger role to government. It pointed out, for instance, that some Asian countries rode the banking crisis better than others, but that the more successful ones used a variety of approaches. China, which had in any case been cautious about deregulations, adopted Keynesian policies; India, too, had paced and sequenced capital market deregulation carefully; and Malaysia imposed capital movement controls. All did better in the crisis than those like Thailand, which had followed the IMF model.[20]

For these reasons, the revisions in the deregulatory model which came to be the new orthodoxy, which were led at the World Bank by Joseph Stiglitz as Chief Economic Adviser, focused on the role of *institutions*, and especially *governments*. The key to sound monetary policy was the relationship with the banks, as the suppliers of loans to individuals and firms, to give them the right incentives as well as provide an adequate regulatory framework. In this, the new model saw itself as a contribution to the new institutional economics – 'institutions matter'[21] – but one in which many aspects of institutions could be explained 'by looking at transactions-cost technology or the imperfections and costs of information. This . . . [approach] argues that financial institutions – banks – are critical in determining the behaviour of the economy, and that the central features of banks and bank behaviour can be understood in terms of (or derived from) an analysis of information imperfections'.[22]

Derived as it was from the theory of contract, information and incentives, the model purported to supply a balanced system for credit which would, in combination with other government macro-economic institutions and policies, provide long-term growth with stability.[23] In retrospect, it is easy to see where it all went wrong. The model pitted banks – huge, sprawling, international organizations, with enormous wealth and power – against governments, which had been enfeebled by the privatizations and deregulations of the Washington Consensus era.

It was for these puny national authorities to set the terms, through their central banks, under which those organiza- tions created credit, within a vast, transnational, electronically operated system, in which the global reach and speed of trans- actions actually increased risks.[24] It was governments, too, which were to appoint and empower regulators, at a boom time, when it was impossible to attract the ablest candidates because of the scale of rewards within the private financial sector.[25]

Furthermore, the theory behind the model itself acknowl- edged that governments were, at best, riding a tiger. Their aim was to influence the supply of credit and the level of risks taken by banks. But – especially once a bubble began to develop – the incentives for banks to take unwarranted risks tended to increase, because the private costs associated with the danger of a bank failure are always less than the social costs. Societies, through their governments, must pay both the bailout costs and the costs to the real economy of redundancies, falling incomes and rising benefits.

Government had to try to offer insurance for deposits (by savers), but not create the moral hazard of insurance schemes that were too high and unconditional – a very difficult bal- ance to strike.[26] In the event, the limitations of the model were exposed by the failure of Lehman Brothers and Northern Rock, which showed that 'There are two kinds of govern- ments, those that have [explicit] deposit insurance and know it, and those that have [implicit] deposit insurance and don't know it'.[27]

The reasons why governments were drawn into repeated rounds of bailouts, capital injections, loan guarantees and even 'quantitative easing' (printing money) after the crash demonstrated how inadequate they had been for the role allot- ted them by the model. Since governments and regulators had only imperfect information, and could control banks only indirectly, under the principal–agent formulation, they could try 'to *control* or *affect* the behaviour of the bank (the agent) to make the bank act *more* in accord with social obejectives'.[28] But, once a bubble of credit had been created, using loans from money raised in the Far East and the Gulf, the consequences of bank failures were well beyond the scope of the model's control (or influence) mechanisms.

Not only were massive quantities of taxpayers' money required to refloat failing organizations, but the whole system's ability to supply credit was stalled. Banks in the USA and UK could no longer borrow from Asia and the Middle East, both because they had lost credibility, and because of the poor prospects of their national economies. This in turn meant that firms which would otherwise have been profitable could not raise credit, and went to the wall, in turn making loans riskier, and requiring more government intervention.

In the dominant model, the government itself could not take responsibility for the supply of credit, even if the banks failed to function. This was because of 'differential information' and 'differential incentives' – the government had a better 'big picture', but the banks alone had detailed knowledge of the kind required to make good loans.[29] But in the aftermath of the crash, when the banks had been revealed as being short-sighted, greedy and far too risk-tolerant, there was an urgent need for alternative suppliers of credit. The crash should discredit the contract model's specific prescriptions, but its emphasis on institutions, and the relationships between them, remains important. Above all, how might a better *international* architecture of institutions create a framework for development with stability and growth worldwide?

Since the crash, the power relations within global interdependences have shifted. Wall Street and the City of London can no longer pose as the epicentres of financial wizardry, turning global savings into hugely profitable derivatives. Many of their intermediary functions are now recognized as redundant or harmful. By contrast, the sovereign wealth funds of countries like China, the Middle Eastern oil-rich states and Norway are far stronger forces than before, and will drive the future direction of global economic change. These shifts in turn have important implications for national governments and social policy options.

Fiscal federalism, public finance and political authority

The crash created huge problems for public finance. First, already heavily indebted regimes, such as the USA, Italy, Hungary, Latvia and Greece, were forced to borrow on unprecedented scales to bail out their banks. Then global money markets did not supply the funds for banks to start to make new loans. All this further undermined the viability and authority of governments, making them look even more helpless than they were during the months of the original 'credit crunch'. Finally, the need to respond to crises in employment, income and housing supply reduced the scope for constructive innovations in social policy, even leading to cutbacks in existing provision.

For example, in the UK, falling revenues for local authorities led them to shed 10,000 jobs in the early months of 2009, despite the rise in redundancies in the private sector. Although they claimed that these were mainly 'back room' staff, and that the motive was to make long-planned 'efficiency savings', a spokesperson for one local authority admitted that there would also be cuts in 'soft targets', such as libraries and swimming pools.[30]

All this exposed the shortcomings of the model of macroeconomics and development which the Word Bank's leading theorists had claimed would provide 'stability with growth' in an interdependent, integrated global economy – and would 'maximise long-run societal *well-being* in an *equitable* and sustainable manner'.[31] They insisted that this model recognized the choices open to governments, and the trade-offs between priorities, drawing on the work of Kalecki[32] to rehabilitate the role of governments, armed with a wider range of instruments and a better awareness of risks (i.e. 'no more boom and bust'): 'Models based on more realistic assumptions give rise to firm and household behaviour, that is more in accord with actual observed behaviour – and provide an additional rationale for government to intervene in the economy, and additional tasks for government and central banks to stabilize the economy'.[33]

But – as we have already seen (see pp. 118–25) – none of this took proper account of the massive increase in mobility of money, technologies and people brought about by the integration of the world economy, or the way in which governments had facilitated this, by stripping away the controls they exercised in the twenty-five years after the Second World War. When the crash came, their 'wider range of instruments' proved puny indeed, because the collective life of even the strongest economies had been transformed so as to allow individuals and firms to sort themselves into groupings, organizations, service providers and jurisdictions of their own choices, and to switch and shift rapidly between them. They had also been encouraged to fund all this out of bank credit, which now had suddenly run dry.

Public finance in the years when the state was the dominant collective actor had been relatively easy to define and manage. Those needs which were not adequately met by markets, because people who did not pay for them could not be excluded from their benefits (such as police protection), were supplied by public authorities, out of compulsory taxation.

The fundamental difference between this and the market method of finance is that there is no relation between tax liability of any individual and the share of collectively provided services that he will be able to enjoy. Nor, save in very exceptional circumstances, can the revenue from any particular tax be regarded as paying for any particular service. Taxes are paid into a pool; entirely separate decisions govern the distribution of revenue between the public services.[34]

A quite different tradition, which constructs political authority on another economic basis, has become dominant in academic analysis and real-world public finance in the sixty years since this was written. Drawing on the work of Wicksell,[35] public choice and fiscal federalist theories have consolidated this approach to public finance, in which political authority is constructed from the full consent of members, who also agree the tax rate. Because they move to (or stay in) a jurisdiction, they can select the particular infrastructure of services they desire – the quantity, the quality and the costs, reflected in the level of taxation. The model was elegantly reformulated in an influential article by Charles Tiebout in 1956,[36] one of the foundational texts of a school which became an orthodoxy in the Anglophone countries.

The idea that collective goods can indeed be supplied exclusively, as long as non-paying individuals can be locked out, was developed by Buchanan, in his theory of economic clubs.[37] Here again, a range of amenities, shared among contributing members, can allow the public to choose between (in his example) swimming clubs, according to the fees they are willing and able to pay. In the same tradition, this can in turn be applied to a range of social services – schools, hospitals, clinics, care homes and social housing units – or to whole 'gated communities', in which a bundle of such facilities is offered at an overall price.[38]

In this extension of the theory, and unlike the definition

of public goods and tax-based finance for them given above, particular services can be paid for separately, by specific tax contributions. Different collective schemes for health, education or social care can operate over a number of political jurisdictions, while particular aspects of the physical and social infrastructure can be supplied by different levels of political authority. In this way, it is by choosing among these units that individuals achieve an efficient allocation of public funds, and create the membership systems which make up the political order. It also implies that many of the goods and services supplied by national governments under the post-war model are more efficiently provided by firms, public–private partnerships or smaller jurisdictions, under a set of overlapping 'clubs' and territorial authorities.[39]

The current period might be compared with the late medieval age, when compact, market-orientated 'city states' won considerable autonomy from the sprawling feudal empires which encompassed them,[40] or with the later nineteenth century, when administrators and soldiers from the affluent European nations established colonies in Africa, Asia and the Pacific. Given a regime of 'subsidiarity' – that the monopoly power of national governments should be limited, and that all collective provision should be located at the lowest level of administration encompassing the relevant benefits and costs[41] – the budgets for public services should be devolved to local units, even if (as in the UK) the taxation powers are not.

Theorists of this school distinguish between the advantages of fiscal federalism which stem from its *political* potential for transformation, and those which come from its *economic* dimension, though the two are linked through the concept of *membership*. The idea of chosen units of political authority is claimed to foster participation, collective action, civic qualities and virtues, and respect for human rights – all important components of well-being. This points towards small polities, such as city states, as in the civic republican tradition of Greece, Rome and the Renaissance.[42]

But to gain the full advantages of these forms of political devolution (including those for well-being), these 'city states' must be highly accountable to their citizens, and have very substantial autonomy from the national polity. In reality, only Switzerland, a confederacy established over 600 years ago, which allows local and national referenda on many public policy issues, comes close to this model. (Research on well-being has suggested that this accounts for high overall life-satisfaction in this country.)[43]

In the UK, despite token gestures such as having elected mayors in some cities, this political rationale for devolution of powers to local authorities has not been heeded. Indeed, with the exception of the Scottish Parliament and Welsh Assembly, lower levels of political authority have made few gains in their sovereignty since the very strong centralizing measures of the Thatcher years. This may help to explain the high levels of cynicism and apathy about politics in the UK.

But the second aspect of fiscal federalism has been very influential in the UK, as well as the other affluent Anglophone countries. In the economic rationale for self-selecting membership, organizations and jurisdictions supplying specific, or bundles of, goods and services, to be shared among members, compete to attract these by the quality and price on offer. This gives gains in efficiency through specialization and competition, both between suppliers of a single service and between devolved local authorities. For every level of output of a collective good, 'there is a technically-efficient population size that minimises the average cost per household of providing that service'.[44]

However, whereas the political benefits of devolution and participation are likely to be greatest where populations, once they have selected a city state or rural district, remain stable and interact frequently, the economic benefits are likely to be greatest where people move frequently between fluid, temporary, contingent groupings. 'Voting with the feet' becomes the public-choice counterpart to market consumption,[45] and welfare gains from privatization and decentralization stem from sorting populations into units in terms of their preferences concerning collective goods, and their abilities to pay for them. It also implies that rich people are largely segregated from poor, and that the least mobile will be concentrated in jurisdictions and membership systems with the worst services.[46]

What this indicates is that decentralized and privatized regimes consistently undersupply the resources for poverty alleviation, for achieving social cohesion and harmony, and also for environmental protection[47] (see chapter 5), as a result of tax competition between local authorities, and the selection processes of economic 'clubs'. Up to now, it has been left to national governments to arrange income transfers and to make intergovernmental grants, using their own tax revenues to offset the fragmentations, conflicts and inequalities generated by those processes, as well as to offset environmental damage. For the sake of balanced development, cohesion and inclusion, this redistributive function (for instance in the large grants made by the German federal government to the Länder) smooths over some of the disruptions to social relations.

The crash threatens the fragile viability of all these arrangements. Not only will many people no longer be able to afford the mortgages, fees and contributions required to belong to organizations providing commercial services, or the local taxes for their neighbourhoods; the consequent disruptions, divisions and downward spirals will also be beyond the scope of governments to remedy with falling revenues and rising debts. But the international economic crisis, and the reductions in aid from affluent countries, will also expose the fact that this model has never worked for developing ones. In many parts of the world, and especially in Africa, the state has simply withdrawn from large parts of its territory, making no attempt to integrate them into the economy or polity. Because the inhabitants are too poor to provide education, health care or a basic infrastructure for themselves, they have been left to the mercies of warlords, or have become active in resistance or secessionist movements, as in Sudan, Somalia, the Democratic Republic of Congo, Liberia, Sierra Leone and so on.

The fiscal federalist approach does not provide the clear blueprint for political authority and public finance it claims. Even at the theoretical level, although it can indicate the optimal membership size and composition of a 'club' for the supply of health and social care, or the elements in an efficient jurisdiction supplying an infrastructure for firms and residents, it cannot indicate how functional and territorial units can best be joined into a system of overlapping clubs and political authorities.[48]

Since the crash, the governments of the USA and UK can no longer set the agenda for social policy programmes and public sector restructurings worldwide. Their model of global development, led by Wall Street and the City of London, is described. The increased power of China, India, Brazil, Russia and other industrializing states is symbolized in the replacement of the G8 by the G20 as the main global economic forum.

This is why Barack Obama and Gordon Brown have been required to put their weight behind attempts to regulate global money markets and bank activities, and to subjugate their previously all-powerful financial centres to international institutions and rules. Domestically, as Obama struggled to widen health care coverage and Brown to survive in government, leaders not experiencing public finance crisis, such as Angela Merkel in Germany, have gained additional authority.

The attempts to re-assert some political control over the forces of the global economy will have to operate at early level, from international to regional and local, if governments at any of these levels are to gain leverage over social policy issues. But they will only slowly, and with difficulty, be able to reclaim powers from the financial and commercial interests to which they were handed under the discredited Anglophone model.

Mobility, migration and membership

The deafening silence from the international financial organizations during the crash belied their official responsibilities for the overall stability of the world economy, and their active role in using the transformative power of markets to reshape the collective life of the planet, during the Washington Consensus and its successor regime. The IMF is responsible for global financial stability; the World Bank makes loans to governments, and sets conditions on these concerning their systems of governance, fiscal arrangements and institutional order. The WTO governs international trade relations, promoting free exchange of goods and services across borders. Collectively, they seek economic growth and human development; recently, the World Bank has concerned itself directly with 'attacking poverty'.[49]

The crash signals a catastrophic failure in their exercise of these functions, and in this section I shall review the shortcomings of the model under which they were acting, and start to sketch how it might be fixed. I shall argue that the process of globalization promoted mobility of the factors of production, as well as products, across organizational and political borders of all kinds, but it lacked an adequate theory of how membership organizations (which created such boundaries in order to share risks among contributors) benefited from their interdependence. Even under the revisions to the Washington

Consensus neo-liberal, deregulatory and privatizing agendas that have occurred since the mid-1990s, there is no coherent account of how these can promote human development and well-being through social policies, either within or between nations.

Since the early 1980s, the dominant approach to these issues applies microeconomic principles to the whole world, as one big market. In theory, equilibrium is reached in markets when money, machines and people move to wherever they can be most productively deployed. But in a world with national borders, trade between countries specializing in certain kinds of production is claimed to be an alternative to migration of workers as a way of achieving the optimum allocation of resources for global efficiency.[50] Whereas the IMF and the World Bank were established after the Second World War to correct failures in capital markets, and to stop crises in one country spreading to others, during the Washington Consensus they shifted their focus to 'government failure' – the 'overregulation' of national economies, and 'excessive' taxation and redistribution, leading to distortions and barriers to mobility and trade. However, restrictions on immigration were not a target of their policies.

Despite attempts by national governments to limit inward (and sometimes outward) flows of population, the period of neo-liberal dominance was also an 'age of migration'.[51] After the Second World War, when huge numbers of refugees moved (or were moved) across borders, rates of migration had slowed by the 1970s. Since then the mobility of money and technology, promoted by the opening of national economies to global market forces, has led to accelerated movement of managers and professionals (within the new, transnational corporations which dominated global finance and production), of skilled workers (in search of the best returns on their expertise), of students and trainees, as well as of refugees from regional conflicts, such as those of Central Africa, the Middle East and (after the collapse of the Soviet Bloc) the Balkans and Caucasus.

In some cases, these flows of population were simply from poorer countries to richer ones, as in the (often irregular) immigrations from Central and North Africa to France, Italy and Spain, or from Mexico, Central America and the Caribbean to the USA and Canada, or from the post-communist Central and East European states to the older EU countries. In other cases, they took the form of migrations from former colonies to the colonial power, as from the Indian subcontinent to the UK. In others still, workers were recruited for a sudden boom in construction, extraction and services, as in Sri Lankan and Indian migrations to the oil-rich Gulf states; and in others, domestic or unskilled service workers moved, for instance from the Philippines to Japan, in search of more adequate wages.

Theorists of these phenomena pointed out that they also often followed patterns related specifically to other processes of globalization. Saskia Sassen found that the migration pathways of people from the countries in which export-orientated production zones had been established in the early 1980s (in Brazil, Puerto Rico and South-East Asia) followed the reverse route to investment flows from affluent North American and Asian states.[52] From this research, she developed her analysis of 'global cities' – cosmopolitan financial centres like New York, London and Tokyo, made up of concentrations of banking and business services, and served by immigrant workers in low-paid, insecure and irregular employments.[53] In her account, these were the nerve centres of the global financial system, which had largely replaced that of nation states in the new world order.[54]

Such analyses linking transnational movements of people with economic integration, through mobile global elites and their minions, suggested that this constituted an alternative regime of 'top-level management and control operations' in 'central places where the work of globalization gets done . . . [I]nformation industries require a vast infrastructure containing strategic nodes with hyper-concentrations of facilities'.[55] To enable the supply of expertise and low-paid service workers for these centres, there has been 'the emergence of a new, privatised transnational regime for cross-border transactions which now also includes certain components of cross-border labor mobility, notably service workers'.[56]

In Sassen's view, these concentrations of technology and power in the strategic headquarters cities of global capitalism give possibilities for a 'new politics' which transcends national states. But it is unclear from her work, or that of others in the field of mobility and migration, what the rationale for these new claims and contestations might ultimately be. The global crash, which has disproportionately impacted on global cities, as the centres for financial services to the world economy, has revealed that this prosperity was a kind of pyramid fraud.[57] Many of the huge temples to international banking and credit now house bankrupt companies, or ones which have been taken into the ownership of their host states; reverse migration of both their high-flying acolytes and the cleaners and *au pairs* who serviced them is under way.

The current World Bank model attempts to set out the relationships between monetary systems, shareholders' property rights, fiscal regimes and public finance instruments, with chains of accountability throughout the system, and with international organizations themselves at the top of a hierarchy, guaranteeing 'good governance'.[58] The model maintains continuity with the neo-liberal path of market reforms, but with much more emphasis on institutional design and functioning, and a range of regulatory and redistributive measures. In all this, the theme is still one of decentralization

and fiscal devolution. States in the developing world are supposed to make a 'social contract' with their citizens, under
which they will share in growth through integration in global
markets. This is seen as the outcome of a negotiation process
between civil-society organizations, public partnerships and
commercial firms, often at a local level: 'Sound governance,
competition and markets – and free entry for multiple agents,
whether government, non-government or private – are essential for effective service delivery, especially to poor people'.[59]

But the incoherence of the model stems from its inability
to say when organizations, as systems of membership, are
conducive to human development and well-being, and when
they are barriers to efficiency and equity. Behind the whole
approach to the analysis of governance, institutions and collective life lies the concept of 'rent-seeking' – the collective
actions by which agents can gain extra incomes for their
services, above those which would have been available under
competitive market conditions.[60] Although most commonly
applied to the activities of trade unions, cartels, criminal con-
spiracies and the professionals, it can also be used to analyse
the distortions caused by corrupt politicians, or bureaucrats
who expand their budgets by over-supplying public services.[61]

Yet *all* organizations, and *all* forms of political authority,
are derived from attempts to restrain competitions between
members, and gain benefits from their interdependence,[62]
while excluding unorganized others. This includes firms,
co-operatives, federations and nation states. And it is no con-
tradiction to say that many organizations and polities are also
ways of mobilizing their members to compete with other
organizations and authorities, and to break down other coalitions and confederacies built around rents for their members.
For this reason, collective life is always a flux, and principles
for equity among membership systems cannot be derived
from the theory of rents and rent-seeking.

Instead, to fix global social policy it is necessary to recognize some general principles under which risks and benefits can be equitably shared, among populations, some of whom are settled, both territorially and in terms of communities, and others of whom are short- or long-term migrants. Such membership systems will be a mixture of political, commercial and voluntary organizations, from local to global in scope. The World Bank model of governance has lamentably failed to provide 'stability with growth'. Above all, it has failed to lift the majority of the world's 6 billion inhabitants out of abject poverty.

'Attacking poverty': social capital and the international trade in services

Mobility provides the dynamic for gains in economic efficiency; but it is community which supplies the basis for democratic political authority. This does not imply a uniform culture with a single set of standards. Democratic political communities can and should uphold diversity. But they should also consist of a sustainable set of relationships, capable of reproducing a society over a number of generations. To achieve this, they must command the loyalty and solidarity of members, sharing in an identifiable collective project, and contributing to its practices.

In the World Bank's model, democracy and cohesive social relations are always secondary to economic efficiency within an integrated global system. While the IMF, under the Washington Consensus, favoured such clearly dictatorial regimes as Chile and Argentina as models of institutional rectitude, and post-Soviet Russia's approach to market transformation, the World Bank's protagonists admire China for its 'pacing and sequencing' of reforms and deregulations, despite its human rights record;[63] its massive and growing inequalities within populations and between them are seen as less significant than the growth which is supposed to lift the poor out of their disadvantages.

All this can be recognized in the way in which 'social capital' theory is deployed in the World Bank's literature. Originally developed in the late 1980s,[64] and coming to prominence in social science research in the mid-1990s,[65] the concept of social capital was almost immediately taken up by the World Bank's research and analysis organization,[66] to the extent that some 800 researchers and 3,000 other professionals were employed on projects incorporating its framework by 1997.[67] This helped to boost the notion to the status of a 'master idea' in the social sciences by the first decades of the new century.[68]

Social capital denotes 'norms and networks of reciprocity and trustworthiness'[69] which underpin both economic and political exchanges, helping them to function better. As already argued (see pp. 78–9), it is often unclear from the concept's definition and use whether it refers to a particular way of doing things collectively, involving intensive face-to-face interactions (as an alternative to markets and the third-party enforcement of property rights through law); or whether it is supposed to reside in whole communities as a generalized and accessible resource, but one which is depleted if it is not used. Some authors treat it as a private good, which 'belongs' to individuals,[70] others as a collective good; others still insist, confusingly, that it is both.[71] Especially in the work of economists like Becker[72] and sociologists like his colleague Coleman,[73] it is a way of extending economic theory to embrace cultural, social and political interactions, and hence to subsume the latter into an economic approach to public policy.

Social capital theory is a very important part of the World Bank's (failed) strategy for 'attacking poverty'. Because poor people's patterns of behaviour are orientated towards subsistence and survival, they do not participate in wider networks which might give them access to better opportunities, both through markets and through political processes. Although states in developed countries are still responsible for the overall institutional frameworks for health and education, the implementation of the World Bank model relies on NGOs, both international and indigenous, for the inclusion of marginal groups and districts. Poor people are disadvantaged by not sharing in the norms, networks and practices of the more successful in the mainstream; in effect, they have the wrong kind of social capital, 'bonding' social capital, which ties them into reciprocities with their own small kinship and tribal circuits, rather than 'bridging' social capital,[74] linking them to national and global networks. NGOs should connect them into these wider systems, both 'making markets work better for poor people',[75] and linking them to official agencies.

The claims that this approach 'empowers' and 'includes' poor people in developing countries, giving them 'opportunity' and 'security',[76] are contradicted by the record. Above all, the strategy of affluent states, under the terms of the World Trade Organization's General Agreement on Trade in Services (GATS), has created a huge differential between the health education and welfare services available to the more affluent members of the mainstream in these countries, and the conditions of life in impoverished districts.[77] Along with growing inequalities in incomes, it has meant that sophisticated hospital care, and access to college education, have become the prerogatives of better-off citizens, while states have been doing less for the basic health, literacy and well-being of their poorest members.[78]

One major purpose of the GATS was to open up the public sectors of nation states worldwide to the incursions of international companies marketing health, education and welfare services. Since most of these were based in the affluent countries, and especially in the USA and UK (where they already had experience of privatization and 'public–private partnerships' in their own regimes since the 1980s), and the most accessible (and vulnerable) public services were in the developing countries, this had meant that the most pervasive transformations of that sector took place in poorer societies, without an infrastructure of inclusive, universal provision. But even countries with much better basic health and education institutions for their whole populations, such as China, have experienced a marked change towards a polarized system, with expensive health care and exclusive schools for the better-off, and fewer affordable basic services for impoverished districts.

In the field of global trade in social services, we can see the ideology and policy programme of the affluent Anglophone countries meshing with the strategy for development adopted by the World Bank. The former, under the influence of Third Way theorists such as Giddens,[79] favoured policies which promoted the interests of multinational companies, backing the global plans of pharmaceutical and biotech firms for new drugs and genetically modified (GM) crops, on the grounds that these would improve the situation of the world's poorest.[80] They also applied the logic of their championing of private service companies in their domestic health, education and welfare sectors to the promotion of competition in these fields worldwide, boosting the profits of firms whose experience and expertise had been gained in the USA and UK.

Meanwhile, the IMF and World Bank, as well as the WTO, created the conditions in which this strategy could prosper. In Argentina, for example, the restructuring of the public sector was one of the conditions for the loans which followed the fiscal and financial crises of the late 1990s.[81] Social-insurance funded health care was cut back, in favour of commercial provision and schemes requiring co-payments from patients, in which promotional costs made up 20 per cent of the former, and fees 41 per cent of the latter.[82] Argentina experienced a re-appearance of epidemic illnesses such as cholera, measles and typhus.[83] Multinationals penetrated the health care systems of other Latin American countries,[84] ending rights to universal treatment for all citizens, and introducing market principles, with state care reserved for the very poor.

In China, such changes were not enforced by international financial authorities; the government shifted from policies for labour-intensive basic public health care for all (the 'barefoot doctors' approach of the Mao era) to World Bank-style developments as part of its market reforms. Only 10 per cent of the rural populations in the provinces (which have not benefited directly from rapid growth) are now covered by state schemes.[85]

Among the more prosperous inhabitants of the cities where 80 per cent of doctors are located,[86] an increasing proportion of health costs are met by patients, as the pharmaceutical industry has become the fifth largest in China, and over 50 per cent of China's health care spending now goes on drugs,[87] compared with 14 to 40 per cent in other developing countries. Expensive Western medical equipment has been purchased by hospitals and used to diagnose and treat rich patients, and to raise revenue for these institutions through fees.[88]

The idea that commercial expansion in health care can benefit the economies of developing countries, and remove barriers to efficiency, has been promoted by the World Bank's Development Plan, as a part of its Poverty Reduction Strategy. Through the International Finance Corporation (IFC), it has funded projects for helping private companies to access financial markets for this purpose.[89] Because the IFC expects a reliable return for its investments of around 5 per cent, there is a strong bias towards high technology and private health schemes for the better-off.[90] This is supposed to leave governments to focus on the problems of their poorest citizens, mainly infectious diseases and (especially in Africa) HIV/AIDS. However, a great many developing countries have seen a deterioration in the health and life-expectancy of their populations, in child mortality, access to immunization and the containment of diseases such as tuberculosis, malaria and yellow fever, particularly in sub-Saharan Africa.[91]

In the field of education, the WTO has a business-minded approach to the 'knowledge market', in which large international companies, based in the USA, UK and Europe, have (under the terms of the GATS) been given access to developing countries' systems.[92] Especially in India, Latin America and Africa, the World Bank has promoted fee-paying schooling.[93] This business agenda for education worldwide has been sponsored by international banks, and supported by the OECD and the European Union. In the model these organizations support, public spending on citizens' education is often a hindrance for enterprise and growth. Under the commercial approach, the curriculum should encourage business and improve competitiveness.

Whereas basic literacy, especially for women, was the goal of policies in countries such as China, Sri Lanka and Brazil in the years after the Second World War, achieving rates of over 80 per cent for the population as a whole,[94] the business model focused on the educational needs of those parts of the economies of developing countries which contributed to global markets, aiming at a minority of highly skilled workers and managers. All this further reinforced inequalities both within these countries, and between them and the affluent ones.

Conclusions

What's wrong with social policy globally can be traced to the IMF, World Bank and WTO. Instead of guarding against market failure, they have pursued an aggressive programme targeting what they defined as 'government failure', under a grandiose plan to manage global growth through the integration of world markets. These pretensions have turned out to be delusional. The three organizations, while claiming to set out a model of 'stability with growth' for the global economy, took their eye off the ball that they were supposed to be watching. They have presided over a world financial crisis, leading to a world economic crash.

This is why the construction of a 'new financial architecture' for the global economy is now a top priority in any attempt to fix social policy. These organizations should revert to their original roles in relation to banking, credit and trade; in the meantime, during that period of market hubris, other ideas about global governance have emerged from international organizations and academic analysis, and the IMF, World Bank and WTO might redirect their efforts towards the support of new orientations in human and economic development, rather than trying to set the whole agenda for the world's future.

All the alternative approaches canvassed in the literatures argue that the larger interdependences brought about by the integration of the world economy demand transnational institutions, and ultimately some system of 'global governance'. This rests on the view that, just as in the past the growth of trade and the new, wider divisions of labour which came with complex processes of production caused larger-scale collective action problems,[95] so globalization demands more encompassing political units. But – as we have seen – this leaves open the question of how functions such as social welfare provision would be organized: for instance the possibility of overlapping 'clubs' and jurisdictions on every scale.

The range of proposals includes a Global Compact promoted by Kofi Annan, UN Secretary General, in 1999, which would combine universal ethical principles to include all in the benefits of global growth with 'corporate leadership';[96] the Monterey Consensus of 2002, establishing a Finance for Development perspective and an ethical prospectus for global governance;[97] and those theories which postulate a 'global public sphere', in which NGOs with a more ethically informed and qualitative view of well-being and development can influence governance and decision-making.[98] Still others insist that globalization simply demands that governments act together to create global institution for solving collective problems.[99]

The first two perspectives do not really break with the liberal-communitarian or World Bank models of social policy, mainly extending it in a new institutional framework, under explicit principles for human rights, equality and justice. The third rests its hopes on 'cosmopolitan citizenship', under which universal rights might be recognized, and redistribution in favour of poor people negotiated, through discursive democratic processes.[100] A cosmopolitan constitution, transcending nationalism, might underpin these processes. Delanty sees this as possibly arising from a blend of political participation and global cultural community;[101] others see it as stemming from a democratized, deliberative United Nations.[102]

These somewhat abstract debates, taking place before the economic crash, will be resumed with urgency in its aftermath. More successful models for social policy, based on export-led industrialization in China and South-East Asia,[103] are unlikely to be suited to Africa; the innovations of those South American countries which have been influenced by Venezuela also seem to be specific to that region. Income redistribution schemes pioneered in Brazil and South Africa will be discussed in the next chapter (pp. 176–9). But no one version seems to fit all developing countries, while policy dilemmas in the affluent ones are fundamentally challenged by fiscal and financial crises.

Throughout this book, I have argued that what is wrong with social policy can be traced to a model in which money (finance capitalism) shapes the policies of collective authorities at all levels, through contracts, with the banks and commercial firms as the drivers of collective organization. The alternative approach, which I shall develop further in the next chapter, sees the basis for risk sharing and the benefits of interdependence as being unavoidably located in *communities* of some kind, and in their cultures and practices.

Political authority, in this view, can shape and enable these processes, by designing institutions which engineer solidarities among larger collectivities, and by resolving conflicts of interest. But their aim should not be to replace political and social action, debate and contestation, by 'voting with the feet', or by shifting between collective facilities, on an analogy with market choice. Social policy structures should encourage and reward participation, solidarity and loyalty, and should do so through interactions which give esteem and respect to those who contribute to meeting social needs. They should also foster resources for supportive social relations among members of diverse societies.

All this implies that mobility, which will continue to be required for the achievement of economic efficiency, and migration, through which the beneficial effects of world economic integration are partly achieved, will continue to be features of global society; but that social policy should seek to offset their negative effects, rather than try to harness them for an accelerated growth of privatized social provision. The vast majority of the world's population continues to live out its life in communities, where interdependences of many kinds rely on longstanding bonds of kinship, occupation or faith. While collective authority should enable members to travel for education and work, and stable communities to absorb outsiders, the overall aim of social policy should be to improve the quality of life of settled populations.

The G20 meeting in London in early April 2009 represented an extension on a global scale of the policies deployed
by national governments to rescue their financial sectors.
Perhaps the most surprising decision taken at the meeting
was to entrust to the IMF the task of making massive new
loans to failing national governments. This was consolidated
by the meeting of the G20 in September of the same year.

The way that these global shifts played out at the national
level can be illustrated in two examples of public policy
developments in the UK. There, the post-crash debt crisis
demanded alternatives to the reliance on the City of London
for tax revenue, employment growth and the credit to fund
individual life projects. The decline of London's position in
the global economy required new approaches to incomes,
industrial development and tax–benefit issues.

The most trenchant denunciations of the City's excesses
came from the newly appointed head of the Financial Services
Authority, Lord Adair Turner. As well as declaring many of its
activities and employees 'socially useless', he criticized them
for creating financial instability through abuse of their power
over credit, and suggested tighter rules on capital ratios.[104] The
implication was that a viable future for tax revenues, earnings
and prosperity demanded a stronger industrial sector, and an
increase in outputs of other marketable services. But at the
same time government minister for the City, Lord Myners,
bemoaned the fact that such companies were being taken over
by foreign interests (firms and sovereign wealth funds), and
that UK institutional owners of shares (notably pension funds)
were insufficiently active in corporate governance issues.[105]

Meanwhile, shifts in the global economy were having an
immediate effect on the labour market, and hence on the
income maintenance system. With the rise in unemployment
and the decline in prospects for secure, better-paid jobs for
school, college and university leavers, a think tank linked with

that Conservative Party published a radical set of proposals for integrating the income tax and means-tested benefits systems. Finally accepting that the combination of bank credit and welfare-to-work measures could not supply adequate incomes or incentives for those with low earning power, or living in regions with few opportunities, the Centre for Social Justice's report aimed to smooth the impact of benefits withdrawals and tax payments, in order to reduce the social exclusion of the poorest UK citizens.[106]

The report focused on the rising costs of these benefits, their failure to lower numbers outside labour markets or to reduce poverty, and their harmful effects on saving, family stability and social order. Blaming fragmented schemes (fifty-one in all) of income support, it recommended an approach with just two elements (work credit and life credit), to be assessed in terms of a single calculation of resources and needs, with higher disregards of earnings, and withdrawals at the steady rate of 70 per cent to be made through PAYE deductions.

This simplified form of automatic entitlement and easy access, with its emphasis on social integration and the promotion of participation in the mainstream, represented a first step towards the basic income approach outlined elsewhere in this book (pp. 28–9 and 173–9). I shall return to the implications of this shift in income maintenance policies in the final two chapters.

5

Sustainability – communities and the environment

The crash had an ambiguous effect on policies for the environment; recession meant that there was a danger that major projects (on carbon emissions or renewable energy) might be postponed or abandoned. But the shuddering halt in growth, and the need to rethink development, offered opportunities for green initiatives. In the programme he announced in the days before taking office as US President, Barack Obama promised that his public works measures to combat the fall in economic activity and loss of employment would include an ambitious plan to create a 'green energy grid', through renewable electricity generation projects. Such bold innovations led commentators to wonder whether 'we might enter the recession in the red, and come out of it green'.

The enormous potential of the USA for such initiatives, arising from its vast expanse of unoccupied or sparsely inhabited territory, and its potential for solar, water and tidal power generation, make programmes like Gordon Brown's for loft-insulation in the UK, also projected as a measure to combat unemployment, seem extremely tame. But new technologies, and the harnessing of natural resources, are not the only elements in policies for sustainability.

In this chapter, I shall argue that the link between social and environmental policies for sustainability should be *communities* and their mobilization. In the final analysis, climate change will only be contained, depletable fuels conserved and natural diversity protected if people learn to act in ways consistent with a sustainable economy. The economics of growth has encouraged cultures of greed, waste and disrespect for the world of nature, treated as free goods, and valued only for its contribution to human consumption and wealth. This was not the attitude of our ancestors, or of surviving simple societies of hunter-gatherers, who regard natural phenomena, including plants and animals, as sacred.

I have argued in chapter 3 (pp. 86–7) that human well-being depends on social interactions in which social value is produced and distributed, and that this value is also 'sacred', in the sense that it deals in what is meaningful in human life. We gain emotional closeness, support, friendship, respect and the sense of belonging through communications using cultural resources, which in turn embody our standards and beliefs about what is valuable in our society's relationships. Even in the highly individualistic cultures of the affluent Anglophone countries, where the self is seen as the holy temple of value, and each person claims the right to self-realization and self-fulfilment,[1] this notion of sacredness in relationships and communications is omnipresent – albeit often in a tragi-comic, distorted form.[2]

Sustainability demands that we recognize the value, not only of nature's resources, of other species and of the inter-dependent elements in the ecology of the planet, but also of each other. It is very difficult to imagine how the world would change the course on which it is at present travelling, with rising carbon emissions leading to irreversible and fatal global warming, without abandoning the consumerist, self-regarding individualism which constitutes the affluent Anglophone culture. The principles of self-realization through choice and lifestyle, on which the model of contractual relations and governance rests, demand a right to squander and destroy, which can lead only to the destruction of life on this planet.

I have argued that a different culture could provide the

restraints which would allow greed and waste to be contained, and supply the resources for enjoying a life more attuned to the natural environment – a culture which values its diversity. But this in turn requires communities which practice respect and conservation, and a collective life which shares and fosters resources in a sustainable way. To move towards these cultures and practises, a very different public policy framework must recognize and support relations of mutuality, care and conviviality. This follows from the idea of services consistent with viable social reproduction over several generations (see pp. 88–90).

Such a paradigm shift requires inspirational leadership. Here President Obama's visionary rhetoric, combined with his subtle and pragmatic political skills, could play a key role. His public works programme reflects the need to rebuild the physical infrastructure of the USA – the roads, bridges and levees – as well as to invest in green initiatives. Since President Reagan's neo-liberal revolution defined the goals of cutting back federal government responsibilities and expenditures, devolution of powers and budgets to states and localities, and privatization of services, these infrastructural features had deteriorated alarmingly in many parts of the country. Hurricane Katrina and the collapse of the road bridge at Cleveland bore witness to this dilapidation. Obama's programme could be justified in terms of efficiency and productivity as well as employment.

But the wider significance of these and his environmental measures could be the sense of renewal of collective life that they enable, and the participation in projects which symbolize commitment to a sustainable future, based on a unified purpose. In all this, Obama's words can help to supply the cultural resources and set the policy course for an improved quality of social relations through collective action – a dynamic political community.

The USA may be more in need of this kind of leadership for change than any other country in the world, because of its great inequalities in income, housing standards and health care, but it is probably also more capable of such a shift than any other country. It has a history of embracing opportunities for self-renewal as a political community, from the War of Independence to the Civil War and the New Deal.[3]

In the rest of the affluent Anglophone countries, and notably in the UK, where the country's economic plight is even more perilous, culture shifts are not so readily achieved. In Europe, too, there are huge issues to be faced, as sustainability – more seriously addressed in Germany, for instance, than in the USA or UK – still demands a more radical orientation towards the whole purpose of economy and society. Germany in particular has a strongly 'productivist' basis for all its political and social policy institutions; its structures are derived from an idea of 'social partnership' between the state, employers' federations and trade unions, and its entitlements to income transfers and services closely linked to contributions by all the members of this productive triumvirate. Germany's education and apprenticeship systems still perpetuate its high technological standards, it still exports industrial products in large volumes, and its reputation for excellence in these fields is a source of national identity and pride as well as national income.

The questions raised in this chapter are whether sustainability is consistent with productivism of this kind, and how the foundations of social policy might be shifted to a 'non-productivist' basis.[4] Productivism of the kind which characterized the UK and the advanced North European economies during the period from the industrial revolution to the 1960s was, of course, the basis for welfare states there and in the so-called 'White Dominions' of the British Empire.[5] It is likely to remain as the organizing principle of social policy in the newly industrializing countries of Asia, including China.[6] Any attempt to re-orientate these countries towards environmental sustainability will require leadership and the commitment of resources from the affluent countries (this will be discussed towards the end of this chapter).

Non-productivist approaches to social policy can learn from the developing world, because of the priority given to communal and mutual systems of activity, and the balance between human life and nature, found in many of these societies. In these, cultural and social reproduction are more important aspects of the life of communities than consumption and growth. How might such ways of life be applicable to the rich world?

The versions of productivism which dominated the advanced economies during the boom (variants of the liberal-communitarian model of social policy) defined and analysed informal care and the human services within the methodologically individualistic and contract-based terms of its underlying economic theory. Services (and environmental protection) could generate employment and, as long as the demands of cost-efficiency and management control were observed, could be positive factors for economic growth.[7] Women enter the labour market mainly in service roles, but this contributes to gender equality overall, and advances household income as well as women's autonomy;[8] feminists are ambivalent about this development, but in general favour it, especially in its Scandinavian, social democratic form.[9] The crash brings all this under fresh scrutiny.

In particular, the collapse of the financial services sector, where most income and employment growth occurred during the boom, raised questions about how the buoyancy of productivism could be maintained in its aftermath – the example of super-productivist Japan being a prominent warning here. Especially in the UK, where the bursting of the bubble in the

City of London left it looking like 'Iceland-on-Thames', the extreme version of the individualistic, contract-based, time-productivity constrained economy needs replacement sources of dynamism. If the UK in particular is to emerge from the crash with a new sense of purpose, it needs to engage the purposeful participation of its population in a new project. Instead of the narrow idea of 'UK Plc' canvassed by all government departments under New Labour, a vision of a society in which members contribute to a better quality of life is required – one in which employment is not simply concerned with earning for consumption, and the role of citizen is no longer to 'earn, shop, save and pretty much shut up'.[10]

I shall argue that a non-productivist alternative must fuse together ideas and policies from the environmentalist agenda with ones from the ethic-of-care and the quality-of-life approaches. This is not original – it has been canvassed by other analysts of social policy.[11] What I hope is distinctive in my recommendations about how to fix social policy is the combination of institutional and cultural aspects that are outlined in what follows.

Drawing on the examples of music and sport,[12] I shall argue that a sustainable mixture of these elements could provide a new basis for human development and social justice in the affluent countries, and eventually in the whole world. The point about these activities is that they combine cosmopolitanism with locality-based traditions, highly paid professional work with a huge informal field of participation, activity with appreciation and following, and individual with group and communal identification and achievement. Furthermore, they are valued for themselves – for the intrinsic worth of doing them, hearing and watching them, and supporting them in loyal and continuous ways. They are perceived as meaningful and as giving meaning to the lives of cultural groups, cities and whole societies. They generate enthusiasm and mass belonging, but they also require discipline and restraint to perform and to appreciate.

The notions of sustainable communities, environmental protection or politics might seem idealistic or fanciful, were it not for a few charismatic leaders and visionaries who have achieved such mobilizations. Social policy has had the experience of being made subservient to a very instrumental, materialistic and grubby version of politics and social relations; at a time of crises, when that model has collapsed, it is not entirely implausible to see an opportunity to link it with a new and exciting agenda for change.

Communities and the environment

On the face of it, the attempt to link the idea of fostering purposeful participation in the quality of life of communities and the project of protecting and valuing the environment involves two different priorities. There would appear to be circumstances – for instance, under conditions of severe constraints on public spending – when the demand for health, education and social care spending, or for transport and the infrastructure provision, might compete with that for environmental projects. Why might the crash, following which there are crises in the public finances of several countries (including the UK) be an opportunity for reconciling these tensions, and fusing them into a non-productivist approach to public policy?

Part of the answer to this question stems from some of the weaknesses of productivism[13] already identified in the previous chapters of this book. Although the model based on methodological individualism and contract is only one version of productivism (the Soviet system being historically its great rival, and many post-war regimes containing a mixture of elements from these two models), it is this extreme version which has driven the integration of the world economy, and which stands in greatest need of transformation after the crash. The Chinese regime, with its odd mixture of authoritarian collectivist government[14] and unrestrained capitalist dynamics, along with major elements of familialism and communal cooperation, is likely to prove the most enduring and successful form of productivism among the newly industrializing countries, for many reasons to do with history, human capital and location on the world economic map. But it is scarcely a model for the developed world.

The crash has shown that much of the apparent complementarity and reciprocity between China, India, Brazil, Russia and the oil-rich Gulf states, on the one hand, and the affluent countries (particularly the USA and UK) was deceptive. Funds from savers, and from the rich, in the former group will no longer flow through financial markets into the banks and insurance companies of the West, because the fabulously high returns on these flows have been shown to come from unsustainable trickery. In future, these funds will be invested in their countries of origin, and will consolidate their growth in manufacturing production and commercial services.

The affluent countries will rely even more on their investments in the newly industrializing and developing world, and on research and technological innovation for production there. But they will also have to discover some new purposes for their populations, who can neither engage in the business of making money out of money, nor borrow large sums at low interest rates to support consumerist lifestyles.

So, the attention of policy makers and political entrepreneurs will shift towards two sets of issues, once the immediate economic crisis is over. On the one hand, the threat of climate change will be both a challenge and an opportunity; if there are to be scientific innovations to allow renewable energy sources to power the continued growth of the global economy, this will be the time to develop them. On the other hand, some of the ablest young people in these countries, who had been drawn into the financial services sector from the mid-1980s onwards by high salaries and golden prospects, will be unemployed, and looking for a career. Scientific research and public policy can supply a new direction for this generation.

But the crash will also affect those whose employments and incomes – in retailing, leisure, hospitality, personal services and a range of other activity supporting the consumerist lifestyles of the better-off – have been created through a combination of the bubble and state policy. The logic of productivism is to convert informal activities, such as child care and self-provisioning, domestic work and gardening, into paid employment, and to reinforce these processes by state authority, in the conditions around welfare-to-work programmes. Workfare in the USA, the New Deals for employment in the UK, and 'activation' policies in the Continental European countries have reinforced the incentives for low-paid, part-time and short-term service work with penalties on beneficiaries who refuse it; in the Anglophone countries, low wages have also been supplemented by tax credits,[15] to 'make work pay'.

This dynamic in productivism has been supported by some feminists, who argue that both better-paid women, and those whose paid services enable them to enter the labour market, have gained through their access to the formal economy, in terms of value for their contributions, and access to the public sphere.[16] Others suggest that all this confirms that only economic contributions through employment are counted as valuable in the productivist system.[17] These issues will be further analysed in the next section.

The underlying point here is that, in adapting its principles to the post-industrial circumstances of the affluent countries after most manufacturing has been transferred to Asia and Latin America, productivism has not in fact changed its criteria for valuing either people, their relationships or natural resources. The motivations for having children, supporting each other in partnership, caring for elders, helping neighbours and being active in community projects are fundamentally emotional and relational. We do them because we value other people and our bonds with them.[18] Productivism distorts some of these feelings and relationships by putting them on a contractual basis, as part of a calculative rationale for economic gain.

Much the same can be said of productivism's approach to the environment. What I have called social value (see pp. 78–87), which includes aesthetic and cultural elements in our resources for giving meaning to our relational and social environment, can be extended to include the natural world. Here again, we experience and interpret nature (which has been transformed by our interactions with it) through cultural resources. But the productivist approach denies value to any elements which cannot supply land or raw materials for commodities, and it puts a pure accessibility and scarcity value on those which can. This leads to the non-productivist demand that the components of the natural environment should be given values, and that their contribution to well-being should be recognized in public policy.[19]

This leads Tony Fitzpatrick to argue that emotional and ecological value should be regarded as the basis for all value, and combined as 'reproduction':

> Reproductive value refers to the ecological foundations of economic value, that upon which economic value is founded, but which it can never fully incorporate or commodify, since care and sustainability imply forms of activity so extensive that they can never be completely quantified or reduced to economic criteria. . . . Economic value depends on reproduction of its conditions, but cannot acknowledge this dependency, since no economy is wealthy enough to fully

compensate for the emotional and ecological costs that it creates: the ethics of affluence and growth are undermined the moment we render visible the foundations upon which they rest, because it is these foundations which they are gradually eroding.[20]

This leads to the next increasingly evident weakness of productivism – that it is undermining its own basis in material resources, because it cannot value the natural environment properly. Productivism has allowed human populations to increase, but at the expense of the delicate balance between life-forms which sustains the planet's ability to support our own and other species. A report on climate change forecasts that half the world's population could face severe food shortages by the end of this century as rising temperatures make agricultural production impossible over much of the tropics and the sub-tropical regions.[21]

This report estimates that harvests of staple food crops (like rice and maize) could fall by 20 to 40 per cent as a result of excessive temperatures during their growing seasons, with an added risk due to droughts. These dangers are greatest in the densely populated equatorial belt of Latin America, Africa and Indonesia, where the numbers of inhabitants are growing fastest, putting strains on food production and increasing prices. These forecasts, which emphasize that Europe too could experience damaging temperature rises, take no account of the effects of climate change on water supplies. In all, the combination of temperature rise and population increase requires a complete rethink of food production, soil fertility and human development for some of the poorest people in the world, the authors of the report argue.[22]

The point here is that the scale of the problem will overwhelm such technological innovations as GM crops; only a huge, international effort to stem carbon emissions and slow global warming, together with the re-establishment of sustainable communities (in terms of their populations and farming practices), offers any hope. There is no productivist way out of a situation caused by productivism itself, through the reckless discharge of carbon into the atmosphere from vastly increased industrial production worldwide.

So we turn back to the positive reasons why the crash might afford an opportunity to shift towards non-productivist approaches. Obviously, the downturn in output worldwide is in itself a factor – emissions and depletions will be moderated by falls in activity. But in addition to this, the crisis comes at a time when new arguments for change and new evidence of alternatives might be combined with new political and social mobilizations around agendas of sustainability.

The term 'sustainability' refers to a system of interactions which meets 'the needs of the present without compromising the ability of future generations to meet theirs'.[23] This implies that we recognize limits on what the natural world can supply, and adopt human systems of reproduction which are consistent with these limits. It entails a set of attitudes and practices in relation to the natural environment which respects the value of other species and the resources which support them, and acknowledges the interdependence of all forms of life.

Ideas and practices of this kind can only be created, maintained and updated through the cultures of communities. They do not necessarily involve extreme forms of nature worship, or communing with birds, flowers, trees and the moon. But they do imply that humans have a constant awareness of their reliance on the rest of the living world, and restraints which operate at the level of standards and values, affecting everyday beliefs and behaviours, which translate this into action.

In the non-productivist literature, attempts have been made to link these standards and values to the ethic of care, and to the caring activities of women.[24] Undoubtedly, because women have less of an involvement in technology-led productivism than men, and more with the emotional aspects of reproductive work, they are less responsible for the damages inflicted on the environment, but not necessarily more aware of the need to reduce our demands on it, or how to achieve this. Furthermore, the women's movement is deeply divided about the implications of the ethic of care and emotional work for their emancipation. For these reasons, as I shall argue, it seems to be a mistake to link the non-productivist agenda to women's role alone.

In the next section, I shall argue that sustainability should instead be seen as a matter of recognizing the benefits of interdependence, both between humans and between our species and the rest of the natural world. This distinguishes the non-productivist approach from the productivist one, which primarily aims to reduce the costs of interdependence,[25] and to maximize the scope for individual, private gain, through free choice. This does not involve a 'green police', or the totalitarian imposition of joyless, fustian traditionalism; it can be achieved through democratic processes.

Interdependence, sustainability and democracy

The most difficult theoretical and policy issues faced by a non-productivist approach to sustainability concern the fear that individual rights must be curtailed to achieve the necessary controls on consumption and waste. This is not simply a matter of regulation – for instance, of pollution. It also concerns the idea that more community and interdependence will make individuals accountable to others (their neighbours, as well as officials) over every aspect of their lifestyles.

Women are suspicious that they would be most affected by such a shift – they are centrally concerned with social reproduction, both in the home and in the kind of paid work they tend to do, and hence that they would be the ones required to be self-denying, puritanical or just poor. This echoes the approach adopted by feminist thinkers to issues of quality of life and well-being, and how emotional and relational components of this are to be analysed. As we saw in the work of Martha Nussbaum (pp. 84–5), universal human rights to resources and liberties seemed to provide a more reliable basis for the social minimum standards of the good life; cultures have often restricted women's capabilities, under-educating them, and confining them to subordinate, dependent, traditional roles.[26]

Indeed, one whole stream of feminist thought trusts the rights and choices characteristic of markets more than those of politics or social movements to set women free of these restrictions.[27] In this view, women must gain the sovereignty over their bodies, their possessions and their decisions to be truly self-realizing and self-responsible, in order to escape their domination and oppression by men. This means that liberal productivism is a safer option than interdependence, and that contract, the relationship that can be most specifically defined and that leaves the parties least involved with the details of each others' lives, is the least damaging for women's interests. On this account, non-productivism would be a step backwards for women, which would risk miring them in the obligations of cultural bondage.

I want to make it clear that this is not what I am advocating. Non-productivist interdependence does not imply enslavement to others' wills, or turning back the clock through women's resubordination. It does involve the *balancing* of individuals' freedoms and choices with their accountability to others, through *democratic* processes. This would apply equally to men and women, who would be equally free to assert their rights to autonomous choices, but equally part of systems of sustainable social relations in *political* communities.

By democratization I do not mean that sustainability must

become the business of government – though it could certainly become an important part of the rationale of public policy. I want to argue that sustainability can only be achieved through processes of self-rule, both turning individual liberty into a more far-reaching aspect of responsibility (responsibility for self-in-society, not simply 'self-realization' or self-fulfilment), and self-government in groups, associations and communities. In feminist literature, this view has been developed by Carole Pateman,[28] but it is also reflected in Green political theory.[29] The common theme here is more active participation, not in formal representative democracy, but in collective action of many kinds for improving a sustainable quality of life.

It is here that the examples of music and sport seem instructive. Although government interests itself in the overall structures in which the arts and sport take place in most societies, it does not provide the institutions, rules, forms and practices through which they are organized and performed. People learn and do these things for the love of it, and their individual commitment and group organization are largely spontaneous (most learning and training take place in private homes, clubs or public spaces, rather than schools or colleges, or specially provided state facilities). The vast majority of activity is informal and unpaid, and it is well recognized that the vigour and flourishing of professional music and sport depends on that of these informal spheres, both in terms of audiences and crowds, and in terms of new blood and new creativity. Similarly, the health of less prestigious and celebrated levels of performance is recognized as supplying the lifeblood for the highly paid elites in both fields.

Self-organized activities are co-ordinated into complex patchworks of amateur and professional events by various bodies – in the case of music, a diversity of commercial companies and impresarios, and various elite cultural organizations;

in that of sport, by tiers of local, national and international associations, which regulate participation and organize competition. There are also, in both cases, festivals in which the diversity of music and sport are celebrated, bringing together fans and followers of different branches, traditions or styles.

Music and sport are certainly not immune to the ills that stem from extreme individualism: greed, self-indulgence, drug and alcohol abuse, and so on. Their commercial sectors are rife with the exploitation, corruption and cults of celebrity which are features of the culture at large; in some respects, they even exaggerate them. But neither can thrive on purely market-driven methods; both need inspiration from sources in human effort, creativity and the celebration of collective joy. And they are both able to create and sustain kinds of loyalty and solidarity, across racial, religious and geographical boundaries, which few political movements are now able to achieve.

They also inspire self-mobilization of groups and communities, to innovate as well as to preserve traditions through their interactions, and to create bonds among audiences, spectators, followers and unpaid officials as well as skilled participants. Their capacities for self-financing and self-government must be envied, and should be emulated, by those in other services, and in political authority.

The relevant contrasts are therefore with politics, in which individuals and parties compete for control over the provision of formal collective goods (including laws and regulations), and with markets, where producers and suppliers compete to influence and meet the desires of individuals. Social policy has been sucked into the battle between these two organizing principles, with voluntary action appearing mainly as backward-looking charity and self-help, or in the guise of an alternative source of formal provision, under contract to government.

Yet there are, in fact, other examples of activities which lie somewhere between music and sport on the one hand, and politics and markets on the other. Activities such as angling (which has more participants in the UK than any other recreation or sport) are organized in clubs mainly for licensing purposes, and only secondarily for those of competition. Although anglers are not federated into tiers, or governed by layers of authority, they are well able to take collective action, either in defence of their traditional rights and practices, or in constructive contributions to environmental causes (such as promoting the purity of water in rivers). Although gardening is mostly conducted inside people's private property, or on allotments in a shared field, it generates a culture of appreciation which is expressed in clubs and competitions, and in visits to humble and grand gardens, where ideas, displays and produce are compared and shared. Gardening is highly commercialized, both in retail outlets and in media broadcasts, but it retains a committed membership of knowledgeable, enthusiastic practitioners, in several different branches of expertise.

All these examples raise the question of whether, with a different kind of leadership, and the development of new cultures of participation, there could be a more diverse and pervasive social movement towards sustainability within communities. The crash has meant, as I argued in chapter 1 (p. 40), that people have been forced to pause in their projects for self-development through property and consumption, and look for others with whom to share risks and resources. Any such increase in spontaneous interdependence is an important first step in the direction I am suggesting, and potentially a basis for an important part of fixing social policy, broadly conceived.

The sustainability agenda widens the scope of social policy, to include a whole range of activities which substitute non-productivist rationales for productivist ones. The goal of these is neither to create employment, nor to improve economic efficiency, nor to achieve growth, nor even to meet the needs of those who cannot meet market criteria of employability and income adequacy. It is rather to mobilize people to iden- tify and pursue activities which *both* enhance their quality of life, *and* create a collective social and physical environment which makes demands on natural resources such that it can be enjoyed by future generations. This involves the creation of ideas, images and practices which are shared among and developed by members, and can be passed on to younger par- ticipants, who will modify and enhance them further.

The obvious instances of this happening in the UK in recent years concern food, cooking and eating. Celebrity chefs, par- ticularly Jamie Oliver and Hugh Fearnley-Whittingstall, have conducted campaigns to improve standards in food production and marketing, preparation and cooking, and appreciation. Jamie Oliver's TV programmes devoted to converting school canteens to producing healthy meals were remarkably suc- cessful;[30] his even more ambitious attempt to get a whole community (Rotherham) to cook and eat family meals was more ambiguous in its outcomes,[31] but it had some success in mobilizing a group of enthusiastic individuals and companies.

Where a charismatic media personality gives a lead, and communicates a message about quality of life and sustain- ability, it appears to be possible to bring about cultural shifts, and mass participation. This might be contrasted with many failures in government policy, where attempts to define tar- gets for change, and deploy professionals, experts, regulators or enforcement staff, have demonstrated the shortcomings of a top-down approach, derived from a contractual rationale. For instance, when the New Labour government wanted to try to catch up with Continental European countries' record on recycling waste, its chosen method was to propose that those who recycled a higher proportion of their rubbish would pay less council tax, and those who put out more waste would pay more. This provoked a furious media campaign of opposition, much of it focused on the enforcement measures which were taken by council officials under existing local authority schemes. The result was that, when the government looked for councils to pilot its approach, none came forward.[32]

Yet there are in fact many examples of voluntary recycling schemes, which flourish in the absence of state or local authority involvement. In the village where I live, one such, even though it does not engage the whole population, is able to dispose of several types of organic and non-organic waste in sustainable ways, using volunteer labour. The paternalism of government, and the 'clientalization' of citizens[33] in most of its interventions, actually create barriers for bottom-up collective action in many such cases, making the wider significance of issues less recognizable, and masking community members' interdependence.

This implies that the role of government should not be to try to modify *individual* behaviour, by changing the costs of various kinds of actions so as to provide incentives for those which are socially desirable. Nor should it be to contract with local authority agencies or voluntary organizations, in order to get them to 'deliver' the collective outcomes it wants, through targets and incentives, under regimes of inspection. It is more important for government to ensure that the framework in which collective action takes place contains sufficient rights and resources for individual autonomy and self-rule, and that the *ethical* and *social* principles underpinning such collective action (social value, environmental value, diversity, equality, etc.) are explicit and upheld.

If those two goals are achieved, it is likely that sustainable communities will be better served by grants to collective bodies of several kinds, to be spent by them through their members' democratic decisions. This would encourage grassroots and wider community organizations to emerge,[34] and to form coalitions, identifying a broad range of issues for improving quality of life. Far from imposing oppressive control, it could enhance collective investment in chosen projects, through the exercise of community self-rule.

Individual autonomy and the quality of life

A non-productivist approach to sustainability and human development demands a radical reorientation of collective life, but also requires the protection of individual autonomy. Those who advocate 'eco-welfare' or Green social policies are often also supporters of a redistributive measure – 'basic income' or 'citizen's income' – which would, they claim, enhance the rights of individuals, completing the promises of the Enlightenment philosophers on moral sovereignty.[35] This proposal, achieved through an integration of the tax and benefit systems,[36] or through an annual demogrant,[37] would provide all residents (or all citizens) in each society with an unconditional sum, not tied to work roles, or to domestic arrangements. This would leave each free to choose how to combine paid and voluntary work, self-provisioning and leisure. It would also allow couples and groups (or communes) to negotiate their division of labour in the household, or – for example – to take turns in paid employment, study or volunteering, on the basis of security and equality.[38]

There is some dispute among advocates of basic income (BI) as an approach to distributive issues over whether it is *intrinsically* favourable to a non-productivist, sustainable model of society, or whether the transformations in public policy needed for sustainability and community would require other measures to be realized. This in turn reflects a deeper theoretical debate about whether BI is to be seen as in principle an enhancement of the liberty of individuals, or as fundamental for a transformation in social relations.

The most influential theorist of BI, Philippe Van Parijs, based his case for the scheme on a guarded justification of capitalism and global economic integration as the most plausible roads to the dynamic efficiency needed to sustain maximum feasible BIs for every human being, and justice between them. His arguments used a strict methodological individualism, insisting that each individual should be left to live as he or she might like to do, to do whatever he or she might want to do. Since such individuals are, by assumption, diverse, markets will give the best results by this criterion. He rejected any 'particular substantive conception of the good life' as 'perfectionist';[39] by implication, therefore, he accepted the orthodox economic model of development, growth and productivism, or at least prioritized liberal neutrality over sustainability and community as political principles, though he conceded that ethical goals other than justice might require policies based on different values.

Others have argued that BI would, by its very nature (if it was both unconditional and adequate for basic needs) transform social relations, to allow the expression of principles and practices quite different from those which prevail under productivist capitalism. For instance, Brian Barry claimed that these transformations could be analogous to those sought by socialists and feminists, that they would 'go back to Marx's utopian vision' in a way 'more plausible . . . than anything Marx himself came up with'.[40] If the BI was adequate, this would end exploitation, 'however low the pay . . . for the job is freely chosen in preference to an acceptable alternative of not having a job',[41] enabling the reorganization of employment for socially desirable ends, such as transport system maintenance, health and social care, urban environmental conservation, education and training.

In the same vein, Erik O. Wright claimed that BI would alter the balance between the classes, reducing the workers' dependence on capitalists for their subsistence. It would allow non-market activity, and 'the collective struggle', because it would provide 'a guaranteed strike fund for workers'.[42] He included in his 'socially productive' activities caregiving, the arts and politics.[43] Finally, Carole Pateman argued for the BI as the basis for the freedom and self-rule denied women by previous political settlements, by 'breaking the link between income and employment' and ending 'the mutual reinforcement of the institutions of marriage, employment and citizenship'.[44] As noted earlier, the goal of this transformation could be the democratization of social interactions of all kinds, for instance in workplaces and households, and the guarantee that 'feminist arguments are taken seriously',[45] with social reproduction a focus for reforms, addressing 'social relations and institutions, rather than atomistic individuals'.[46]

All these views suggest that the adoption of a BI approach to income distribution (or, indeed, a demogrant one, involving lump sum transfers) would enable a radical reassessment of society's priorities and goals, including certain tasks and activities given little recognition or reward under present conditions. Above all, because the BI would be neutral between paid and unpaid activity (unlike the present model of productivism, which uses the threat of withholding benefits to drive claimants into employment), it would allow individuals to reflect and negotiate over how to divide time and energy between their earning endeavours and volunteering or purely creative or recreational ones.

But there is no obvious reason why a principle which framed its justification in terms of *individual* autonomy, and in negotiations between individuals, should enable *collective* action. On the contrary, the examples given in Van Parijs's account, of surfers and exhibitionists with names like Lazy and Lovely, emphasize that 'real freedom for all' is understood as self-realization, much as in the current version of liberal individualism.

So it makes more sense to see the BI principle as one which could balance a new form of collectivism, which would be a central feature of non-productivism, under this approach to transforming social relations and fixing social policy. The BI would leave individuals free to hold back from collective action, or to leave if their views were not heeded by the rest of the group, or to move to another, more congenial community. These exit opportunities would stem from the autonomy which came with an income that was not linked to the community's collective projects, any more than to the household's roles and resources.

Indeed, despite his opposition to 'perfectionism', Van Parijs seemed to recognize this towards the end of his celebrated analysis. Just because BI is so strongly rooted in the value of individual autonomy, it might need to be offset by other institutions, to achieve even the necessary solidarity for a sustainable level of BI, let alone for a set of sustainable social relations of solidarity. Van Parijs made this concession in the context of a discussion on how a *global* BI, distributing a subsistence minimum income to the whole world's population, might feasibly be organized. He acknowledged that it could need the underpinning of certain attitudes and institutions fostering equal respect and equal concern for all humanity. These he called 'strategies' of 'democratic scale-lifting' for global redistributive schemes, and 'solidaristic patriotism' for social justice within national polities – 'dispositions' which find an 'emotional basis' in the interactions between people 'from all categories in society'.[47]

Van Parijs, at the very end of his book, conceded that such relationships among interdependent collective units, and within an integrated world economy, and promoted by institutions and authorities (if necessary with compulsory powers), were necessary to achieve 'a sufficient level of social cohesion' to sustain global transfer mechanisms.[48] He admitted that these measures might sound more communitarian than real-libertarian. But – as other advocates of BI have acknowledged[49] – what is really at stake in the transformation of the collective life of communities, societies and the world's population is sustainability, which itself requires cohesion and a sense of common purpose for its achievement. The autonomy supplied by BI, and the collective will to improve the quality of life over the generations, can be mutually reinforcing, so long as an extreme individualism and consumerism is replaced by a non-productivist political and moral culture.

Indeed, the guarantee of individual autonomy supplied by a BI is not in itself sufficient protection for liberty without free movement between collective units, including nation states. Van Parijs has opposed open borders, on the grounds that some countries would 'dump' their poor, disabled and elderly citizens on others.[50] But free movement is an exit right which complements the BI, allowing people who do not subscribe to the dominant rationale for social reproduction in one country to move to another.[51]

The question, of course, is how entitlement to a national BI scheme for the citizens of one state (a CI, or citizen's income) could be meshed with a worldwide GBI (global basic income). One obvious solution would be to have an organization (such as the United Nations or IMF) which distributed a GBI to all the world's population, but that this was 'topped up' with national, regional or local sums. This would mean that international migrants might have to apply for the CI of the country they entered, and could take time to qualify.[52]

The other side of this would be that, in the aftermath of the crash, national governments are going to have stronger incentives to hold on to their citizens. Many regimes had become over-reliant on global money markets to cover their budget or trade deficits. The UK was a clear example of this. Its nation's banks had increased their borrowing from abroad from about

£6 billion in 2000 to £750 billion in 2008.[53] In that year, the government's annual account deficit had doubled over that of 2007, to 8 per cent of GDP, even before its second-stage bail-out of the banks.[54] With foreign lenders unwilling to supply the UK banks, and increasingly reluctant to lend to the government, the important question began to focus on UK savers – were they willing to buy government debt ('gilts')?

Countries with high volumes of private savings – like China, Japan and other Asian states – or large sovereign wealth funds – like many of the Gulf states – are in any case still in productivist mode, and can absorb extra funds for industrial investment. But those which, like the UK, Spain, Greece, Ireland and Iceland, had bubbles in financial services and housing, would have to turn to their citizens to fund rising annual account deficits (see pp. 64–5). So it was important to them that neither these citizens, nor their savings, moved abroad.

In the post-crash situation, although the first reaction of governments might be to try to stem immigration, to limit claims on public resources such as housing and health care,[55] a more considered approach would focus on improving cohesion, to conserve private assets and eventually harness them to national purposes. A non-productivist rationale for sustainable reproduction could mobilize these resources, in a project of regeneration – on the lines of the one that President Obama is seeking to set up in the USA, where he has a similar level of public and trade deficit, but much more national wealth potentially at his call.

A non-productivist agenda for sustainability therefore involves the adoption of institutions and policies which balance individual rights with collective mobilizations and political democracy. But – as the examples of music and sport show – it need not be solemn or dutiful, self-denying or intrusive. If autonomy and exit are safeguarded, it can combine justice and an approach to efficiency which takes account of social and natural value.

Intergenerational relations, technology and culture

A non-productivist version of human development implies a system of social reproduction which is sustainable (with suitable modifications) over several generations. The idea of being able to improve the quality of life of future generations was one of the characteristics of Enlightenment modernity. Progress, through science, would give rise to greater well-being; this was the promise of productivism, implicit in the economic model for increasing overall welfare which dominated public policy up to the crash.

Environmental degradation, climate change and resource depletion all place newly recognized constraints on this approach, and demand that we acknowledge the claims of natural diversity and sustainable lifestyles. But what about the claims of future generations? Some theorists have argued that unborn people cannot have claims against us (they cannot enjoy rights) because they cannot reciprocate. Hence there cannot be said to be a coherent notion of intergenerational justice.[56] But this seems merely to indicate that relationships between present and future generations cannot be adequately analysed in terms of individual rights or liberal justice. The unborn future inhabitants of the planet are in much the same position as the members of other life-species – they depend on living humans to create the conditions in which they may flourish, because we have the political and technological means to ensure that they can exist. (Of course, given modern weaponry, the same can be said about the great majority of the world's living population, in relation to the political and technological capabilities of the relatively few inhabitants of the affluent countries.)

So a more meaningful way to frame questions about future generations' relationships with ourselves is to ask how much we should *discount* potential future costs and risks in making decisions about our quality of life.[57] Because we can never quantify these accurately, to take account of cosmic disasters or transformative beneficial discoveries, there is an almost inbuilt human propensity to favour present advantages over possible future dangers. The idea of a discount rate asks how much of our investment in present and future resources should value the interests of future generations in relation to our own. As Fitzpatrick points out, 'If we set a discount rate that is too high (profligacy), then we might not be able to create and maintain a sustainable eco-system; if we set a rate that is too low (asceticism), then the present generation may be called upon to make sacrifices that are politically and culturally unrealistic'.[58]

His solution is to make trade-offs between present and future needs on the basis of a non-material conception of well-being,[59] respecting reproductive values (social and natural). Keeping the discount rate low, but finding ways of consuming, and investing, which are geared to sustainability (though not necessarily lower than at present).[60] The crash provides an opportunity to switch to this approach.

In practice, this means that, while we take the threats of depletion and pollution seriously, and aim to reduce global poverty, we should (for example) pursue growth through investment in energy-saving and climate-change-reducing technologies, as well as changing lifestyles through less wasteful and polluting cultures of consumption. Policies to improve the well-being of today's poor could be reconciled with those to protect the well-being of future generations through trade-offs under which justice (greater equality of incomes and freedoms) converges with sustainability over time.[61] The tax–benefit regime should ensure that the utilization of resources both contributes to just distribution among present populations and encourages the development of substitutes for those depletable resources (such as fossil fuels), which can potentially be used for present benefit without long-term harm (such as increased carbon emissions).[62]

The crash offers an opportunity to identify and pursue such trade-offs, as President Obama's programme seems to recognize. Some measures which could slow global warming are unsophisticated and would be inexpensive, such as growing strains of wheat with more reflective leaves, or painting buildings white. The scientist Hashem Akbari has calculated that, if all urban environments were painted to reflect the sun's rays, this would avoid the need to cool cities with air-conditioning, and cool the Earth enough to cancel out the warming caused by 44 billion tonnes of CO_2 pollution, wiping out the expected rise in global emissions over the next decade.[63] Together with other simple fuel-saving measures like roof insulation, these low-tech approaches would provide employment for less-skilled workers, and hence be consistent with social justice and sustainability.

Other high-tech measures for sustainability raise more complex issues, because they involve expensive investments which will only pay for themselves over a long period. Wind, tidal and solar sources of renewable energy, and the capture of carbon emissions from coal- and gas-powered generators, are in this category. But here, too, there are potential trade-offs. It has been calculated that a million people will be employed in the world wind-power industry alone by 2010 – even allowing for the crash – through the 30 per cent growth rate of the renewable energy sector set in 2008. Increases in the USA and China in particular have been dramatic.[64]

With the affluent Anglophone countries looking for new kinds of high-tech economic activity to replace their over-reliance on financial services, these industries are an

obvious opportunity. They might provide a way of offering new knowledge and investment goods to trade against
manufactured commodities from the newly industrializing
countries of Asia and Latin America. But the needs of developing countries would require them to be assisted by the
affluent states, if their attempts to catch up with China, India
and Brazil are not to cancel out gains in sustainability among
those countries which have already become centres of global
industrial production. It is in the early stages of industrialization that pollution, depletion and despoliation are most
damaging to sustainability,[65] so developing countries would
need assistance and support from affluent ones to avoid these
outcomes.

All in all, then, there should not have to be a 'tragic choice'
between policies for greater equality and social justice among
present populations of the planet and the well-being of future
generations. So long as the goal of long-term sustainability
frames measures to improve the incomes and living standards of poor people today, the two should be able to converge,
towards the point where conflicts arising from depletion and
irreversible damage are minimized. Because the crash has
removed the illusion of super-profits and breakneck growth
through financial wizardry, there are strong incentives for
countries like the USA and UK to focus on environmentally
friendly innovations, which will safeguard future generations'
interests *and* allow developing economies to grow in sustainable ways.

But all this will rely on encompassing cultures of respect
for ecological values, and concern for those most vulnerable
to depletion of resources (water, as well as oil) and climate
change. Such cultures can be fostered by courageous and
inspiring leadership, by clear policy priorities within an
explicit ethical framework and by empowering democratic
communities to improve their long-term quality of life.

Conclusions

During the long years between the neo-liberal revolution of the late 1970s and the crash of 2008, a very narrow conception of the basis for social policy prevailed. It was assumed that property and markets would supply the dynamic for social relations of all kinds, and that utility-maximizing individuals would, given the right opportunities and incentives, be able to provide for most of their needs as independent agents, and that interdependence over collective goods could also be efficiently constructed out of their choices.

The model derived from these principles is busted. Much of the value of the property rights (in houses, shares, private pensions, etc.), which were supposed to give people independence and security has disappeared. But their indebtedness – and that of the banks and governments which were supposed to have created permanent boom conditions – is all too real. So ordinary citizens, organizations and political leaderships are casting around for new ideas, institutions and directions.

In this chapter, I have argued that there is already evidence that all of them are coming to recognize more of the benefits of interdependence – the sharing of risks, the pooling of resources, and co-operation over new ways forward. Some societies were already in a better position to fall back on forms of interdependence which had never been allowed to wither – for example, family mutual support in China[66] and Latin America,[67] or kinship and communality in Africa. In the affluent countries, it is having largely to be rediscovered, and needs to be fostered and given a sense of purpose through new kinds of organization and mobilization.

This will be a painful and difficult process, especially in the affluent Anglophone countries, because people's very psychology has been transformed, along with the collective landscape, under the regime of individualism, private property, incentives and contract. The ruling idea is that we should all pursue 'projects of self',[68] to realize our personal potential, linking identity with property, credit and choice, in the public services as well as consumer markets. It is a big step to realize how our individual fates are intertwined with those of others, and how little we can do to preserve our cherished autonomy in the face of global economic forces. The very banks, which were supposed to provide us with the means to realize our projects, have dragged us down with them in their reckless greed.

The threat to the future of the planet offers a new focus for our interactions, along with the effort to preserve the quality of our lives. As all suffer declines in incomes and many far more serious loss of prospects, we look to leaders like President Obama for inspiration, and to public policy for collective expression of the potential advantages of acting together in a common purpose.

But I have argued that many of the clues as to how collective action might be galvanized by the crash are all around us, waiting to be recognized. Using the examples of music and sport, I suggested that our quality of life would be best served by engagement in groups and communities, in activities which we can identify and pursue simply by meeting and discussing with others. These interactions will go a long way to overcoming the barriers that have been created by the culture of individualism, and open communications that can give rise to new cultural resources, new ideas and new values.

The examples of music and sport are instructive because they are inescapably collective, and produce recognizable interdependences. Their value to participants and those who appreciate their performances is self-evidently in shared experiences, images and identities, whose value arises from interactions within cultural traditions. But they are not exclusive, or confined to specific localities, nations, ethnicities or faiths – they thrive on diversity and innovation, within the constraints of rules and disciplines.

Nor are they immune from all the problems in their surrounding cultures. They do not offer an escape from the wider collective life of societies, but they do give a hint of what a broader agenda for social policy might look like. In particular, they show that people can and do organize themselves around activities which give them a sense of excitement, creativity, mutuality, membership and belonging.

Although I have drawn on the work of theorists of non-productivism and sustainability, I have argued for a broader conception of social policies for human development and well-being than the ones they usually include. To focus on caregiving and environmentalism invites the response that what is required by the shift to sustainability is altruism (especially from women) and a certain puritanism (green fastidiousness). Yet the social reproduction systems, embodied in cultures, include all the elements which make life meaningful and valuable, and allow it to be enjoyed and celebrated. Because we can only experience, interpret and reproduce our collective world through cultures, and these are built out of exchanges involving social value, the transformations required for truly sustainable social relations should involve all these aspects of interactions. So music, sport, gardening and walking become as important for social policy as caring for children and disabled people, or for the natural environment.

I have also argued that, to fix social policy in an integrated world economy, the non-productivist agenda must be balanced by institutions and policies which uphold individual autonomy and freedom of movement. The ones outlined in this chapter were an unconditional basic income (BI) for all, and free movement across borders. These would allow individuals to criticize, withhold their participation and, ultimately, exit from the projects and directions chosen by groups and communities, and to innovate and initiate projects of their own. This would also allow them to choose how to combine formal (paid) and informal (voluntary) activity, and to be economic and social entrepreneurs.

Unlike the current liberal-communitarian approach, which is the social policy counterpart to the model of governance derived from the theory of information, incentives and contracts, the balance I am proposing does not leave community as an afterthought or fall-back for failures in the mainstream system. Nor does it require the values of social relationships and the natural world to be protected in an ethical framework which does not itself enter into the political decision-making process, as in the cost-benefit approach.[69] Community and sustainability are central to social policy, because it is the grassroots democratic process which deals in the issues which are of the core of quality of life and the meeting of needs. Instead of the government or international organizations setting targets and deciding ways to bring about desirable outcomes, people themselves both govern and adopt the means to their ends.

The crash has had about it echoes of almost all the events on Wall Street in October 1929, when a stock market collapse triggered over 2,000 local bank failures in the USA, the supply of credit dried up and output fell all over the world. As in 2008, that crash followed a bubble, in that case in stocks, after large sections of the US citizenry had been drawn into 'buying on the margin' – borrowing from banks or brokers to purchase shares for a 10 per cent deposit – and the market had risen 50 per cent in 1928. Here again, bankers had manipulated the markets to make super-profits, only to miscalculate through greed, causing the collapse.[70]

In the ensuing decade, as people turned to the state for a solution to the collapse of markets, totalitarianism replaced individualism in a rapid cultural transformation. Only the UK, its Empire and the USA escaped the cruelties of communism, fascism or some form of military dictatorship, but at the cost of massive unemployment and destitution. The hope is that today's world may avoid a slide into ethnic or religious conflicts, and wars over scarce resources. The 1930s should serve as a warning of how quickly political ideologies and group loyalties can be transformed in a real depression, and of how the consequences can be truly global.

If we have not moved far from those days in terms of economic wisdom and foresight, the symbolism of a black US President, bearing a Muslim second name, whose father was an African, and who grew up in Hawaii and Indonesia, is a powerful pointer towards global approaches to the aftermath of the crash. Social policy can be part of a broader programme to fix economies and societies if the new ideology and solidarity are formed around sustainability in social reproduction.

6

Conclusions – transforming social policy

My diagnosis of what is wrong with social policy, and my prescription for how to fix it, rest on two separate but linked analyses. The first concerns the economic model of social relations, public policy and politics derived from the theory of information, incentives and contracts. The second concerns the approach to human well-being and development in which other aspects of social, collective and natural life are sacrificed to individual gains in utility.

The link between these two strands of the orthodoxy which prevailed in international organizations and affluent Anglophone governments before the crash of September–October 2008 is that collective arrangements are supposed to be explained and justified in terms of individual choices among agents with different tastes, and the abilities to pursue their interests through selected strategies and projects. This in turn is supposed to give rise to a set of mechanisms and laws, which apply to societies as a whole, and indeed to the whole world, and not simply to economic life.

The crash made this whole theoretical enterprise absurd, since it was the very epicentre of its grandiosity, the world's banking citadel, which imploded. Yet the shock is still being felt as much in the academic social sciences as in stock exchanges, boardrooms and cabinet offices. A replacement analysis for the institutions to sustain collective life has still not been found.

Part of the problem is that political leaders are as yet unsure how much of the architecture derived from the old model can be rescued and reconstructed for the post-crash challenges. An obvious example has been the decision to entrust the IMF with newly funded crisis loans to destitute governments, made at the G20 meeting in London. The idea that the IMF could discover a 'new culture' for the administration of these missions was wildly optimistic.

I have argued that the model was to blame for a very wide range of failures in public policy generally, and social policy in particular, and that these failures stemmed from general features of the model, rather than specific weaknesses. This may seem to be an overstatement of the problems arising from the application of economic analysis to government, but it is based on equally radical criticisms from inside the economics profession itself.

These focused on the micro-foundations of the discipline itself,[1] on the predictability of future economic patterns,[2] and on the use of cost-benefit analyses in policy decisions.[3] They indicate the need for a major overhaul and revision of economic theory, and above all a greater modesty about what economics can offer to the other social sciences, and what it needs to learn from them.

The crash has simply confirmed these doubts and criticisms. First, it has shown that much of what passes for 'information' in global markets is speculative and nebulous, and cannot be relied upon to 'reveal' opportunities for efficiency gains. In reality, predictions about global market trends are more like weather forecasts, because the situation in which decisions are made is more like shifting flows of air than like a machine, by analogy with which the dominant model is constructed.[4]

Small events (such as the mortgage defaults in the USA which triggered the crash) can shift the overall path of change, so development of the whole system depends on tipping points and thresholds to non-linear reactions, as in complex mathematical and computer modelling. Hence organic and evolutionary analyses, using complexity theory, may be more appropriate than mechanical ones, and explaining events more feasible for economics than predicting them.[5]

Second, the notions that banks are the best-informed agents in the economic system, and that they have the strongest incentives to use this information rationally, has been the main factor in the genesis of the crash. Banks suffered from the collective delusion that they had discovered completely new ways to manage risks, and to make money out of money. What passed for a golden age of financial innovation was self-deception on an epic scale.

The challenge for regulators and governments in future is not so much one of finding the right degree of control over the financial system as of ensuring that bankers can never again make decisions within an insulated, self-referential circle, untouched by the influences of common sense.[6] With the active encouragement of economic theorists, central bank authorities and governments, they had convinced themselves that their slicing and dicing of debt was an exact science, and that they could go on generating enormous profits with borrowed sums for ever.

In fact, neither bankers nor economists are particularly good at spotting the really significant factors in economic development or decline. This is because opportunities for efficiency gains and sustainable growth are not 'out there', waiting to be recognized, but latent in certain configurations which give rise to potentially increasing returns, as in Silicon Valley in the early days of the microelectronic revolution. Equally, the collapse of whole industries and regional economies can be sudden, more like biological extinctions than the gradual running down of a mechanism.[7]

Third, the whole model's reliance on the cornerstone of the individual maximizer of utility, following rational strategies, based on consistently ordered preferences, is delusional and misleading. In the real world, advertisers (including those selling financial products and promoting credit cards) act as if people are irrational fantasists, who live on dreams of personal fulfilment and public celebrity. They used the long boom to lure them deep into debt, on the basis of an illusion of ever-rising asset values and sustainable long-term growth of the global economy.

The governments of affluent Anglophone countries have been willing partners in this deception. Because they relied on their financial sectors for such a high proportion of their tax revenues, they entrusted them with the main responsibility for guiding citizens' choices over such crucial issues as pensions and care in old age. But they also encouraged the habit of indebtedness, through the student loans system, by which half of each cohort of young people was drawn into a net of long-term borrowing for ordinary living expenses.

With the crash, the folly of that policy has been revealed. Those leaving universities in 2009 face very poor prospects of getting the type of jobs and pay associated with graduate employment, and are unlikely to be able to repay their loans for many years. Governments have peddled debt in much the same way as banks, on the back of what turned out to be false optimism.

All this links with the second major theme of this book – that social policy has allowed itself to be hijacked by a version of individual self-realization which subverts the whole basis of a viable collective life and social order. The supposed rationality of the individual in the economic model is contradicted by the cultivation of a fantasy of the independent, self-improving person, who is engaged in a project of self-fulfilment.

Individualism, inequality and well-being

Social policy is based on the sharing of resources and risks, through systems which gain the benefits of interdependence as well as reducing its costs. This requires relations of trust and solidarity among members of a political community. The evidence increasingly points to the corrosive effects of the individualism which is fundamental to the economic model adopted by the affluent Anglophone countries, and exported throughout the world through international financial organizations.

The basis for individualism in economics is itself shaky. Markets stimulate demand for the things they produce, but under conditions of affluence these increasingly rely on image and branding – the creation of mental associations which titivate the imagination and the emotions, but which are fragile and easily destabilized.[8] Marketing does not so much influence tastes as build whole fantasy worlds of bodily self-perfection, located in the beautiful home and garden, with the car as the expression of assertiveness and expertise.

The dominant model of government requires individual citizens to 'invent themselves', and sustain a constantly updated narrative of their own self-development.[9] Far from being a rational project, this elaboration of the self draws on cultural resources from the media and advertising, as well as family and community traditions, to construct ways of reconciling ambitions with responsibilities, insecurities with needs, and dreams with realities.

These social constructions enter the economy and the collective life of society as consumers and citizens, with inconsistent and confused expectations that are easily disappointed. Small disillusionments can sum together into major behavioural changes,[10] as when people suddenly shifted from buying cars as exaggerated status symbols to not buying cars at all.

Part of the role of social policy should be to protect the collective life of societies from the potential destabilization to well-being caused by human fickleness. But instead, affluent Anglophone governments have made fickleness ('choice', 'independence', 'mobility') the very badge of good citizenship. The big exporting economies, such as Japan, Germany and China, paid an equally heavy price after the crash for having geared their economies to providing the material commodities and the funding to boost these fragile self-delusions.

Economists themselves are making the link between individualism and the hidden costs of Anglophone regimes – rivalry, stress, insecurity, inappropriate aspirations, waste, debt, environmental degradation – in their analyses of the widening gap between welfare (measured in terms of GDP) and well-being.[11] The finding that the UK came bottom of a league table of the well-being of children and young people in twenty-one affluent OECD countries (see pp. 106–9) led to particular concern. In the report on an eighteen-month enquiry into the experiences of childhood in the UK, conducted by a panel of experts, and chaired by the economist Richard Layard, the conclusion was that 'there is one common theme that links all these problems [family breakup, commercial pressures, risky lifestyles, etc.]: excessive individualism'. This was also identified in the Joseph Rowntree Foundation's consultation on 'social evils'.

> By excessive individualism we mean the belief that the prime duty of the individual is to make the most of her own life, rather than to contribute to the good of others. . .. [I]ndividuals will never lead satisfying lives except in a society where people care for each other's good as well as their own. The pursuit of personal success *relative* to others cannot create a happy society, since one person's success necessarily involves another's failure.[12]

The report highlighted the rise in the percentages of young people suffering emotional and behavioural problems, in tandem with the rise in consumerism, obesity and alcohol and drug consumption. It emphasized the importance of relationships with parents and peers as factors in well-being; the

UK and USA fared worst on these measures, among the rich countries. This is scarcely surprising, given that the definition of excessive individualism given above is almost exactly the wording of the first duty of citizenship provided by the New Labour government in its version of rights and responsibilities in its Social Contract.[13]

I have argued that these features of individualism have become central to the cultures of these societies. They now serve as the means by which young people make sense of their social worlds, and orientate themselves to the actions of others. They aim to explain and justify their behaviour in terms of an effort to realize their personal potential, to develop distinctive identities based on commercial opportunities and the ownership of consumer goods. In the logic of the market, there is no requirement on them to take account of the actions of others (all of whom are conceived as involved in similar projects of self-realization) except to negotiate specific – ideally contractual – exchanges.

One paradoxical feature of this culture is that, as recorded levels of anxiety have risen, so have levels of self-esteem.[14] The obligation, in any individualistic account of oneself, to take a line on having achieved a successful version of one's personal potential, requires members to claim that they are proud of themselves, and are owed respect for what they have made of themselves. Research in the USA has shown that people under stress because their social evaluation was at stake seek to defend their self-image more actively, even desperately.[15] In other words, the assertion of high self-esteem can signal threats to a sustainable level of social value, as when an individual feels shamed, isolated or excluded.

Other US research indicates that rising levels of anxiety in all sections of society are related to the prevalence of self-promotion and narcissism in everyday social interactions, and that this in turn can be traced to conditions of increased individualization

and the absence of reliable intimacy, social support and community membership.[16] In comparison with Japan, where incomes
are far more equal, and the culture restrains expressions of
boastfulness or self-enhancement, the US social environment
demands the vigilant defence of fragile egos.[17]

These findings form part of the controversial claims, by
the UK researchers Richard Wilkinson and Kate Pickett, that
more equal societies almost always do better, in terms of a
whole range of indicators of health and well-being, and worse
in terms of an even longer list of social problems. Comparing
both nations and states of the USA, they produce statistical
evidence that greater equality is closely correlated with higher
life expectancy, with greater happiness, child well-being and
trust between citizens, and with low scores for a large cluster
of social problems, whereas higher average incomes are not.
They conclude:

> The assumption is that greater equality helps those at the
> bottom. As well as being only a minor part of the proper
> explanation, it is an assumption which reflects our failure to
> recognize very important processes affecting our lives and
> the societies we are part of. The truth is that the vast majority
> of the population is harmed by greater inequality. . . .
>
> Across *whole* populations, rates of mental illness are five
> times higher in the most unequal compared to the least une-
> qual societies. Similarly, in more unequal societies people
> are five times as likely to be clinically obese, and murder
> rates may be many times higher. The reason why these dif-
> ferences are so big is, quite simply, because the effects of
> inequality are not confined just to the less well-off; instead
> they affect the vast majority of the population.[18]

The USA and UK come out very badly from these findings,
performing consistently worse than other affluent societies,
in both Europe and the East, and worse than many poorer
countries also. Although the New Labour government in the

UK tries to rebut such evidence by claiming it is out of date, the figures on inequality for 2007–8 (i.e. before the crash) showed a continued rise in inequality, to the point where it is now greater than at any time since the 1960s,[19] and the government has even been forced to admit that it will not achieve its much-vaunted targets on reducing child poverty by 2012.

All this indicates that, in line with the central arguments in this book, the affluent Anglophone model for social policy, derived from its economic theory of society, politics and public administration, has failed, and that it has not been addressing the right goals. In the UK in particular, the New Labour government has focused on re-jigging the tax–benefits system to achieve better targeting and incentives, and on re-organizing the public services and their relationships with the business and financial sectors to improve efficiency through new contractual approaches.

The returns on these investments, in terms of improvements in well-being, health and the reduction of social problems, especially those associated with inequality, have been paltry. It is time to shift to policies which address social relations, quality of life and the civic culture. The recent evidence of systems failures and disappointing outcomes has proved the inability of presently configured services to sustain the social value that alone can allow people to enjoy their interactions as family members, neighbours, associates and citizens.

Such cultural resources are easy to destroy, as has been proved since the early 1980s, but much harder to rebuild. This process of reconstruction cannot start until these problems are properly acknowledged. Then the challenge will be to try to rediscover mutuality and solidarity, so that redistribution and service provision can become sustainable, and act as the institutions supporting risk-sharing and a viable collective life.

This cannot be achieved by clever adjustments to the 'choice architecture' of collective life, as a fashionable theory of public policy claims. That approach, derived from 'behavioural economics', aims to 'nudge' citizens towards more restrained or socially responsible decisions, simply by framing everyday decisions more cunningly.[20] I am arguing for a politics which motivates them to take collective action for change.

The big new question is how states will mobilize their populations, so that families, districts, communities and whole societies act to provide for each other in ways which complement government programmes. Already there are signs that lessons can be learnt from what is happening in the newly industrializing and developing countries.

In China, family mutuality and communal solidarity will have to absorb a good deal of unemployment and poverty as growth rates fall; will the Communist Party leadership be able to put enough resources into rural areas, and to maintain the loyalty of these marginal regions by allowing more participation and voice? In India, can the commercialized symbolism of unity conveyed in Bollywood films and 20–20 cricket override the threats of inter-faith strife and terrorist subversion? And can the mechanisms for investing the wealth generated by twenty years of rapid growth (in huge personal fortunes in India, sovereign wealth in China) in global economic development now fund human development and well-being at home in reliable ways?

Elsewhere, too, new approaches to these issues are being tested. Also on 26 January 2009, President Evo Morales of Bolivia announced that the referendum on a new Constitution for the country had endorsed new full rights of citizenship for the indigenous populations, mainly living in the highland regions.[21] But could his regime overcome the resentment of the mainly white, more prosperous inhabitants of the lowlands (most of whom opposed the Constitution), and could it redistribute enough of the returns from the recently nationalized oil and gas resources to indigenous communities to ensure new forms of economic and political participation?

Finally, on the same day, a conference of the United Nations Food Poverty Programme in Madrid heard pleas from an executive of the World Bank for the affluent countries to spend 0.7 per cent of the money going to bail-out the banks (i.e. £5 billion) on aid to the 1 billion people worldwide living in hunger or at risk of starvation.[22] Would any such transfers be forthcoming, in the face of rising food prices and climate change?

Social rights and the moral order

In chapters 4 and 5, I suggested that the kinds of interdependence created by global economic integration have generated problems requiring international collective action, both to capture the benefits of new complementarities, and to combat the risks of global degradation and other negative externalities. Ideas about global social policy are often framed in terms of human rights[23] – universal entitlements, some of which are liberties, and others claims to shares of the fruits of human endeavour and our natural heritage. Can human rights steer social policy worldwide?

It is now well recognized[24] that social rights – to income, health, education and care – have been the most problematic of these entitlements. This is because it is highly contested whether they can ever be universal, unconditional entitlements, with the same status as rights to life, to self-ownership (freedom from enslavement) and to freedom from inhuman and degrading treatment, by others or the state. In part, this is because liberals doubt whether 'positive freedoms' can ever be guaranteed, upheld and enforced as can 'negative freedoms' (from interference or coercion).[25]

But it is also a dispute about whether rights to private ownership of property, in land and material goods, can ever be trumped by common rights to ownership of natural resources, minerals, or more generally of nature itself (the 'wild woods', mountains, rivers, etc.);[26] and whether the state can legitimately sequester or tax away owners' rights to an income from material wealth more generally. These arguments seemed to have been settled after the Second World War, both through the nationalization of key industries in wartime, and through redistributive welfare state regimes.

But they soon reappeared,[27] and the failures of Keynesian economic management to deliver reliable growth, and of social insurance systems to eradicate poverty, allowed neo-liberalism to achieve a comeback, and indeed to gain global hegemony by the end of the 1980s. It was no coincidence that this shift marked a change from unconditional versions of social rights (for instance, in pensions and child benefits) to increased conditionality, first for unemployed people and lone parents, and then increasingly for disabled people and those with long-term illnesses.[28] Workfare and welfare-to-work measures proclaimed that rights to income support for low earners and those outside the labour market were *not* like property rights, or rights to self-ownership. Indeed, those who received benefits had a responsibility to strive hard to support themselves, to prove to those who supported them through taxes that they too were worthy of full membership of the community.[29]

I have argued that the crash opens up the debate about these issues once more. On the one hand, the property rights which generated the wealth that was supposed to benefit all (bank profits, bank loans, private pensions, mortgages, owner occupation) have proved to be the products of a speculative bubble. Countries like China, whose high savings rate allowed the accumulation of a sovereign wealth fund, turned out to be in a far better position in the longer run than ones like the USA and UK, where government and households borrowing against illusory riches left even the apparently wealthy vulnerable. If state assets in China, Dubai, Qatar and Kuwait proved more reliable sources of the wealth that allowed economic leverage in the global marketplace, would not the nationalization of banks and industries be a good strategy during the aftermath of the crash? And if the nation's wealth belonged increasingly to the government, why should not citizens have a share in it, in the form of a basic income (BI)?

The same questions arise in the developing world, through issues about the ownership of land and mineral rights. In Latin America, the nationalization of oil and gas resources has provided a source of government revenue which can be used for distributing income to indigenous households and communities. In Guyana and Brazil, the protection of tropical forests and their indigenous inhabitants is a potential source of revenue from governments worldwide, because of their huge importance for reducing carbon accumulations in the atmosphere. Land redistribution, and various kinds of communal land-holdings, are alternative forms in which property rights can be redistributed, to provide reliable incomes.[30] In South Africa and Namibia, black people often own mineral rights on the land of wealthier white farmers, and here too steps towards BI have been taken.[31]

So the possibility of converting social rights to income or wealth into something like property rights, which then become analogous to self-ownership or to freedom from coercion, could be part of a global agenda of transformation in the new situation. As free-market capitalism reveals its frailties and contradictions, there is a far stronger case for approaches which root income and wealth in a sustainable economy, which values human and natural resources, and gives them a material basis for their reproduction and conservation.

But the other kinds of social rights, to health, education and care, cannot be treated as if they were like property or self-ownership, not just because they involve claims on others, but because they are necessarily interactive and communicative in their realization. The support and expertise people need in illness (or to stay healthy), in childhood (or in periods of retraining) and if they rely on others for everyday assistance (either permanently or for shorter times), all involve *social* interactions, as well as specific skills. They entail the nego-tiation of the meaning of health, knowledge and well-being, how they relate to morality, culture and social relations, and to power and the political order.[32] As I argued in chapter 3, the notions of services which are 'delivered', in costed 'packages', according to target strategies for managerially determined outcomes, under contracts to governments, all distort these features of such interactions.[33]

In chapter 5, I argued that the crash offers an opportunity for a transformation of the social relations of affluent countries, through the adoption of approaches to social reproduction which embrace principles of sustainability in communities. This would mobilize people for the democratic determina-tion of how to improve the quality of their shared lives, and make those staff who provide expert services accountable to such movements. Already the social policy literature contains a recognition of the weaknesses of the contract model of serv-ices, and of the legalistic approach to rights, including human rights, in relation to these needs.

Many authors argued that professionals must negotiate with service users about the meaning of their experiences and locate them in a moral and political framework.[34] This inter-pretative and interactive approach recognizes that practice is a social–political process.

I have also argued for a much broader conception of social policy than has been orthodox within the academic discipline. Using music and sport as models, I suggested that people will participate in self-organized activities if they can run them according to their own ideas and images of what is enjoyable and meaningful, and that this kind of engagement is highly relevant for well-being. This means that the frameworks

under which activities are regulated should not only be democratic, but also enable cultures of appreciation and standards
of excellence to flourish, rather than managerial controls.

Although music and sport show that voluntary involvement can mesh with commercial profit, they also indicate the
gains in quality of life available through such an approach.
For example, even using existing cost-benefit analysis, the
UK Audit Commission has reported that youth projects in leisure, music and sport are cost-effective, especially in terms of
savings in criminal justice expenditures.[35] The Commission
bemoaned the fact that government funding systems required
inordinate amounts of time to be spent making applications,
taking staff and volunteers away from face-to-face activities.
As an instance of success, they quoted a golf club in North-
East England which, after suffering expensive vandalism and
theft at the hands of local youths, invited them into its facilities and gained over 100 new members.

Sources of resistance to a new social policy agenda

The most obvious arguments against the new approach to
social policy outlined above come from those who think that
the model of governance derived from the theory of information, incentives and contracts can be repaired, and (eventually)
both national and global economic growth can return to their
previous upward trajectories. On this analysis, banks can be
restructured so as to remove the perverse incentives under
which those making loans had no stake in their repayment,
since they were selling them on to others at a profit. If banks
returned to their traditional role in assessing credit-worthiness
and monitoring repayment of loans, the whole of the rest of
the system could return to normal functioning.

This view ignores the fact that most of the growth achieved

in the affluent Anglophone countries during the boom years since the early 1990s was based on bubbles of one kind or another (dotcom companies, house prices, derivatives, etc.).[36] For example, in the UK, aggregate personal wealth (in houses, shares, pension rights and savings) had grown to eight times GDP, historically a high level, and since the crash had much reduced in value.[37] The low interest rates set by central banks (especially the US Federal Reserve) made borrowing seem cheap, but the casino practices of the commercial banks allowed them to give good returns on foreign borrowing. Now none of this can continue, the foundations for growth in the contract model have subsided, so – in the absence of funds from Asia and the Middle East – the financial sector cannot supply the dynamic for the success of these economies.

So the whole approach to social policy – in which individual sovereignty and choice shape the forms of collective life, allow the stability of public finances and construct the basis for political authority – ceases to be viable. Together with the imperatives of ecological sustainability, this demands a new rationale for credit, employment, taxation, collective action and political institutions. But inevitably there will be losers in this transformation – not just bankers and hedge fund managers, builders of speculative housing estates and shopping malls, and traders in gas-guzzling SUVs, but also those with a stake in the 'pre-crash' order, and especially in the service sector.

This is because the interests of professionals and managers in the public services have become intertwined with those of entrepreneurs and financiers in the commercial services, through the innovations of the boom years. On the one hand, the contract model favoured the introduction of private suppliers and private finance into health, education and social care, and into social housing provision, often making new state funding conditional on 'partnership' with these organizations.

On the other, the World Trade Organization has insisted that these sectors be open to competition from firms from all over the world, so many large commercial companies have a strong interest in global trade in these services, and in keeping a contractual, business approach to their organization, in which neither communities nor democratic processes can have much influence.[38]

This means that there are cadres of professionals and managers whose careers have been made in these organizational systems, and whose expertise lies in a commercial approach to their provision. They are likely to oppose the transformations advocated in this book, as will the theorists who supplied the analyses on which the model was developed.

In the way in which social policy is taught in universities in the UK, for example, there has inevitably been an adaptation to the thinking and the structures adopted by the New Labour government, and although a critical and comparative perspective is maintained in textbooks on the subject, the orthodoxy of the contract model shapes the learning agenda. For instance, in a popular text, the chapter on 'public expenditure decision-making' moves quickly from a general outline of the management of government spending to an account of Public Service Agreements in the UK, and how they set out 'the broad objectives of the policies of [each spending] department and specific targets to be delivered in the next three years'.[39] On the next page, it illustrates this with the Public Service Agreement for the Department of Health, 2005–8, giving the 'objectives and performance targets' to 'produce faster, fairer services that deliver better health and tackle health inequalities'.[40]

This means that, even as students, future administrators, managers and practitioners learn to think in terms of the contract model, and understand what social policy is in these terms. Their roles and relationships with front-line staff and service users are understood as exchanges within a frame-work of government-set priorities and outcomes, evidence-led, measurable and costed in line with these principles. The textbook retains a critical perspective on these approaches, pointing out for instance that, 'Typically the individualised mode of dealing with problems in the social policy sphere leads people to experience deprivations as individuals. . . . This has an isolating or fragmenting effect, and reduces the probability of group action among those involved. However, this does not rule it out altogether. The effectiveness of the movement of disabled people is a case in point'.[41]

In other instances, the influence of the orthodoxy is more subtle. For example, in a volume of essays on *New Agendas for Women*, in which leading theorists argue for better access to public life and citizenship for women, the editor, Sylvia Walby, in her introduction, wrote of 'a new social contract between women and men' which was emerging under New Labour in the UK, which was 'potentially more equitable, productive and socially inclusive'.[42] This involved 'a different way of thinking about resources', specifically *time*: 'The lens of time enables the competing needs and contributions to be assessed in a more symmetrical way, more in tune with the vocabularies and concepts of the actors involved'.[43]

As we have seen (pp. 116–17), the productivity of time is indeed part of the policy orthodoxy in which decisions are supposed to be made, by individuals and service managers, in the contract model. This has undoubtedly influenced how service users perceive the services they receive, as well as how managers 'deliver' them. For example, parents who have been involved in New Labour's flagship programmes for pre-school children, SureStart and the Children's Centres, are more likely to want a good child care service and environment than to want to be involved in, and committed to activities and groups. Despite the rhetoric of participation, the dominant logic of social relations and economic needs pulls them towards evaluating the uses of their time in terms of utility – income, expenditure and rationing of time in the most productive way.

The real question is whether the post-crash social environment will bring about a change in the ways that both staff and service users in such facilities evaluate their interactions. In chapter 5, I argued the case for a radical transformation in social relations, in which a non-productivist approach to services allowed people to mobilize around issues of the quality of their lives. My sense is that people are likely to form groups and movements for collective action of this kind before managers and professionals in services are ready to embrace this new orientation. It will be harder for those trained and experienced in the contract model to change their organizations and practices than it will be for ordinary citizens to begin to adapt.

I have suggested that there are already signs that people will recognize that, instead of making all their decisions as individuals realizing their projects of self-development, they can do better by acting with others in similar situations to gain the benefits of interdependence and risk-sharing. An awareness of the significance of these possibilities may be dawning in British politics (see below pp. 208–9).

This need not mean that the technical expertise and knowledge gained in recent years is devalued and eroded. It simply implies that it is put to the service of people's self-defined collective demands, and made democratically accountable, instead of being deployed for the purposes of achieving government-decreed targets and outcomes.

Unfortunately, it is an iron law of professionalism in the human services that status, prestige and money attach to more esoteric forms of knowledge and practice, which least involve communication and negotiation with ordinary people. Those roles which require professionals to work in informal settings (rather than deploy expert jargon), and to engage with self-selected groups and communities (rather than people defined by their neediness), carry little kudos. This is another reason why the movements for change in these organizations will be resisted – and why, for the sake of well-being and sustainability, these objections should be overcome.

The way forward

The crash has changed the collective landscape of our planet. As politicians struggled to save the world's banking system, it began to dawn on those with the luxury of being able to stand back from the immediate demands of the crisis that things would never be the same again. The collapse in incomes and employment showed that what was wrong was structural, not just cyclical, and structural change was needed. For one thing, the international loans from which the bubbles were created, and which funded the explosive growth in credit, would not be coming back. For another, the reputations of free-market economists and deregulatory policies were fatally damaged; the state had been drawn into fields which it would not be able to leave for many years, even if governments wanted this.

All this clarified that the urgent requirement for a 'new financial architecture' for the global economy included a much better-resourced IMF and World Bank, to lend to the developing countries of the world, not so much because of the plight of their populations, but because they were integral to a whole system in danger of grinding to a halt. Unless they continued to build, produce and spend, there would be no demand for the credit, investment and technology with which the richer nations traded for raw materials, or for the manufactured goods from the newly industrializing countries.

Another indication of the growing importance of the latter states for the global economy was the purchase of large tracts of agricultural land in the developing world. Whereas the previous decade saw a huge growth in the services, especially health and education, exported from affluent to poor countries, this trend signified a form of 'food colonialism', through which low-cost production of basic agricultural commodities was assured.

So, for instance, 'agri-investment' in North Cambodia and Southern Sudan by individuals, corporations and governments from Libya, Kuwait, China, Saudi Arabia, South Korea and the USA, saw local authorities (or warlords) in those and other poor countries sign agreements to allow 'development' of areas where land had been lying fallow, or cultivated by archaic methods.[44] This land-grab could result in peasants with ancestral ties to their districts being evicted.

But such new manifestations of globalization are being accompanied by other signals of retreat into national or local protectionism. On the one hand, China and the UK have been accused of covert devaluations of their currencies (by the USA and France respectively), as a way of gaining competitive advantage in trade. And both French trade unionists and Greek and Mexican farmers have reacted against their governments' unfavourable treatment of their interests. In the UK, construction workers in the power industry took strike action over contracts going to firms employing Portuguese and Italian workers.

At the national level, pressures for protectionist measures are intensifying in all kinds of states, as would be predictable in terms of Polanyi's 'two movements' (see below p. 122). Social policy is ambivalently poised between these forces for universalization and for collective conservation. On the one hand, it warns of the dangers of self-defeating retreats into protectionism, and (worse still) of ethnic and inter-faith strife or fascism. On the other, globalization has weakened the solidarities on which welfare states drew for their sustenance, and the turn of the tide against individualism and markets represents a new opportunity.

In the UK, the radical overhaul of the tax–benefits system recommended by the Centre for Social Justice (see pp. 153–4) has not been unequivocally adopted as official policy by David Cameron, the Conservative Party leader in the period before the 2010 general election.[45] This would be to reject New Labour's whole strategy of welfare-to-work conditionally and counselling, in favour of more generous disregards of resources and slower withdrawal of income support for those with low earning power. It would recast the task of increasing economic participation by poor people during the 'job crisis' in terms of improved access and social inclusion, rather than individual self-responsibility and obligation to be 'independent'.

It is intriguing to speculate how this shift in thinking about a great issue in social policy might be linked with the iconoclastic speculations of another influential thinker in Cameron's circle, Phillip Blond. On the face of it, Blond's critique of oppressive monopoly capitalism (both financial and industrial), his pleas for redistribution of wealth to localities and communities, and for the strengthening of associational, kinship and personal ties,[46] are all seemingly compatible with many of the arguments of this book. If the tax–benefits integration now accepted by the Conservatives can be seen as a first step towards the basic income approach which is my other main recommendation, could UK social policy be taking a surprising new direction under a 'Red Tory'[47] administration?

One virtue of such a shift would be the possibility of reconciling more equal citizenship status and more inclusive collective membership with an open economy, and with the overall aims of global sustainability. These changes might allow well-being and human development to replace gains in individual utility at the heart of social policy. The next stage in the worldwide debate about how to fix social policy (at all levels of human association) promises to be both intriguing and important.

Notes and References

INTRODUCTION

1 BBC Radio 4, *Today*, 25 November 2008.
2 Kahneman, Diener and Schwartz (1999); Huppert et al. (2005);
  Helliwell (2003); Wilkinson and Pickett (2009)..
3 Jordan (2008).
4 Stiglitz (2002); Stiglitz and Greenwald (2003); Stiglitz et al.
  (2006).
5 Department of Social Security (DSS) (1998), p. 80.
6 James (2007).
7 Stiglitz and Greenwald (2003).
8 Macho-Stadler and Pérez-Castrillo (2001); Laffont and Martimort
  (2002); Bolton and Dewatripont (2005).
9 Levitt and Dubner (2006).
10 BBC Radio 4, *You and Yours*, 25 August 2008.
11 BBC Radio 4, *News*, 3 December 2008.
12 BBC Radio 4, *Today*, 28 January 2009.

I THE PROBLEM

1 BBC Radio 4, *News*, 10 December 2008.
2 BBC Radio 4, *PM*, 12 December 2008.
3 Esping-Andersen (1990, 1996); Iversen and Wren (1998).
4 Esping-Andersen (1996), ch. 4.
5 Esping-Andersen (1999); Jordan (2006a).
6 BBC Radio 4, *News*, 15 December 2008.
7 Esping-Andersen (1990, 1996, 1999).
8 'Welcome to Britain – so long as you're an engineer, maths
  teacher or sheep shearer', *The Guardian*, 10 September 2008, p. 3.

9 *Financial Times*, 13 November 2008.
10 BBC Radio 4, *News*, 6 February 2009.
11 Newman (2002).
12 BBC Radio 4, *World at One*, 2 December 2008.
13 Pareto (1916).
14 Harris (1992); J. Offer (2006); Carter (2003).
15 Jordan (2008).
16 Buchanan and Tullock (1962); Becker (1976).
17 Clarke and Newman (1997).
18 Jordan (2008).
19 *Ibid.*, chs. 2, 6 and 7.
20 Perkins (2005).
21 S. Milne, 'The seeds of Latin America's rebirth were sown in Cuba', *The Guardian*, 29 January 2009, p. 33.
22 Ku and Jones Finer (2007).
23 BBC Radio 4, *Open Country*, 6 December 2008.
24 *Ibid.*
25 BBC Radio 4, *You and Yours*, 5 December 2008.
26 'Philanthropist loses £550m. in Madoff Fraud', *The Guardian*, 17 December 2008, p. 25.

2 INCOME, CREDIT AND REDISTRIBUTION

1 Buchanan and Tullock (1962), p. 4.
2 Stiglitz and Greenwald (2003), pp. 3–4.
3 Tett (2009), ch. 2.
4 *Ibid.*, p. 154.
5 Interview with Professor John Kay, former head of the Institute for Fiscal Studies, BBC Radio 4, *Today*, 20 December 2008.
6 John Varley, interviewed on BBC Radio 4, *Today*, 20 December 2008.
7 Stiglitz and Greenwald (2003), p. 204.
8 Macho-Stadler and Pérez-Castrillo (2001); Laffont and Martimort (2002); Bolton and Dewatripont (2005).
9 Stiglitz and Greenwald (2003), pp. 203–4.
10 *Ibid.*, pp3–4.
11 Stiglitz et al. (2006), p. 47.
12 Becker (1996), p. 4.

13   Rose (1996); Department of Social Security (hereafter DSS) (1998), p. 80.

14   *National Income Statistics* (2008).

15   Anderloni et al. (2008).

16   Blake and de Jong (2008).

17   Marshall (2004)

18   Erdemir and Vasta (2007); Datta (2007); Vasta (2006).

19   Gough (2004); Barrientos (2004).

20   Jordan and Düvell (2002).

21   Isaacs (2008).

22   Datta (2007).

23   Buchanan (1965); Cornes and Sandler (1986); Buchanan and Tullock (1980).

24   Leonard (1994, 1999, 2004).

25   BBC Radio 4, *News*, 6 February 2009.

26   BBC Radio 4, *Today*, 11 February 2009.

27   Hart (1995), pp. 29–44.

28   *Ibid.*, p. 57.

29   'People rush for government bonds – but experts fear they will become part of the problem', *The Guardian*, 4 December 2008, p. 17.

30   Jim Rogers, former partner of George Soros.

31   DSS (1998), p. 80.

32   'Labour tightens rules on benefits', *The Guardian*, 11 December 2008, p. 12.

33   Van Parijs (1995); Jordan (1987, 1996, 2006a, 2008); Fitzpatrick (1999, 2003).

34   Ackerman and Alstott (1999); Nissan and Le Grand (2000).

35   BBC Radio 4, *News*, 6 December 2008.

36   Bowles and Gintis (2002).

37   'Boost for local authority mortgages after government cuts borrowing rate', *The Guardian*, 2 February 2009, p. 27.

38   'Bank plan for Post Office', *The Guardian*, 2 February 2009, p. 27.

39   Gesell (1958 [1920]).

40   Monbiot (2009).

41   Blunkett (2004).

42   Blunkett (2003).

43   Huber and Stephens (2001); Seeleib-Kaiser, Van Dyk and Roggenkamp (2005).

44 Milner (1919).
45 C. H. Douglas (1974 [1920]).
46 Cole (1920).
47 Meade (1938).
48 Macmillan (1938).

3 SERVICES AND WELL-BEING

1 See Van Praag and Ferrer-i-Carbonell (2004); Layard (2005, 2006). The psychologist, Daniel Kahneman, was awarded the Nobel Prize for Economics for his work in this field – see Kahneman et al. (1999).
2 Frey and Stutzer (2002); Bruni and Porta (2005); Helliwell (2003).
3 Easterlin (2005); Di Tella, MacCulloch and Oswald (2003); A. Offer (2006); Helliwell (2003).
4 Bradshaw, Hoelscher and Richardson (2007); Bradshaw (2008); Jordan (2006b and c).
5 David Cameron, Leader of the Opposition of the UK, made a speech introducing this debate in Hertfordshire on 22 May 2006.
6 Veenhoven (1989, 1999); Van Praag and Frijters (1999); Frey and Stutzer (2002).
7 Veenhoven (1999); Layard (2005).
8 Griffin (1986), Nussbaum (2000).
9 Adler and Posner (2006).
10 For instance Mueller (1997), Cullis and Jones (1994) and Davies (1992) Wicksell (1958 [1896]); Tiebout (1956); Buchanan (1965).
11 Doyal and Gough (1991); Dean (2009).
12 Nussbaum (2000); Dean (2009) Goodrich and Cornwell (2008); Wilkinson and Pickett (2009).
13 BBC Radio 4, *News*, 30 December 2008.
14 McKinnon and Hampsher-Monk (2000).
15 Putnam (2000), p. 19.
16 World Bank (1998, 2001); Dasgupta and Serageldin, 2000).
17 World Bank (2001); for criticisms of this approach, see Harriss (2001); Fox and Gershman (2000); Fine (2001).
18 Adler and Posner (2006).
19 Jordan (2008), ch. 10.

20 Jordan (2006a and b, 2008).

21 M. Douglas (1982 [1978], 1987).

22 Durkheim (1912); Goffman (1967a and b).

23 Jordan (2005, 2006a and b, 2007, 2008).

24 Jordan (2008).

25 Davies (1992).

26 Cullis and Jones (1994); Mueller (1997).

27 Pareto (1909); Pigou (1920), p. 11; Robbins (1932).

28 Layard (2006).

29 Van Praag and Ferrer-i-Carbonell (2004), p. 4.

30 Layard (2005) claimed that he was returning to the utilitarianism
    of Jeremy Bentham in public economics.

31 Huppert et al. (2005).

32 Van Praag and Ferrer-i-Carbonell (2004), ch. 4.

33 *Ibid.*, p. 10.

34 Easterlin (1974, 2005); Veenhoven (1989, 1999).

35 Layard (2006), p. PC24.

36 Layard (2005), chs. 10 and 11 and pp. 23–4.

37 Layard (2006), p. C31.

38 Nussbaum (2000), p. 74.

39 Sen (1984).

40 Nussbaum (2000), pp. 75–82.

41 *ibid.*, p. 82.

42 *Ibid*, pp. 16–17.

43 *Ibid*, pp. 41–51.

44 *Ibid.*, p. 74.

45 Ormerod (2007).

46 Veenhoven (1999).

47 Jordan (2008), p. 21.

48 Bertrand and Kalafatides (2002), pp. 204–14.

49 M. Douglas (1982 [1976]); Sahlins (1974); Firth (1950).

50 M. Douglas (1987).

51 Durkheim (1912).

52 Goffman (1967a and b).

53 M. Douglas (1978), p. 181.

54 Durkheim (1898); M. Douglas (1987), pp. 98–9.

55 M. Douglas (1987), p. 99.

56 Smith (1976 [1776]), p. 330.

57 Begg, Fisher and Dornbusch (1997), p. 2.

58 Smith (1976 [1776]), p. 331.

59 Esping-Andersen (1990, 1996, 1999).
60 Buchanan and Tullock (1962), p. 13.
61 Buchanan (1968, 1978); Olson (1965, 1982).
62 Wicksell (1896).
63 Buchanan (1965); Cornes and Sandler (1986); Foldvary (1994).
64 Tiebout (1956).
65 Cullis and Jones (1994), pp. 300–3; Jordan (1996).
66 M. Douglas (1982 [1978], 1987).
67 BBC Radio 4, *News*, 27 January 2009.
68 *Ibid.*, 4 December 2008.
69 *Ibid.*, 27 January 2009.
70 BBC Radio 4, *Today*, 27 January 2009.
71 'Philanthropist loses $550 million in Madoff fraud: charities halve grants after losing funds', *The Guardian*, 17 December 2008, p. 25.
72 Jordan (1996, 1998, 2004, 2006b, 2008).
73 Fletcher (1998); Thompson (2002), p. 101.
74 Clarke and Newman (1997); Clarke, Cochrane and McLaughlin (1994).
75 Channel 4 TV, 'Can Jerry Robinson Fix the NHS?' October 2007.
76 '50 injuries, 60 visits – failures that led to the death of Baby P.', *The Guardian*, 12 November 2008, p. 1.
77 'We failed over Haringey – Ofsted head', *The Guardian*, 6 January 2009, p. 1.
78 Commission for Healthcare Audit and Inspection (2009), p. 11.
79 *Ibid.*
80 *Ibid.*
81 *Ibid.*, p. 4.
82 *Ibid.*, pp. 5–6.
83 *Ibid.*, p. 6.
84 *Ibid.*, pp. 6–7.
85 *Ibid.*, p. 8.
86 *Ibid.*, p. 9
87 *Ibid.*, p. 10.
88 *Ibid.*
89 BBC Radio 4, *News*, 19 March 2009.
90 Channel 4 TV, *Dispatches*, 'How They Squandered Our Billions', 9 March 2009.
91 P. Kingston, 'A painful death and a £42m debt', *The Guardian*, Education Section, 28 April 2009, p. 3.

92 *Ibid.*
93 BBC1 TV, *Panorama*, 4 May 2009.
94 'Flaws, flak and falling morale', *The Guardian*, Society Section, 19 November 2008, p. 3; 'Only a matter of time. . .', *The Guardian*, Society Section, 26 November 2008, p. 1.
95 'Child protection staff stifled by £30m computer system – report', *The Guardian*, 19 November 2008, p. 7.
96 BBC1 TV, *Panorama*, 4 May 2009.
97 'Ofsted accused of complacency on child protection', *The Guardian*, 11 December 2008, p. 4.
98 Jordan (2008).
99 Smith (1948 [1759]).
100 Pareto (1916), pp. 196, 244.
101 Pigou (1920), p. 21.
102 Bradshaw et al. (2007).
103 Innocenti Report card 7 (2007).
104 Layard and Dunn (2009), p. 6.
105 *Ibid.*, p. 151.
106 Helliwell (2003).
107 Layard and Dunn (2009), p. 3.
108 Pateman (1988), on Locke, Rousseau and others.
109 Pateman (1989), and (1988), pp. 16, 96, 100–1.
110 Tronto (1994); Sevenhuijsen (2000); Williams (2002).
111 See, for instance, the account of female supervisors of contract drawing workers in Ehrenreich (2002).
112 Argyle (1999); Helliwell (2003); Frey and Stutzer (2002).
113 Department of Health (2005).
114 *Ibid.*
115 Jordan (2008), pp. 207–9.
116 North Devon Parents' Group (2006).
117 Gambetta (1988); Platteau (1994a and b); Putnam, 1993, p. 174.
118 Durlauf and Fafchamps (2004).
119 BBC Radio 4, *News*, 2 December 2008.
120 North Devon Parents' Group (2006).
121 Bunting (2008).
122 Bowles and Gintis (2002), p. F423.
123 *Ibid*, p. F433.
124 BBC1 TV, *Panorama*, 4 May 2009.
125 Jordan (2007), ch. 8.

126 Jordan with Jordan (2000).
127 Becker (1976), p. 87.
128 Offer (2006), p. 147, fig.7.2.
129 Baumol (1967); Baumol, Batey-Brakeman and Wolf (1985).
130 Rose (1996).
131 *Ibid.*
132 Veenhoven (1999).
133 Rothstein and Stolle (2008).
134 Jordan (2006c).

4 GLOBAL SOCIAL POLICY

1 BBC Radio 4, *PM*, 30 January 2009.
2 Bevan (2004a and b); Wood (2004).
3 C. Pierson (1991); P. Pierson (1994, 2000).
4 Polanyi (1944).
5 Oates (1972, 1999).
6 Polanyi (1944).
7 World Bank (2001).
8 Fine (2001); Durlauf and Fafchamps (2004); van Staveren (2003).
9 World Bank (1998, 2001).
10 Putnam (1993, 2000, 2002).
11 Estimated by the Bank of England, *The Guardian*, 1 January 2009, p. 14.
12 *Ibid.*, p. 23.
13 BBC World Service, *News Briefing*, 19 January 2009.
14 Stiglitz and Greenwald (2003), pp. 284–5.
15 Stiglitz (2002).
16 Stiglitz and Greenwald (2003), pp. 205–6.
17 Stiglitz et al. (2006), p. 4.
18 Caprio (1997), p. 96.
19 Stiglitz (2002).
20 Stiglitz et al. (2006), p. 7.
21 Stiglitz and Greenwald (2003), pp. 3–4.
22 *Ibid.*, p. 4.
23 Stiglitz et al. (2006).
24 Stiglitz and Greenwald (2003), p. 286.
25 *Ibid.*, p. 221.

26 *Ibid.*, p. 208.
27 Caprio (1996).
28 Stiglitz and Greenwald (2003), p. 209.
29 *Ibid.*, p. 208.
30 BBC Radio 4, *You and Yours*, 14 January 2009.
31 Stiglitz et al. (2006), p. 11.
32 Kalecki (1971).
33 Stiglitz et al. (2006), p. 47.
34 Hicks (1947), p. 2.
35 Wicksell (1896).
36 Tiebout (1956).
37 Buchanan (1965).
38 Foldvary (1994).
39 Casella and Frey (1992).
40 Spruyt (1994).
41 Oates (1999).
42 Inman and Rubinfeld (1997), pp. 73–4; Bauböck (1994), p. 14; Coase (1937).
43 Frey and Stutzer (2002).
44 Inman and Rubinfeld (1997), p. 81.
45 Cullis and Jones (1994), pp. 300–2.
46 *Ibid.*, p. 303.
47 Brueckner (2000); Jordan and Düvell (2003), ch. 2.
48 Casella and Frey (1992); Jordan and Düvell (2003) pp. 54–5.
49 World Bank (2001).
50 Roemer (1983); Van Parijs (1992).
51 Castles and Miller (2003).
52 Sassen (1988).
53 Sassen (1991).
54 Sassen (1998).
55 *Ibid.*, p. xxii.
56 *Ibid.*, p. 5.
57 Akerlof and Shiller (2009).
58 World Bank (2001), pp. 6–7.
59 *Ibid.*, p. 85.
60 Buchanan and Tullock (1980); Begg et al. (1997), p. 187.
61 Niskanen (1975).
62 Jordan (1996), ch. 2; Olson (1965, 1982); Jordan and Düvell (2003), pp. 34–5.
63 Stiglitz (2002).

64 Coleman (1988).
65 Putnam (1993).
66 World Bank (1997, 1998, 2001).
67 Fine (2001), p. 146.
68 Bowles and Gintis (2002); Bjørnskov (2006); Van Staveren (2003).
69 Putnam (2000), p. 19.
70 Glaeser, Laibson and Sacerdote (2002).
71 Putnam (2000), p. 19.
72 Becker (1996).
73 Coleman (1992).
74 Putnam (2000), pp. 22–3.
75 World Bank (2001), ch. 4.
76 *Ibid.*, pp. 34–41.
77 Bertrand and Kalafatides (2002); Hatcher (2002).
78 Jordan (2006a), Part 1C.
79 Giddens (1998).
80 Blair (1998).
81 Iriart, Waitzkin and Trotta (2002).
82 Iriart, Merhy and Waitzkin (2001).
83 Stocker, Waitzkin and Iriart (1999).
84 Iriart et al. (2002), pp. 245–6.
85 United Nations Development Programme (UNDP) (1999), p. 37.
86 Xing (2002), p. 250.
87 Tomlinson (1997), p. 835.
88 Lipson and Pemble (1992).
89 Dodd (2002), pp. 344–6.
90 Lethbridge (2002).
91 Sanders (2000, 2002).
92 Edinvest (1999).
93 Martin and Schumann (2000); Bertrand and Kalafatides (2002).
94 Sen (1999), pp. 46–8.
95 De Swaan (1988).
96 United Nations (2001).
97 Day (2002).
98 Bohman (1998, 1999); Dryzek (1999, 2000); Delanty (2000).
99 Held (2004).
100 Habermas (1996); Dryzek (1990, 2000); Bohman (1996, 1997).
101 Delanty (2000), p. 141.
102 Held (2004), chs. 9 and 10.

103 Gough (2004); Ku and Jones Finer (2007).
104 Interview with Adair Turner, BBC Radio 4, *Today*, 23 September 2009.
105 'Too many firms fall into foreign hands, warns crusading Myners', *The Guardian*, 24 September 2009, p. 31.
106 Centre for Social Justice (2009).

5 SUSTAINABILITY – COMMUNITIES AND THE ENVIRONMENT

1 Rose (1996); Cruikshank (1994); Giddens (1991).
2 Bauman (2003); Jordan (2004).
3 David Reynolds, *America: Empire of Liberty*, BBC Radio 4, October 2008 – March 2009.
4 Fitzpatrick (2003); Offe (1992); Dean (2006); Holliday (2000).
5 Rimlinger (1971); Higgins (1981).
6 Gough (2004); Ku and Jones Finer (2007).
7 Esping-Andersen (1990, 1996, 1999); Fitzpatrick (2003), p. 99.
8 Orloff (1993).
9 Lewis (2001); Fitzpatrick (2003), p. 100.
10 Fitzpatrick (2003), p. 108.
11 Dean (2006, 2009); Fitzpatrick (2003).
12 Jordan (2006c).
13 Goodin (2001).
14 Holliday (2000), pp. 708–9.
15 Newman (2002).
16 Orloff (1993); Lewis (2001).
17 Elshtain (1981, 1998); Tronto (1994).
18 Fitzpatrick (2003), p. 97.
19 Douthwaite (1992); Pearce (2000); Brennan (2001).
20 Fitzpatrick (2003), pp. 98–9.
21 Battisti and Naylor (2009).
22 Interviews with Naylor, reported in *The Guardian*, 9 January 2009.
23 Brundtland Commission (1987); Fitzpatrick (2003), p. 119.
24 Fitzpatrick (2003), pp. 118–22; Dean (2006).
25 Buchanan and Tullock (1962), pp. 44–6.
26 Nussbaum (2000), pp. 41–51.
27 Orloff (1993); Lewis (2001).

28 Pateman (1988, 1989, 2004).
29 Fitzpatrick (2003), p. 122.
30 Channel 4 TV, *Jamie's School Dinners*, October 2007.
31 Channel 4 TV, *Jamie's Ministry of Food*, October 2008.
32 BBC Radio 4, *News*, 21 January 2009.
33 Fitzpatrick (1999, 2003).
34 Hirst (1994); Dean (2006).
35 Casassas (2007); Pateman (2004).
36 Parker (1988).
37 Ackerman and Alstott (1999); Nissan and Le Grand (2000).
38 Jordan (1987, 1989, 1998, 2006a, 2008); Jordan et al. (2000).
39 Van Parijs (1995), p. 28.
40 Barry (1997), pp. 161–5.
41 *Ibid.*, p. 167
42 Wright (2004), p. 79.
43 *Ibid.*, p. 83.
44 Pateman (2004), p. 90.
45 *Ibid.*, p. 97.
46 *Ibid.*, p. 101.
47 Van Parijs (1995), pp. 230–1.
48 *Ibid.*, pp. 231–2.
49 Birnbaum (2008); Jordan (2008).
50 Van Parijs (1992).
51 Jordan and Düvell (2003), ch. 5.
52 *Ibid.*
53 Channel 4 TV, *News*, 19 January 2009.
54 BBC Radio 4, *World at One*, 23 January 2009.
55 Interview with Immigration Minister, Phil Woolas, *Daily Telegraph*, 18 October 2008.
56 Beckerman and Pasek (2001).
57 Portney and Weyant (1999); Fitzpatrick (2003), pp. 137–8.
58 Fitzpatrick (2003), p. 158.
59 Tacconi and Bennett (1995), p. 218.
60 Fitzpatrick (2003), pp. 139–40.
61 *Ibid.*, p. 144.
62 *Ibid.*, pp. 147–8.
63 D. Adam, 'Paint it white', *The Guardian*, G2, 16 January 2009, p. 6.
64 T. MacAlister, 'One million jobs in wind power by end of 2010', *The Guardian*, 21 January 2009, p. 30, reporting the Green Summit in Abu Dhabi.

65 Panayotou (1995).
66 Gough (2004); Kim (2007).
67 Barrientos (2004).
68 Foucault (1984); Rose (1996); Jordan (2004).
69 Adler and Posner (2006).
70 BBC2 TV, *1929: The Great Crash*, 28 January 2009.

6 CONCLUSIONS – TRANSFORMING SOCIAL POLICY

1 Arthur (1990); Waldrop (1994); Tabb (1999); Sutton (2000); Schwartz (2004).
2 Howkins (2001); Colander (2001); Bronk (2009).
3 Weimer and Vining (1992).
4 Bronk (2009), pp. 68–70 and 128–32.
5 Arthur (1990); Waldrop (1994).
6 Tett (2009), pp. xii–xiv.
7 Bronk (2009), pp. 122–5.
8 Shackle (1979, 1992).
9 Rose (1996).
10 Bronk (2009), pp. 68–70.
11 Layard (2005, 2006).
12 Layard and Dunn (2009), p. 6.
13 DSS (1998), p. 80.
14 Wilkinson and Pickett (2009), p. 36.
15 Dickerson and Kemeny (2004).
16 Twenge (2006).
17 Wilkinson and Pickett (2009), pp. 44–5.
18 *Ibid.*, p. 181.
19 *The Guardian*, 8 May 2009, p. 1.
20 Thaler and Sunstein (2008).
21 BBC World Service, *The World Today*, 26 January 2009.
22 BBC Radio 4, *PM*, 26 January 2009.
23 Dean (2004).
24 R. H. Cox (1998, 2001).
25 Berlin (1951).
26 Blackburn (1999); Roemer (1993).
27 Hayek (1960).
28 Korpi (2003).

29 Schram et al. (2006).
30 Blackburn (1999); Roemer (1993).
31 Standing (2009).
32 Jordan (2004, 2006a, b and c, 2008)
33 Jordan (2007, 2008).
34 Borowski (2007); Ife (2001); Witkin (1998).
35 BBC Radio 4, *Today*, 28 January 2009.
36 Fleckenstein and Sheehan (2008).
37 BBC Radio 4, *PM*, 16 January 2009.
38 Jordan (2006a), chs. 5 and 6.
39 Baldock, Manning and Vickerstaff (2006), p. 280, box 10.1.
40 *Ibid.*, p. 281, box 10.2.
41 *Ibid.*, p. 678.
42 Walby (1999), p. 1.
43 *Ibid.*, p. 7.
44 BBC Radio 4, *Today*, 14 January 2009; Channel 4 TV, *News*, 29 January 2009.
45 Centre for Social Justice (2009).
46 Blond (2009).
47 *Ibid.*

Bibliography

Ackerman, B. and Alstott, A. (1999), *Liberalism and Social Justice*. New York: Columbia University Press.

Adler, M. D. and Posner, E. A. (2006), *New Foundations of Cost-Benefit Analysis*. Cambridge, MA: Harvard University Press.

Ahrne, G. (1990), *Agency and Organisation: Towards an Organisational Theory of Society*. London: Sage.

Akerlof, G.A. and Shiller, R.J. (2009), *Animal Spirits: How Human Psychology Drives the Economy, and Why it Matters for Global Capitalism*. Princeton, NJ: Princeton University Press.

Anderloni, L., Bayot, B., Bledowski, P., Iwanicz-Drozdowska, M. and Kempson, F. (2008), *Financial Service Provision and the Prevention of Financial Exclusion*. Report prepared for the European Commission Director General for Employment, Social Affairs and Equal Opportunities, Brussels: European Commission.

Argyle, M. (1999), 'Causes and Correlates of Happiness', in D. Kahneman et al. (eds.), *Well-being: The Foundations of Hedonic Psychology*. New York: Russell Sage Foundation, pp. 353–72.

Arthur, W. B. (1990), 'Positive Feedback in the Economy'. *Scientific American*, February, pp. 80–5.

Baldock, J. (2007), 'Social Policy, Social Welfare and the Welfare State', in J. Baldock, N. Manning and S. Vickerstaff (eds.), *Social Policy* (3rd edn). Oxford: Oxford University Press, pp. 5–30.

Barrientos, A. (2004), 'Latin America: Towards a Liberal–Informal Welfare Regime', in I. Gough and G. Wood, with A. Barrientos, P. Bevan, P. Davis and G. Room, *Insecurity and Welfare Regimes in Asia, Africa and Latin America*, Cambridge: Cambridge University Press, pp. 121–68.

Barry, B. (1997), 'The Attractions of Basic Income', in J. Franklin (ed.), *Equality*, London: Institute for Public Policy Research. pp. 157–71.

Bass, B. M. (1990), 'From Transactional to Transformational Leadership', *Organisational Dynamics*, 18, pp. 15–31.

Battisti, D. S. and Naylor, R. L. (2009), 'Historical Warnings of Food Insecurity with Unprecedented Seasonal Heat', *Science*, 9 January, pp. 272–5.

Bauböck, R. (1994), *Transnational Citizenship: Membership and Rights in International Migration*. Aldershot: Edward Elgar.

Bauman, Z. (2003), *Liquid Love: On the Frailty of Human Bonds*. Cambridge: Polity.

Baumol, W. (1967), 'The Macroeconomics of Unbalanced Growth', *American Economic Review*, 57, pp. 415–26.

Baumol, W., Batey-Blackman, S. and Wolf, E. (1985), 'Unbalanced Growth Revisited: Asymptotic Stagnancy and New Evidence', *American Economic Review*, **87**, pp. 806–17.

Beck, U. and Beck-Gernsheim, E. (1995), *The Normal Chaos of Love*. Cambridge: Polity.

(2002), *Individualization*. London: Sage.

Becker, G. S. (1976), *The Economic Approach to Human Behaviour*. Chicago: University of Chicago Press.

(1996), *Accounting for Tastes*. Cambridge, MA: Harvard University Press.

Beckerman, W. and Pasek, J. (2001), *Justice, Posterity and the Environment*. Oxford: Oxford University Press.

Begg, D., Fischer, S. and Dombusch, R. (1997), *Economics* (5th edn). London: McGraw Hill.

Bennis, W. G. and Nanus, B. (1985), *Leaders: The Strategies for Taking Charge*. New York: Harper and Row.

Berlin, I. (1951), *Two Concepts of Liberty*. Oxford: Clarendon Press.

Bertrand, A., and Kalafatides, L. (2002), *OMC, le pouvoir invisible*. Paris: Fayard.

Bevan, P. (2004a), 'Conceptualising In/security Regimes', in I. Gough and G. Wood, with A. Barrientos, P. Bevan, P. Davis and G. Room, *Insecurity and Welfare Regimes in Asia, Africa and Latin America*. Cambridge: Cambridge University Press, pp. 88–120.

(2004b), 'The Dynamics of Africa's In/security Regimes', in I. Gough and G. Wood, with A. Barrientos, P. Bevan, P. Davis and G. Room, *Insecurity and Welfare Regimes in Asia, Africa and Latin America*. Cambridge: Cambridge University Press, pp. 202–54.

Birnbaum, S. (2008), 'Just Distribution, Rawlsian Liberalism and the Politics of Basic Income', *Stockholm Studies in Politics*, 122.

Bjørnskov, C. (2006), 'The Multiple Facets of Social Capital', *European Journal of Political Economy*, 22, pp. 22–40.

Blackburn, R. (1999), 'The New Collectivism: Pension Reform, Grey Capitalism and Complex Socialism', *New Left Review*, 233, pp. 3–65.

Blair, T. (1998), *The Third Way: New Politics for the New Century*. Fabian Pamphlet 588, London: Fabian Society.

(2007), 'I've Been Tough on Crime: Now We Have to Nip it in the Bud', *Sunday Telegraph*, 28 April.

Blake, S. and de Jong, E. (2008), *Short Changed? Financial Exclusion: A Guide to Donors and Finders*. London: New Philanthropy Capital.

Blond, P. (2009), 'Rise of the Red Tories', *Prospect Magazine*, 10 Februrary.

Blunkett, D. (2003), 'Active Citizens, Strong Communities: Progressing Civil Renewal', Scarman Lecture to the Citizens Convention, Runnymede, 11 December.

(2004), 'New Challenges for Race Equality and Community Cohesion in the Twenty-First Century', speech to the Institute for Public Policy Research, 20 June.

Bohman, J. (1996), *Public Deliberation, Pluralism, Complexity and Democracy*. London: MIT Press.

(1997), 'Deliberative Democracy in Effective Social Freedom: Capabilities, Resources and Opportunities', in J. Bohman and W. Rehg (eds.), *Deliberative Democracy: Essays on Reason and Politics*, London: MIT Press, pp. 321–48.

(1998), 'The Globalisation of the Public Sphere', *Philosophy and Social Affairs*, 24(2/3), pp. 199–216.

(1999), 'International Regimes and Democratic Governance: Political Equality and Influence in Global Institutions', *International Affairs*, 75(3), pp. 499–513.

Bolton, P. and Dewatripont, M. (2005), *Contract Theory*, Cambridge, MA: MIT Press.

Borowski, A. (2007), 'On Human Dignity and Social Work', *International Social Work*, 43(3), pp. 197–201.

Bowles, S. and Gintis, H. (2002), 'Social Capital and Community Governance', *Economic Journal*, 112(483), pp. F419–36.

Bradshaw, J. (ed.) (2008), *Social Security, Happiness and Well-being*. Oxford: Intersentia.

Bradshaw, J., Hoelscher, P. and Richardson, D. (2007), 'An Index of Child Well-being in the European Union 25', *Journal of Social Indicators Research*, 80, pp. 133–77.

Brennan, T. (2001), 'Which Third Way?' *Thesis Eleven*, 64, pp. 39–64.

Bronk, R. (2009), *The Romantic Economist: Imagination in Economics*. Cambridge: Cambridge University Press.

Brueckner, J.K. (2000), 'Economic Reform and the "Race to the Bottom": Theory and Evidence', *Southern Economic Journal*, 66(3), pp. 287–302.

Brundtland Commission (1987), *Our Common Future*. Oxford: Oxford University Press.

Bruni, L. and Porta, P. L. (eds.) (2005), *Economics and Happiness: Framing the Analysis*. Oxford: Oxford University Press.

Bryman, A. (1992), *Charisma and Leadership in Organisations*. London: Sage.

Buchanan, J. M. (1965), 'An Economic Theory of Clubs', *Economica*, 32, pp. 1–14.

 (1968), *The Demand and Supply of Public Goods*. Chicago: Rand McNally.

 (1978), *The Economics of Politics*. London: Institute for Economic Affairs.

Buchanan, J. M. and Tullock, G. (1962), *The Calculus of Consent: Logical Foundations of Constitutional Democracy*. Ann Arbor: University of Michigan Press.

 (1980), *Towards a Theory of a Rent-Seeking Society*. College Station: Texas A and M University Press.

Bunting, M. (2008), 'From Buses To Blogs, a Pathological Individualism is Poisoning Public Life', *The Guardian*, 28 January.

Caprio, J. (1996), 'Bank Regulation: The Case of the Missing Model', *Policy Research Working Paper*. 1574, presented at conference on 'The Sequencing of Financial Services', Washington, DC, 20 May.

 (1997), 'Safe and Sound Banking in Developing Countries: We're Not in Kansas Anymore', *Research in Financial Services*, 9, pp. 79–97.

Carter, M. (2003), *T. H. Green and the Development of Ethical Socialism*. Exeter: Imprint Academic.

Casassas, D. (2007) *A Political Constitution of the Invisible Hand? Property, Community and the Accomplishment of Republican*

Freedom in Market Societies. Oxford: Centre for the Study of Social Justice, Oxford University.

Casella, A. and Frey, B. (1992), 'Federalism and Clubs: Towards an Economic Theory of Overlapping Political Jurisdictions', *European Economic Review*, 36(2/3), pp. 639–46.

Castles, S. and Miller, M. (2003), *The Age of Migration: International Population Movements in the Modern World* (3rd edn). Basingstoke: Macmillan.

Centre for Social Justice (2009), *Dynamic Benefits: Towards Welfare that Works.* London: Centre for Social Justice.

Clarke, J., Cochrane, A. and McLaughlin, E. (1994), *Managing Social Policy.* London: Sage.

Clarke, J. and Newman, J. (1997), *The Managerial State: Power, Politics and Ideology in the Remaking of Social Welfare.* London: Sage.

Club of Rome (1972), *The Limits to Growth,* London: Earth Island.

Coase, R.H. (1937), 'The Nature of the Firm', *Economica,* 4, pp. 386–405.

Colander, D. (2001), *The Lost Art of Economics: Essays in Economics and the Economics Profession.* Cheltenham: Edward Elgar.

Cole, G. D. H. (1920), *Social Theory.* London: Methuen.

Coleman, J. S. (1988), 'Social Capital and the Creation of Human Capital', *American Journal of Sociology,* 94, pp. 595–621.

  (1990), *The Foundations of Social Theory.* Cambridge: Cambridge University Press.

  (1992), 'The Rational Reconstruction of Society', *American Sociological Review,* 58(6), pp. 898–912.

Commission for Healthcare Audit and Inspection (2009), *Investigation into Mid-Staffordshire NHS Foundation Trust.* London: Healthcare Commission.

Cornes, R. and Sandler, T. (1986), *The Theory of Externalities, Public Goods and Club Goods.* Cambridge: Cambridge University Press.

Cox, E. (2002), 'Australia: The Lucky Country', in R. D. Putnam (ed.), *Democracies in Flux: The Evolution of Social Capital in Contemporary Society.* Oxford: Oxford University Press.

Cox, R. H. (1998), 'From Safety Nets to Trampolines', *Governance,* 18(1), pp. 28–47.

  (2001), 'The Social Construction of an Imperative: Why Welfare Reform Happened in Demark and the Netherlands, but not in Germany', *World Politics,* 53, pp. 463–98.

Cruikshank, B. (1994), 'The Will to Empower: Technologies of Citizenship and the War on Poverty', *Socialist Review*, 23(4), pp. 29–55.

Cullis, J. and Jones, P. (1994), *Public Finance and Public Choice: Analytical Perspectives*. London: McGraw Hill.

Dasgupta, P. and Serageldin, I. (eds.), *Social Capital: A Multifaceted Perspective*. Washington, DC: World Bank.

Datta, K. (2007), *Money Matters: Exploring Financial Exclusion among Low Paid Migrant Workers in London*. London: Department of Geography, Queen Mary, University of London.

Davies, H. (1992), *Fighting Leviathan: Building Social Markets that Work*. London: Social Market Foundation.

Day, A. (2002), 'The Prospects of a Cosmopolitan World Order: Investigating the 2002 United Nations Finance for Development Conference', *Global Social Policy*, 2(3), pp. 295–318.

de Swaan, A. (1988), *In Care of the State: Health Care, Education and Welfare in Europe and the USA in the Modern Era*. Cambridge: Polity.

Dean, H. (2004), 'Human Rights and Welfare Rights: Contextualising Dependency and Responsibility', in H. Dean (ed.), *The Ethics of Welfare: Human Rights, Dependency and Responsibility*. Bristol: Policy Press, pp. 7–28.

(2006), *A Short Introduction to Social Policy*. Cambridge: Polity.

(2009), *Understanding Human Need*. Bristol: Policy Press.

Delanty, G. (2000), *Citizenship in a Global Age: Society, Culture, Politics*. Buckingham: Open University Press.

Department of Health (1998), *Modernising Social Services: Promoting Independence, Improving Protection, Raising Standards*. Cm 4169, London: HMSO.

(2005), *Independence, Well-being and Choice: Our Vision of the Future of Social Care for Adults in England*. Cm 6499, London: Stationery Office.

Department of Social Security (DSS) (1998), *A New Contract for Welfare*. Cm 3805, London: Stationery Office.

Di Tella, R., MacCulloch, R. and Oswald, A. (2003), 'The Macroeconomics of Happiness', *Review of Economics and Statistics*, 85(4), pp. 807–27.

Dickerson, S.S. and Kemany, M.C. (2004), 'Acute Stressors and Cortisol Responses: A Theoretical Integration and Synthesis of Laboratory Research', *Psychological Bulletin*, 130(30), pp. 355–91.

Dodd, R. (2002), 'Health in Poverty Reduction Strategy Papers: Will the PSBR Process Mean Better Health for the Poor?' *Global Social Policy*, 2(3), pp. 343–8.

Douglas, C. H. (1974 [1920]), *Economic Democracy*. Sudbury: Bloomfield.

Douglas, M. (1970), *Natural Symbols: Explorations in Cosmology*. London: Barrie and Rockliff.

(1982 [1973]), 'The Exclusion of Economics', in her *In the Active Voice*. London: Routledge and Kegan Paul, pp. 174–82.

(1982 [1976]), 'Goods as a System of Communication', in her *In the Active Voice*. London: Routledge and Kegan Paul, pp. 48–73.

(1982 [1978]), 'Cultural Bias', in her *In the Active Voice*. London: Routledge and Kegan Paul, pp. 183–254.

(1983), 'Identity: Personal and Socio-Cultural', *Uppsala Studies in Cultural Anthropology*, 5, pp. 35–46.

(1987), *How Institutions Think*. London: Routledge and Kegan Paul.

Douthwaite, R. (1992), *The Growth Illusion: How Economic Growth has Enriched the Few, Impoverished the Many, and Endangered the Planet*. Dublin: Recurgence/Liliput.

Doyal, L. and Gough, I. (1991), *A Theory of Human Need*. Basingstoke: Macmillan.

Dryzek, J. (1990), *Discursive Democracy: Politics, Policy and Political Science*. Cambridge: Cambridge University Press.

(1999), 'Transnational Democracy', *Journal of Political Philosophy*, 7(1), pp. 30–51.

(2000), *Deliberative Democracy and Beyond: Liberals, Critics, Contestations*. Oxford: Oxford University Press.

Durkheim, E. (1898), 'Individualism and the Intellectuals', *Revue Bleu*, 4(10), pp. 7–11.

(1912), *Les Formes élémentaires de la vie religieuse: le systéme totemique en Australie*. Paris: Alcan.

Durlauf, S. N. (2002), 'On the Empirics of Social Capital', *Economic Journal*, 112(483), pp. F459–79.

Durlauf, S. N. and Fafchamps, M. (2004), 'Social Capital', *Working Paper*, 10485, www.nber.org/papers/W10485.

Easterlin, R. (1974), 'Does Economic Growth Improve the Human Lot? Some Empirical Evidence', in P. David and M. Reder (eds.), *Nations and Households in Economic Growth: Essays in Honor of Moses Abramovitz*. New York: Academic Press, pp. 267–89.

(2005), 'Building a Better Theory of Well-being', in L. Bruni and P. L. Porta (eds.), *Economics and Happiness*. Oxford: Oxford University Press, pp. 29–64.

Edinvest (1999), 'Financial Aid to Students in Private Establishments', *Edinvest Bulletin*, October.

Edwards, B. and Foley, F. (1997), 'Social Capital and the Political Economy of Our Discontent', *American Behavioral Scientist*, 40(5), pp. 669–78.

Ehrenreich, B. (2002), *Nickel and Dimed: Undercover in Low-Wage USA*. London: Granta.

Elliot, L. and Atkinson, D. (2008), *The Gods that Failed: How Blind Faith in Markets Has Cost Us Our Future*. London: The Bodley Head.

Ellis, K. (2004), 'Dependency, Justice and the Ethic of Care', in H. Dean (ed.), *The Ethics of Welfare: Human Rights, Dependency and Responsibility*. Bristol: Policy Press, pp. 29–48.

Elshtain, J. B., (1998), 'Antigone's Daughters', in A. Phillips (ed.), *Feminism and Politics*. Oxford: Oxford University Press, pp. 369–81.

(1981), *Public Man, Private Woman: Women in Social and Political Thought*. Oxford: Martin Robertson.

Erdemir, A. and Vasta, E. (2007), 'Differentiating Irregularity and Solidarity: Turkish Immigrants at Work in London', *Working Paper*, 42, ESRC Centre on Migration Policy and Society, University of Oxford.

Eriksen, E. and Weigård, J. (2000), 'The End of Citizenship? New Roles Challenging the Political Order', in C. McKinnon and I. Hampsher-Monk (eds.), *The Demands of Citizenship*. London: Continuum pp. 13–34.

Esping-Andersen, G. (1990), *The Three Worlds of Welfare Capitalism*. Cambridge: Polity.

(ed.), (1996), *Welfare States in Transition: National Adaptations in Global Economies*. London: Sage.

(1999), *Social Foundations of Post-Industrial Economies*. Oxford: Oxford University Press.

Fine, B. (2001), *Social Capital versus Social Theory: Political Economy and Social Science at the Turn of the Millennium*. London: Routledge.

Firth, R. (1967), *Tikopia Ritual and Belief*. London: Allen and Unwin.

Fitzpatrick, T. (1999), *Freedom and Security: An Introduction to the Basic Income Debate*. London: Macmillan.

(2003), *After the New Social Democracy: Social Welfare in the Twenty-First Century*. Manchester: Manchester University Press.

Fleckenstein, W. A., with Sheehan, F. (2008), *Greenspan's Bubbles: The Age of Ignorance at the Federal Reserve*. New York: McGraw Hill.

Fletcher, K. (1998), *Best Value Social Services*. Caerphilly: SSSP Publications.

Foldvary, F. (1994), *Public Goods and Private Communities – The Market Provision of Social Services*. Aldershot: Edward Elgar.

Foucault, M. (1984), 'The Order of Discourse', in M. Shapiro (ed.), *Language and Politics*. New York: New York University Press.

Fox, J. and Gershman, J. (2000), 'The World Bank and Social Capital: Lessons from Ten Rural Development Projects in the Philippines and Mexico', *Policy Sciences*, 33, pp. 399–419.

Frank, R. H. (2005), 'Does Money Buy Happiness?' in F. A. Huppert et al., (eds.), *The Science of Well-being*. Oxford: Oxford University Press, pp. 461–74.

Frey, B. and Stutzer, A. (2002), *Happiness and Economics: How the Economy and Institutions Affect Well-being*. Princeton, NJ: Princeton University Press.

Gambetta, D. (1988), 'Can We Trust Trust?' in D. Gambetta (ed.), *Trust: Making and Breaking Cooperative Relations*. Oxford: Blackwell, pp. 213–38.

Gershuny, J. I. (1983), *Social Innovation and the Division of Labour*. Oxford: Oxford University Press.

Gesell, S. (1985 [1920]), *The Natural Economic Order*. London: Peter Owen.

Giddens, A. (1991), *Modernity and Self-Identity: Self and Society in the Late Modern Age*. Cambridge: Polity.

(1998), *The Third Way: The Renewal of Social Democracy*, Cambridge: Polity.

Glaeser, E., Laibson, D. and Sacerdote, B. (2002), 'An Economic Approach to Social Capital', *Economic Journal*, 112(483), pp. F437–58.

Gneezy, U. and Rustichini, A. (2000), 'A Fine is a Price', *Journal of Legal Studies*, 29, pp. 1–17.

Goffman, E. (1967a), 'On Face Work: An Analysis of Ritual Elements in Interaction', in *Interaction Ritual: Essays in Face-to-Face Behaviour*, New York: Doubleday Anchor, pp. 1–46.

(1967b), 'The Nature of Deference and Demeanor', in *Interaction Ritual: Essays in Face-to-Face Behaviour*. New York: Doubleday Anchor, pp. 47–96.

Goodin, R. (2001), 'Towards a Post-Productivist Welfare State', *British Journal of Political Science*, 31, pp. 13–40.

Goodrich, J. and Cornwell, J. (2008), *Seeing the Person in the Patient*. Point of Care Review Paper, London: King's Fund.

Gough, I. (2004), 'East Asia: The Limits of Productivist Regimes', in I. Gough and G. Wood, with A. Barrientos, P. Bevan, P. Davis and G. Room, *Insecurity and Welfare Regimes in Asia, Africa and Latin America*. Cambridge: Cambridge University Press, pp. 169–201.

Griffin, J. (1986), *Well-being: Its Meaning, Measurement and Moral Importance*. Oxford: Oxford University Press.

Haagh, L. (2007), 'Developmental Freedom, Unemployment, and Poverty: Restating the Importance of Regulation to Agency', in O. Neumeier, G. Schweiger and C. Sednak (eds), *Perspectives in Work: Problems, Insights, Challenges*. Munster: LIT Publishing.

Habermas, J. (1996), *Between Facts and Norms: Contributions to a Discourse Theory of Law and Democracy*. Cambridge: Polity.

Harris, J. (1992), 'Political Thought and the Welfare State, 1870–1940: An Intellectual Framework for British Social Policy', *Past and Present*, B5, pp. 116–41.

Harriss, J. (2001), *Depoliticising Development: The World Bank and Social Capital*. New Delhi: LeftWord.

Hart, O. (1995), *Firms, Contracts and Financial Structure*. Oxford: Clarendon Press.

Hatcher, R. (2002), *The Business of Education: How Business Agendas Drive Labour Policies for Schools*. Stafford: Socialist Education Association.

Hayek, F. A. (1960), *The Constitution of Liberty*. London: Routledge and Kegan Paul.

Held, D. (2004), *Global Covenant: The Social Democratic Alternative to the Washington Consensus*. Cambridge: Polity.

Helliwell, J. F. (2003) 'How's Life? Combining Individual and National Variables to Explain Subjective Well-being', *Economic Modelling*, 20, pp. 331–60.

Hicks, U. K. (1947), *Public Finance*. Cambridge: Cambridge University Press.

Higgins, J. (1981), *States of Welfare: Comparative Analysis of Social Policy*. Oxford: Blackwell and Robertson.

Hirst, P. (1994), *Associative Democracy*. Cambridge: Polity.

Hix, S. (2008), *What's Wrong with the European Union, and How to Fix It*. Cambridge: Polity.

Holliday, I. (2000), 'Productivist Welfare Capitalism: Social Policy in East Asia', *Political Studies*, 48, pp. 706–23.

Howkins, J. (2001), *The Creative Economy: How People Make Money from Ideas*. Harmondsworth: Penguin.

Huber, E. and Stephens, J. (2001), *Development and the Crisis of the Welfare State*. Chicago: University of Chicago Press.

Hupport, F.A., Baylis, N. and Keverne, B. (eds.) (2005), *The Science of Well-being*. Oxford: Oxford University Press.

Ife, J. (2001), *Human Rights and Social Work: Towards a Rights-Based Practice*. Cambridge: Cambridge University Press.

Inman, R. P and Rubinfeld, P. H. (1997), 'The Political Economy of Federalism', in D. C. Mueller (ed.), *Perspectives in Public Choice: A Handbook*. Cambridge: Cambridge University Press, pp. 73–105.

Iriart, C., Merhy, E., and Waitzkin, H. (2001), 'Managed Care in Latin America: The New Common Sense in Health Policy Reform', *Social Science and Medicine*, 52(8), pp. 1243–53.

Iriart, C., Waitzkin, H., and Trotta, C. (2002), 'Global Policies, Health Care Systems and Social Movements in Latin America: A Lesson from Argentina', *Global Social Policy*, 2(3), pp. 245–8.

Isaacs, L. (2008), *Research on Migrant Remittances and Linkage to Broader Access to Financial Services*. Report prepared for UK Remittances Task Force, London: University College.

Iversen, F. and Wren, A. (1998), 'Equality, Employment and Budgetary Restraint: The Trilemma of the Service Economy', *World Politics*, 50(4), pp. 507–46.

James, O. (2007), *Affluenza*. London: Ebury Press.

Jordan, B. (1987), *Rethinking Welfare*. Oxford: Blackwell.

(1989), *The Common Good: Citizenship, Morality and Self-Interest*. Oxford: Blackwell.

(1996), *A Theory of Poverty and Social Exclusion*. Cambridge: Polity.

(1998), *The New Politics of Welfare: Social Justice in a Global Context*. London: Sage.

(2004), *Sex, Money and Power: The Transformation of Collective Life*. Cambridge: Polity.

(2006a), *Social Policy for the Twenty-First Century: New Perspectives, Big Issues*. Cambridge: Polity.

(2006b), 'Public Services and the Service Economy: Choice, Order and Well-being', *Journal of Social Policy*, 35(1), pp. 143–62.

(2006c), *Rewarding Company, Enriching Life: The Economics of Relationships and Feelings*, www.billjordan.co.uk.

(2007), *Social Work and Well-being*. Lyme Regis: Russell House.

(2008), *Welfare and Well-being: Social Value in Public Policy*. Bristol: Policy Press.

Jordan, B., Agulnik, P., Burbidge, D. and Duffin, S. (2000), *Stumbling Towards Basic Income: The Prospects for Tax–Benefits Integration*. London: Citizens Income Trust.

Jordan, B. and Düvell, F. (2002), *Irregular Migration: The Dilemmas of Transnational Mobility*. Cheltenham: Edward Elgar.

(2003), *Migration: The Boundaries of Equality and Justice*. Cambridge: Polity.

Jordan, B. with Jordan, C. (2000), *Social Work and the Third Way: Tough Love as Social Policy*. London: Sage.

Kahneman, D. Diener, E. and Schwartz, N. (eds.) (1999), *Well-being: The Foundations of Hedonic Psychology*. New York: Russell Sage Foundation.

Kalecki, M. (1971), *Selected Essays in the Dynamics of the Capitalist Economy*. Cambridge: Cambridge University Press.

Kelsey, J. (1995), *Economic Fundamentalism: The New Zealand Experiment – A World Model of Structural Adjustment*. London: Pluto.

Keynes, J. M. (1936), *A General Theory of Employment, Interest and Money*. London: Macmillan.

Kim, B.-C. (2007), 'The Livelihoods of Unemployed Households in China: A Case Study', Nottingham: University of Nottingham, Department of Social Policy, unpublished Ph.D. thesis.

Korpi, W. (2003), 'Welfare State Regress in Western Europe: Politics, Institutions, Globalization and Europeanization', *Annual Review of Sociology*, 29, pp. 589–609.

Ku, Y.-W. and Jones Finer, K. (2007), 'Developments in East Asian Welfare Studies', *Social Policy and Administration*, 41(2), pp. 115–31.

Laffont, J. J. and Martimort, D. (2002), *The Theory of Incentives: The Principal Agent Model*. Princeton, NJ: Princeton University Press.

Layard, R. (2005), *Happiness: Lessons from a New Science*. London: Allen Lane.

(2006), 'Happiness and Public Policy: A Challenge to the Profession', *Economic Journal*, 116(510), pp. C24–33.

Layard, R. and Dunn, J. (2009), *A Good Childhood: Searching for Values in a Competitive Age*. Harmondsworth: Penguin.

Lethbridge, J. (2002), 'International Finance Corporate (IFC) Health Care Policy Briefing', *Global Social Policy*, 2(3), pp. 349–53.

Leonard, M. (1994), *Informal Economic Activity in Belfast*, Aldershot: Avebury.

(1999), 'Informal Economic Activity Strategies of Households and Communities', paper presented at the 4th ESA conference, 'Will Europe Work?', Amsterdam, 18–21 August.

(2004), 'Bonding and Bridging Social Capital: Reflections from Belfast', *Sociology*, 38(5), pp. 927–44.

Levitt, S. D. and Dubner, S. J. (2006), *Freakonomics*. London: Penguin.

Lewis, J. (2001), 'The Decline of the Male Breadwinner Model: Implications for Work and Care', *Social Politics*, 8(2), pp. 152–69.

Lipson, R. and Pemble, L. (1992), 'China's Medical Equipment Purchases', *China Business Review*, 19(4), pp. 18–21.

Macho-Stadler, I. and Pérez-Castrillo, J. D. (2001), *An Introduction to the Economics of Information, Incentives and Contracts*, (2nd edn). Oxford: Oxford University Press.

Macmillan, H. (1938), *The Middle Way: A Study of the Problem of Economic and Social Progress in a Free and Democratic Society*. London: Macmillan.

Marshall, J. N. (2004), 'Financial Institutions in Disadvantaged Areas: A Comparative Analysis of Polities Encouraging Financial Inclusion in Britain and the United States', *Environment and Planning*, A36, pp. 24–61.

Martin, H. P. and Schumann, H. (2000), *Le Piège de la modialisation*. Arles: Actes Sud.

McKinnon, C. and Hampsher-Monk, I. (eds.) (2000), *The Demands of Citizenship*. London: Continuum.

Meade, J. E. (1938), *Consumers' Credits and Unemployment*, Oxford: Oxford University Press.

Merton, R. (1949), 'The Self-Fulfilling Prophecy', in *Social Theory and Social Structure*. New York: Free Press, pp. 475–90.

Milburn, A. (2002), 'Reforming Social Services', speech to the Annual Social Services Conference, Cardiff, www.doh.gov.uk/speeches.

Milner, D. (1919), 'The State Bonus Scheme: Arguments for a Simple Step Forward', *The Ploughshare*, pp. 155–7.

(1920), *Higher Productivity by a Bonus on National Output: A Proposal for a Minimum Income for All Varying with National Productivity*. London: Allen and Unwin.

Mirrlees, J. (1971), 'An Exploration in the Theory of Optimum Taxation', *Review of Economic Studies*, 38, pp. 175–208.

Mises, L. von (1966), *Human Action*. Chicago: Contemporary Books.

Monbiot, G. (2009), 'If the State Can't Save Us We Need a Licence to Print Our Own Money', *The Guardian*, 20 January 2009.

Mueller, D. C. (1979), *Public Choice*, Cambridge: Cambridge University Press.

(1989), *Public Choice II*. Cambridge: Cambridge University Press.

(ed.) (1997), *Perspectives in Public Choice: A Handbook*. Cambridge: Cambridge University Press.

Myers, D. G. (1999), 'Close Relationships and Quality of Life', in D. Kahneman et al. (eds.), *Well-being: The Foundations of Hedonic Psychology*, New York: Russell Sage Foundation, pp. 374–91.

New Economics Foundation (2008), *Keeping Britain Posted: How Post Office Banking Could Save the Network and Combat Social Exclusion*. Briefing: Financial Inclusion 1, Future Economy.

Newman, A.L. (2002), 'When Opportunity Knocks: Economic Liberalisation and Stealth Welfare in the United States', *Journal of Social Policy*, 32(2), pp. 179–98.

Niskanen, W. A. (1975), 'Bureaucrats and Politicians', *Journal of Law and Economics*, 18, pp. 617–43.

Nissan, D. and Le Grand, J. (2000), *A Capital Idea*. London: Fabian Society.

Nordhaus, W. and Boyer, J. (2000), *Warming the World*. Cambridge, MA: MIT Press.

Nordhaus, W. and Tobin, J. (1972) *Is Growth Obsolete?* New York: NBER / Columbus University Press.

North Devon Parents Group (2006), *Responses to Proposed Changes in Services for Adults with Learning Disabilities*. Barnstaple: North Devon Parents Group.

Northouse, P. G. (1997), *Leadership: Theory and Practice*, London: Sage.

Nussbaum, M. (2000), *Women and Human Development, The Capabilities Approach*. Cambridge: Cambridge University Press.

(2005), 'Mill between Aristotle and Bentham', in L. Bruni and P. L. Porta (eds.), *Economics and Happiness: Framing the Analysis*. Oxford: Oxford University Press, pp. 170–83.

Oates, W. E. (1972), *Fiscal Federalism*. New York: Harcourt Brace Jovanovich.

(1999), 'An Essay on Fiscal Federalism', *Journal of Economic Literature*, 27, pp. 1120–49.

Offe, C. (1992), 'A Non-Productivist Design for Social Policies', in P. Van Parijs (ed.), *Arguing for Basic Income: Ethical Foundations for a Radical Reform*. London: Verso, pp. 61–86.

Offer, A. (2006), *The Challenge of Affluence: Self-Control and Well-being in the United States and Britain since 1950*. Oxford: Oxford University Press.

Offer, J. (2006), *An Intellectual History of British Social Policy: Idealism versus Non-Idealism*. Bristol: Policy Press.

Olson, M. (1965), *The Logic of Collective Action: Public Goods and the Economics of Groups*. Cambridge, MA: Harvard University Press.

(1982), *The Rise and Decline of Nations: Economic Growth, Stagflation and Social Rigidities*. New Haven, CT: Yale University Press.

Orloff, A. (1993), 'Gender and Social Rights in Citizenship: The Comparative Analysis of Gender Relations in Welfare States', *American Sociological Review*, 58(3), pp. 303–28.

Ormerod, P. (2007), 'Against Happiness', *Prospect Magazine*, 133, pp. 1–6.

Panayotou, T. (1995), 'Environmental Degradation at Different Stages of Development', in I. Ahmed and J. Doelman (eds.), *Beyond Rio*. London: Macmillan, pp. 465–82.

Pareto, V. (1966 [1896]), 'Cours d'économie politique', in S. E. Finer (ed.), *Vilfredo Pareto: Sociological Writings*. London: Pall Mall Press, pp. 97–122.

(1909), *Manuel d'économie politique*. Paris: Alcan.

(1916), 'Treatise on General Sociology', in S. E. Finer (ed.), *Vilfredo Pareto: Sociological Writings*. London: Pall Mall Press, pp. 167–331.

Parker, H. (1988), *An Enquiry into Integration of the Tax and Benefit Systems*. London: Routledge

Pateman, C. (1988), *The Sexual Contract*. London: Routledge. Cambridge: Polity.

(1989), *The Disorder of Women: Democracy, Feminism and Political Theory*. Cambridge: Polity.

(2004), 'Democratizing Citizenship: Some Advantages of a Basic Income', *Politics and Society*, 32(1), pp. 89–106.

Pearce, D. (2000), *Blueprint for a Sustainable Economy*. London: Earthscan.

Perkins, J. (2004), *Confessions of an Economic Hit Man*. San Francisco, CA: Barett-Koehler.

Pierson, C. (1991), *Beyond the Welfare State? The New Political Economy of Welfare*. Cambridge: Polity.

Person, P. (1994), *Dismantling the Welfare State*. Cambridge: Cambridge University Press.

(2000), 'Post-Industrial Pressures on Mature Welfare States', in P. Pierson (ed.), *The New Politics of the Welfare State*. New York: Oxford University Press, pp. 1–28.

Pigou, A. C. (1920), *The Economics of Welfare*. London: Macmillan.

Platteau, J.P. (1994a), ' Behind the Market Stage: Where Real Societies Exist. Part I: The Role of Public and Private Order Institutions', *Journal of Development Studies*, 30(3), pp. 533–77.

(1994b), 'Behind the Market Stage: Where Real Societies Exist. Part II: The Role of Public and Private Order Institutions', *Journal of Development Studies*, 30(4), pp. 578–601.

Polanyi, K. (1944), *The Great Transformation: the Political and Economic Origins of Our Times*. Boston, MA: Beacon Press.

Portney, P. and Weyant, J. (eds.) (1999), *Discounting and Intergenerational Equity*. Washington: Resources for the Future.

Putnam, R. D. (1993), *Making Democracy Work: Civic Traditions in Modern Italy*. Princeton, NJ: Princeton University Press.

(2000), *Bowling Alone: The Decline and Revival of America Community*. New York: Simon and Schuster.

(ed.) (2002), *Democracy in Flux: The Evolution of Social Capital in Contemporary Societies*. Oxford: Oxford University Press.

Rimlinger, G. V. (1971), *Welfare, Policy and Industrialisation in Europe, America and Russia*. New York: Wiley.

Robbins, L. (1932), *The Nature and Significance of Economic Science*. London: Allen and Unwin.

Roemer, J. (1983), 'Unequal Exchange, Labour Migration and International Capital Flows: A Theoretical Synthesis', in P. Desai (ed.), *Marxism, the Soviet Economy and Central Planning: Essays in Honor of Alexander Erlich*. Cambridge, MA: MIT Press, pp. 34–60.

(1993), *A Future for Socialism*. London: Verso.

Rose, N. (1996), *Inventing Ourselves: Psychology, Power and Personhood*. Cambridge: Cambridge University Press.

Rothstein, B. and Stolle, D. (2001), 'Social Capital and Street-Level Bureaucracy: An Institutional Theory of Generalised Trust', paper presented at a conference on 'Social Capital', Exeter University, 15–20 September.

(2008), 'Political Institutions and Generalized Trust', in D. Castiglione, J. Van Deth and G. Wolleb (eds.), *The Handbook of Social Capital*, Oxford: Oxford University Press, pp. 273–302.

Sahlins, M. (1974), *Stone Age Economics*. London: Tavistock Publications.

Samuelson, P. (1954), *Foundations of Economic Analysis*. Cambridge, MA: Harvard University Press.

Sanders, D. (2000), 'Primary Health Care 21: "Everybody's Business"', paper for WHO conference, Alma Ata, 27–28 November.

Sanders, D. (2002), 'Globalisation, Health and Health Services in Sub-Saharan Africa', *Global Social Policy*, 2(3), pp. 255–9.

Sassen, S. (1988), *The Mobility of Labour and Capital: A Study in International Investment and Labour Flow*. Cambridge: Cambridge University Press.

(1991), *The Global City: New York, London, Tokyo*, Princeton, NJ: Princeton University Press.

(1998), *Globalisation and its Discontents*. New York: The New Press.

Schram, S. (2006), *Welfare Discipline: Discourse, Governance and Globalisation*. Philadelphia: Temple University Press.

Schwartz, B. (2004), *The Paradox of Choice: Why More Is Less*. London: Harper Collins.

Seeleib-Kaiser, M., Van Dyk, S. and Roggenkamp, M. (2005), 'What Do Parties Want? An Analysis of Programmatic Social Policy Aims in Austria, Germany and the Netherlands', *Working Paper*, 01/2005. Bremen: Centre for Social Policy Research.

Sen, A. (1984), *Resources, Values and Development*. Oxford: Blackwell.

(1999), *Development as Freedom*. Oxford: Oxford University Press.

Sennett, R. (2008), *The Craftsman*. London: Allen Lane.

Sevenhuijsen, S. (2000), 'Caring in the Third Way: The Relation between Obligation, Responsibility and Care in Third Way Discourse', *Critical Social Policy*, 20(1), pp. 5–37.

Shackle, G. (1979), *Imagination and the Nature of Choice*. Edinburgh: Edinburgh University Press.

(1992), *Epistemics and Economics: A Critique of Economic Doctrines*. London: Transaction Publishers.

Smith, A. (1948 [1759]), 'The Theory of Moral Sentiments' in H. W. Schneider (ed.), *Adam Smith's Moral and Political Philosophy*. New York: Harper and Row, pp. 7–280.

(1976 [1776]), *An Inquiry Concerning the Nature and Causes of the Wealth of Nations*. (ed.) R. H. Campbell and A. S. Skinner, Oxford: Clarendon Press.

Spruyt, H. (1994), *Nation States and their Competitors*. Princeton, NJ: Princeton University Press.

Standing, G. (2009), 'Work after Globalisation: A Progressive Agenda', Inaugural Lecture, University of Bath, 28 May.

Starrett, D. A. (1988), *Foundations of Public Economics*. Cambridge: Cambridge University Press.

Stiglitz, J. E. (2002), *Globalization and its Discontents*. London: Allen Lane.

Stiglitz, J. E. and Greenwald, B. (2003), *Towards a New Paradigm in Monetary Economics*. Cambridge: Cambridge University Press.

Stiglitz, J. E., Ocampo, J. A., Spiegel, S., Ffrench-Davis, R. and Nayyar, D. (2006), *Stability with Growth: Macroeconomics, Liberalisation and Development*. Oxford: Oxford University Press.

Stocker K., Waitzkin, H. and Iriart, C. (1999), 'The Exportation of Managed Care to Latin America', *New England Journal of Medicine*, 340(14), pp. 1131–6.

Sutton, J. (2000), *Marshall's Tendencies: What Can Economists Know?* Cambridge, MA: MIT Press.

Tabb, W. K. (1999) *Reconstructing Political Economy: Understanding the Ideas that Have Shaped Our World*. Edinburgh: Ballantine Books.

Tacconi, L. and Bennett, J. (1995), 'Economic Implications of Intergenerational Equity for Biodiversity Conservation', *Ecological Economics*, 12, pp. 209–23.

Tett, G. (2009), *Fool's Gold: How Unrestrained Greed Corrupted a Dream, Shattered Global Markets and Unleashed a Catastrophe*. London: Little, Brown.

Thaler, R. H. and Sunstein, C. R. (2008), *Nudge: Improving Decisions about Health, Wealth and Happiness*. Harmondsworth: Penguin.

Thompson, N. (2002), *Building the Future: Social Work with Children, Young People and Their Families*. Lyme Regis: Russell House.

Tiebout, C. (1956), 'A Pure Theory of Local Expenditures', *Journal of Political Economy*, 42, pp. 416–24.

Tomlinson, R. (1997), 'Health Care in China is Highly Inequitable', *British Medical Journal*, 315(7112), p. 835.

Tronto, J. (1994), *Moral Boundaries; A Political Argument for an Ethic of Care*. London: Routledge,

Twenge, J. M. (2006), *Generation Me*. New York: Simon and Schuster.

United Nations (2001), *The Global Compact: Corporate Leadership in the World Economy*. New York: United Nations.

United Nation's Development Programme (1999), *Human Development Report, 1999*. New York: Oxford University Press.

Van Kersbergen, K. (1995), *Social Capitalism: A Study of Christian Democracy and the Welfare State*. London: Routledge.

Van Parijs, P. (1992), 'Commentary: Citizenship Exploitation, Unequal Exchange and the Breakdown of Popular Sovereignty', in B. Barry and R. E. Goodin (eds.), *Free Movement: Ethical Issues in the Transnational Migration of People and Money*. University Park: Pennsylvania University Press, pp. 155–66.

(1995), *Real Freedom for All: What (if Anything) Can Justify Capitalism?* Oxford: Clarendon Press.

Van Praag, B. and Ferrer-i-Carbonell, A. (2004), *Happiness Quantified: A Satisfaction Calculus Approach*. Oxford: Oxford University Press.

Van Praag, B. and Frijters, P. (1999), 'The Measurement of Welfare and Well-being: The Leyden School Approach', in D. Kahneman et al. (eds.), *Well-being: The Foundations of Hedonic Psychology*, New York: Russell Sage Foundation, pp. 401–33.

Van Staveren, I. (2003), 'Beyond Social Capital in Poverty Research', *Journal of Economic Issues*, 37(2), pp. 415–29.

Vasta, E. (2006), '"The Paper Market", "Borrowing" and "Renting" of Identity Documents', paper presented at 'Paper Tigers or Tiger Papers: The Paper Regime of Modern Societies', Oxford Centre for Migration Studies, Oxford University.

Veenhoven, R. (1989), *Conditions of Happiness*. Dordrecht: Kluwer Academic Press.

(1999), 'Quality of Life in Individualistic Society: A Comparison of Forty-Three Nations in the Early 1990s', *Social Indicators Research*, 48, pp. 157–86.

Wacquant, L. (1998), 'From Welfare State to Prison State: Imprisoning the American Poor', *Le Monde Diplomatique*, July, pp. 1–35.

Walby, S. (1999), 'Introduction', in S. Walby (ed.), *New Agendas for Women*. Basingstoke: Macmillan, pp. 1–16.

Waldrop, M. M. (1994), *Complexity: The Emerging Science at the Edge of Order and Chaos*. Harmondsworth: Penguin.

Weimer, D. I. and Vining, A. R. (1992), *Policy Analysis: Concepts and Practice* (2nd edn). New York: Prentice Hall.

Wicksell, K. (1958 [1896]), 'A New Principle of Just Taxation', in R. A. Musgrave and A. T. Peacock (eds.), *Classics in the Theory of Public Finance*. London: Macmillan, pp. 72–116.

Wilkinson, R. and Pickett, K. (2009), *The Spirit Level: Why More Equal Societies Almost Always Do Better*. London: Allen Lane.

Williams, F. (2002), 'In and Beyond New Labour: Towards a New Political Ethics of Care', *Critical Social Policy*, 21(4), pp. 467–93.

Williamson, O. E. (1975), *Markets and Hierarchies: Analysis and Anti-Trust Implications – A Study in the Economics of Internal Organisation*. New York: Free Press.

Witkin, S. L. (1998), 'Human Rights and Social Work', *Social Work*, 43(3), pp. 197–201.

Wood, G. (2004), 'Informal Security Regimes: The Strength of Relationships', in I. Gough and G. Wood, with A. Barrientos, P. Bevan, P. Davis and G. Room (eds.), *Insecurity and Welfare Regimes in Asia, Africa and Latin America*. Cambridge: Cambridge University Press, pp. 49–87.

World Bank (1997), *Expanding the Measure of Wealth: Indicators of Environmentally Sustainable Development*. Washington, DC: World Bank.

(1998), *The Initiative on Defining, Monitoring, and Measuring Social Capital: Overview and Program Description*. Washington, DC: World Bank (Social Development Fund).

(2001), *World Development Report 2000/2001: Attacking Poverty*. Washington, DC: World Bank.

Wright, E. O. (2004), 'Basic Income, Stakeholder Grants and Class Analysis', *Politics and Society*, 32(1), pp. 79–88.

Xing, L. (2002), 'Shifting the "Burden": Commodification of China's Health Care', *Global Social Policy*, 2(3), pp. 248–52.

Zalenik, A. (1997), 'Managers and Leaders: Are They Different?' *Harvard Business Review*, 55, pp. 67–78.

Index

activism
  among hospital patients 96
  and collective action 14, 122,
    184, 206–9
  environmental 15, 175, 184
  in Obama campaign 1, 67
  post-crash 14
adaptation
  and well-being 83
Afghanistan 123
Africa 38, 120, 134, 137, 148,
    150, 183, 187
  food shortages in 164
  refugees from 140
Akbari, H. 181
Alaska 68
alcohol 9, 169, 193
Al Qa'ida 16, 123
Annan, K.
  and Global Compact 149–50
Argentina 120, 143, 146–7
Aristotle 85
Asia 3, 11, 39, 85, 120, 125, 134,
    162, 178, 182
  banking crises in 127–8
  borrowing from 47, 53, 130,
    203
  kinship in 57
  productivism in 158, 162–3
  South-East 150

associations 11, 168–9, 209
  and well-being 77–8, 110,
    116
Australia 28, 30
  hero from 36
  income redistribution in 30,
    67

Baby P case 94–5, 100–3, 113
Bank of England 12, 23, 65, 69
banks
  bail-out of 30–1, 43, 121, 129,
    131, 200
  and the bubble 5–6, 8, 16,
    42, 79, 90, 119, 140–1, 161,
    186–7, 190, 203
  central 6, 10, 24, 31, 45, 50–1,
    119, 132, 190
  and credit 44–74, 151, 199
  institutions and 128, 149,
    188
  pay in 36
  and social policy 7, 11, 22, 27,
    31, 93, 148, 177–8, 202
Barclay's Bank 47–8
Barry, B. 174
Basic Income (BI) 67, 74, 153,
    173–9, 200, 209
  Global 176–9
Becker, G. S. 52–3, 144

benefits 8, 71
  enforcement of conditions for
    30, 66
  integration with tax system
    74, 173–80, 209
  invalidity 66, 112
  means-tested 66, 196
  payment of 27
  universal 30
Bentham, J. 85
Beveridge, W. 33, 72, 85, 104
Bhutan
  well-being in 85
Blond, P. 209
Bolivia 197
Bosanquet, B. 33
Bowles, S. 113
Bradley, F. H. 33
Brazil 38–9, 67, 85, 125, 137,
    148, 150, 161, 182, 200
  migration from 140
British Broadcasting Corporation
    (BBC) 79
Brown, G. 19, 23–4, 45–6, 63,
    119, 137, 154
Buchanan, J. M. 133
Bush, G. W. 23, 28, 63

Cameron, D. 209
capabilities 83–5
  women's 167
care
  ethic of 159, 165–6
  informal 158–85
  reproductive value of 163–4
Centre for Social Justice 74, 153,
    209
Chávez, H. 38
child protection 34, 93–4,
    100–3

children
  health of 148
  services for 108–9, 201
  well-being of 106–9, 195–6,
    201
Child Trust Funds 68
Chile 38, 143
China 5–6, 15–6, 37, 39, 85, 125,
    128, 137, 143, 146, 148, 150,
    155, 161, 181, 183, 193, 208
  health care in 147
  inequality in 145–7
  sovereign wealth funds in 131,
    178, 197, 199
  unemployment in 197
choice 3, 45, 151, 166, 182, 184,
    188
  architecture 196–7
  by citizens 7, 81
  culture of 87, 155, 203
  political 43
  public 79, 88–90, 105, 114,
    121, 124, 131–7, 203
  and well-being 76–7, 111
Christian Democracy 19–20
cities
  global 140–1
citizenship 4, 54–5, 65–6, 71,
    89, 193–4, 209
  cosmopolitan 150
  of indigenous peoples 197
climate change 2, 126, 154,
    161–4, 180, 182
clubs
  economic 58, 68, 81–2,
    89–90, 121, 133–7, 149
  fishing 170
  sports 168–9
Cole, G. D. H. 33, 72
Coleman, J. S. 144

collective action
  by clubs 170
  and fiscal federalism 134–5
  freedom and 175
  and methodological
    individualism 89, 172
  problems 149
  and rent-seeking 142
  transformative 13–15, 197,
    206–7
  women and 168
common good 9
community 11, 14, 36, 118, 123,
    143, 157–3, 154–73, 176–7,
    182–6, 195, 201, 209
  business 15
  of choice 133
  deprived 33, 58–9, 66, 124,
    09
  of fate 90, 197
  minority ethnic 66
  responsible 71
  and well-being 77, 103, 110–
    15, 117–18
computerization
  in child protection 100–3
  UK projects for 91–2

contract 10, 11–12, 42, 93, 109,
    113, 151, 155, 158, 168, 172,
    184, 201
  firms and 61
  information and incentives in
    50–2, 105, 128
  innovations in 48–9
  in public services 33–4, 78,
    91, 94, 98, 104–5, 111–12,
    201–5
  ritual value of 87
  social 54, 71, 89, 142, 194

  theory of 4, 44, 105, 128, 186,
    188
  and voluntary services 114,
    169
cost-benefit analysis 3, 16, 32–3,
    44, 78, 80, 104, 186,
    189
credit 3–5, 13–14, 24, 43, 44–74,
    89–90, 149, 151–3, 184,
    202–3, 207
  cards 57–8, 127, 191
  global sources of 120
  new forms of 53–70
  and self-realization 116, 184
  supply of 30–1, 49–70, 127,
    130
  unions 58–9, 68
crime 9–11, 16–7, 58–9, 142
Cruddas, J. 28
Cuell, Wes 102
culture
  change in 36–7, 79, 83,
    105–6, 189
  collective 13–14, 36, 77, 80,
    112–3
  commercial 43
  of individualism 11–12, 22,
    80, 87, 109, 117, 155, 169,
    192–5
  of quality and appreciation 62,
    170, 202
  of soundness 47
  traditional 32, 167
  and well-being 79–80, 83,
    103–9, 201
Cyprus 106

Darling, A. 24
debt
  collective 90

government 2, 19, 29–30, 43,
    49, 63–4, 136, 152, 183
private 8, 12–14, 16, 25, 27,
    49, 73, 136, 183, 191
slicing and dicing of 190
sub-prime and 5, 57
Delanty, G. 150
Denmark 56
disabilities 66, 111–13, 120, 177
Douglas, C. H. 72
Douglas, M. 86
drugs 9, 169, 193
dealing 58
Durkheim, E. 86

education 10–11, 32–4, 81, 111,
    121, 137, 160, 167, 174, 198,
    200
computerization in 91–2
finance for colleges 98–100
in Germany 19, 137
inequalities 145–6
and mobility 89–90, 133–4
private 80, 148, 203
trade in 145, 148
and well-being 83–4
employment 18, 20–1, 31, 123,
    131, 158–9, 162, 205, 207
in Germany 20
and income 174–5
manufacturing 26
security of 54
in services 88
environmentalism 15, 26, 37–41,
    122, 136, 155–86, 200
and employment 26, 67, 154
projects 67
equality 3, 13, 20, 85, 160,
    172–3, 180, 182, 209
gender 22, 85

of income 195
of life-chances 120
and well-being 76, 107
European Social Model 28, 157
European Union (EU) 3, 19, 21,
    24, 38–9, 56, 140, 148
exclusion 8–9, 79, 82, 108, 153,
    194
categories of 86
financial 56–8
of non-payers 89
and social value 79, 194
externalities 10, 198

faith 122, 151, 185
family 197
carers 112
customary care in 86, 183
economizing on time in 116
relevance for well-being 11,
    14, 79, 107–8
services for 22
stability of 153
Fearnley-Whittingstall, H. 171
feminism 158, 162, 167–71,
    175
Financial Services Authority
    (FSA) 24, 152
firms
and credit 59–63
and globalization 131–2
as providers 134
theory of 60–1, 142
fiscal federalism 121, 133–7
Fitzpatrick, T. 163–4, 180
food
culture of 171
poverty 198
France 9, 16, 56, 208
banking in 61–2

France (*cont.*)
  migration to 140
  unemployment in 60
Friedman, M. 138
friendship 11, 14, 116

G7 24, 137
G20 24, 36, 137, 152, 189
Gaza Strip 123
Germany
  banking in 61–2, 125
  carbon emissions in 38,
    157
  federalism in 136
  Hegelianism in 33
  industry in 55, 193
  loans from 125
  responses to crash 19, 21,
    125–6, 137
  social model in 19
  unemployment in 60
Gesell, S. 69
Ghana
  well-being in 85
Giddens, A. 146
Gintis, H. 113
globalization 1, 5, 8–9, 11, 18,
    44, 70, 118–25, 140–1, 150,
    174, 198
  and the crash 119
  and welfare regimes 18
Goffman, E. 86
good society
  objective standards for 76,
    80–5
governments, national
  and the crash 119, 129, 131–2,
    191
  and economic management 7,
    127–9

failure of 139, 149
  and migration 177
  role of 7–10, 13, 119–21
  and well-being 75–6
Greece 16, 131, 178, 208
  Ancient 135
Green, T. H. 33

Haringey 93–4, 100–3
health
  choice in 133–4
  computerization in 91–2
  economics of 10–11
  as a factor in well-being 3,
    13, 32–3, 83–4, 105,
    195–6
  inequalities 145–7, 157,
    196
  mental 83, 195
  preventive 81
  private 147–8, 203
  services 22, 35–6, 80, 111, 137,
    160, 174, 178, 198,
    200
  trades in 145
  US system 137
Hicks, A. 32
housing
  affordable 18
  associations 92–3
  finance 5–8, 131, 189
  kinship funding for 58
  price collapse 47
  social 80, 92–3, 111, 133–4,
    178, 203
  as wealth 15
Hungary 131

Iceland 18, 42, 90
  Banks in 93, 178

Idealism 33, 88
income
  inequalities in 157
  redistribution of 18, 39–41,
    44–5, 63–74, 80–1, 119–20,
    136, 141, 150, 173–9
India 6, 15, 39, 85, 125, 128, 140,
    182, 197
  care staff from 22
  education in 148
  massacre in 36
Indonesia 164, 187
inspections 95, 98
  Ofsted 100, 102–3
institutions
  for collective life 14, 26, 52–3,
    168, 175
  design of 29, 72, 105, 117, 141,
    151, 159, 178
  financial 10, 127–8
  global 119, 150, 176
  and individualism 11–12, 43,
    76, 175
  middle-ground 2–3
  national structures of 19–20,
    128
  political 32–3
International Monetary Fund
    (IMF) 8, 12, 38, 70, 119,
    126–8, 138–9, 143, 152, 189,
    207
Iraq 123
Ireland 21, 178
Italy 9, 208
  banking in 61–2
  migration to 140
  public finance in 131

Japan 5, 158, 193, 195
  banking in 61

migration to 140
public debt in 64
saving in 64, 125, 178
service sector in 88
justice
  between generations 179–82
  global 121, 124, 150
  political 84, 174–5
  and rent-seeking 142
  social 8, 14, 17, 67, 72, 80,
    159, 179, 181–2

Kalecki, M. 132
Keynesianism 5, 19, 24, 72, 88,
    126–7, 199
kinship
  and community 77, 151, 183,
    209
  and credit 57, 68
  customary care in 86

Latin America 3, 38, 85, 120,
    162–3, 182
  education in 148
  food shortages in 164
  kinship in 57, 183
  land redistribution in 200
  migration from 140
Latvia 131
Layard, R. 82–3, 85, 107, 193
Learning and Skills Council
    (LSC) 98–100
Lebanon 123
leisure and recreation
  services for 87
Lewes
  local currency in 69
liberal-communitarian model
    71, 150, 158, 186
Libya 208

London
  City of 17, 24, 53, 119, 130,
    137, 140, 152, 159
lone parents 66, 199
loyalty 32–3, 59, 79–80, 105,
    121, 151, 169, 187
  citizens' 65, 197
  ethnic 123
  local 123

Macmillan, H. 72

Maddoff, B. 42, 93
Malaysia 128
Malta 106
managerialism 35, 81, 93–4,
    109–10, 113–15, 201
Marx, K. 88, 174
Meade, J. 72
Merkel, A. 137
Mexico 6, 208
  well-being in 85
Middle East 5–6, 39
  borrowing from 47, 53, 130,
    203
  refugees from 140
  sovereign wealth funds in 131,
    178, 199
Mid-Staffordshire NHS Hospital
    Trust 36, 92, 95–7
migration 56–8, 123, 138–43,
    151, 177–8
  controls on 83
  of refugees 139–40
Millennium Development Goals
    1
Milner, D. 72
mobility 13, 151
  geographical 89, 138–43
  international 9, 138–43

among options 3, 70, 89, 193
  reductions in 83
  social 9, 22
Morales, E. 197
music 117, 159, 168–9, 178,
    184–5, 201–2
Myers, Lord 152

Namibia 67, 200
National Health Service (NHS)
    (UK) 77, 90
  scandals in 92, 95–7
needs 76, 80–5, 174, 192, 201
  of future generations 180
Netherlands 56, 106
New Labour 14, 35, 65, 92–3,
    98, 159, 171, 194–5, 204–6,
    209
New York 16, 140
New Zealand 67
Non-Government Organizations
    (NGOs) 78, 145
  and global governance 150
non-productivism 157–71,
    173–9, 185
Northern Ireland 59
Norway 131
Nussbaum 84–5, 167

Obama, Barack 1–2, 26, 29, 39,
    67, 137, 154, 156, 178, 180,
    184
obesity 9, 193
Oliver, J. 171

Pareto, V. 32–3, 104
Pateman, C. 168, 175
pensions 8, 191, 199, 203
  funds 42, 46–7, 93, 152
  private 66, 71, 199

perfectionism 174–6
Philippines
  care staff from 22
  migration from 140
Pickett, K. 195–6
Pigou, A. C. 32, 104–6
Platonism 84
Poland 38–9
Polanyi, K. 122, 208–9
positional goods 82
Post office (UK) 27
  and credit 68
poverty 3, 8, 22, 28–9, 167,
    198–9
  child 66
  concentrations of 33, 59, 66,
    71
  fuel 18
  global 13, 121, 126, 137–8,
    144–8, 150, 164, 177, 182
  in old age 66, 177
  relief of 30, 136, 209
  resistance and 123
prison 9
productivism 157–70, 174–5,
    179
professionals
  child protection 100–3
  human service 33–5, 43, 98,
    203–7
  managerialism and 94, 101–3,
    203–4
  and private insurance 98
  and well-being 76–7
public finance 63, 122–38, 168,
    203

quangos 98–100
'quantitative easing' 31, 65, 69,
    129

Reagan, R. 14, 22, 156
regulation
  of banks 46–8, 50–1, 54–5,
    119, 128–30, 141
  'external' 46–7, 79–80, 94,
    103–5, 113
  of financial products 66
  'internal' 46, 79, 112–13, 166
  in public services 94
  in simple societies 86
  of society 49–55
  and well-being 79
relationships
  of belonging 78, 103–4,
    107–8, 155, 185
  collective basis for 13
  emotional 78, 103–4, 108, 155
  intimacy in 3, 78, 103–4, 108,
    155
  motivation for 163
  respect in 78, 103–4, 108, 155
  rights in 167
  and well-being 3, 11, 35, 78,
    103–4, 107–8, 116, 155, 186,
    193
rent-seeking 142
retirement
  pensioners 28–9, 191
  savings for 31, 66
rights 84–5, 109, 120, 170, 179,
    201
  human 167, 198, 201
  in individualistic culture 87
  social 198–202
  and sustainability 166–72
risks
  cooperatives and 62
  and globalization 119
  management of by banks
    45–7, 54–5, 57

risk (*cont.*)
  pooling of 49–72, 120, 183
ritual 86
  sacred 84
rivalry 82–3
Roosevelt, F. D. 29–30, 72
Russia 16, 39, 125–7, 137, 143,
    161

Sahara
  solar power project in 41
Sassen, S. 140–1
savings 25, 31, 66, 81, 121, 129,
    153, 161, 178, 203
  rates 64
Scandinavia
  services in 22, 117
  welfare regimes in 20, 29
  well-being of children in
    106
  women in 158
Scotland
  devolution 135
  environmental projects in
    40–1
security
  cameras 9
  military 32
self
  feminism and 167–8
  projects of 116, 184, 192
  -realization 9, 87, 90, 104,
    106, 167–8, 192
  -responsibility 54, 65–6, 71,
    90, 167–8
  sacred 87
  services and 90, 106
Sen, A. 84
services
  cuts in 43

employment in 20–2, 26–7,
    75–6
  financial 21, 54, 203
  global trade in 145–6, 204
  leisure 87
  migrant workers in 140–1
  unemployment in 60
  and well-being 75–90
Sheerman, B. 103
Slovakia 106
Slovenia 106
Smith, A. 24, 32, 87–8, 104
social capital 33, 52, 77–8, 124,
    144–8
  bonding 145
  bridging 145
  and democracy 124
  and well-being 110
social care 22, 32, 81, 111–13,
    137, 160, 174, 198, 200
social insurance 19, 22, 65,
    146–7, 199
  contributions 28, 54
Somalia
  pirates from 16
  poverty in 137
South Africa 67, 150, 200
South Korea 208
Soviet Bloc 76, 127
  migration from 140
Soviet Union 9
  productivism in 160
Spain
  banking in 61–2, 178
  migration to 140
sport 67, 117, 159, 168–9, 184–5,
    201–2
Sri Lanka 120, 148
Steinbrück, P. 19
Stiglitz, J. 4, 51, 128

stigma 3, 30, 33–4, 79, 86, 108
  of claiming benefits 54, 66
sustainability 37–43, 62, 154–86, 201, 209
  and climate change 37–43, 161–4
  and democracy 166–8
  of social relations 88
Sweden 56
Switzerland 135
  well-being in 135

tastes
  differing 45, 76, 188
Tawney, R. H. 33
taxation
  cuts in 24, 27
  increases in 29, 63
  integration with benefits 74, 152–3, 173–80, 209
  rates 20, 89, 134–7, 139
  rationale for 132–3, 199, 203
  revenue from 6, 191
  wartime 64
  on excessive work 83
tax credits 28, 66, 162
  child 29
Tett, G. 46
Thailand 127–8
Thatcher, M. 14, 23, 38, 92, 135
Third Way 2, 13–14, 59, 93, 109, 114, 146
Tiebout, C. 133
time
  allocation of 116
  productivity of 116, 159, 205–6
Titmuss, R. M. 33
Tokyo 140

trade
  in carbon emissions 38
  China–Africa 38
  gains through 45, 182, 208
  imbalances 5–6, 45, 63, 177–8
  by migrants 56–7
  modernization of money 127
  in services 85–6
  world 138–9, 149, 177
trade unions 11, 27, 142, 157, 208
transfers 18, 21, 39–41, 136, 173–9
  in South America 38
  unconditional 43
trust 68, 110–5, 192
  between citizens 77, 117, 195
  and credit 69, 72–3
  and well-being 110–15
Turner, Lord A. 152

Ukraine 126
unemployment 8, 25–6, 60, 66, 69, 152, 154, 187, 199
  in financial services 162
  risks of 48
United States of America (USA) 1, 5–7, 59, 63, 70, 88, 93, 103–4, 110, 115, 119, 125, 137, 148, 156–7, 182, 187, 194–5, 208
  in Africa 38
  crash in 49, 51–2, 186
  employment in 21, 26, 181
  financial exclusion in 56
  income redistribution in 26, 28, 67
  national debt in 64, 199
  Treasury in 6, 64
  unemployment in 56

value
  of capabilities 83–4
  cultural 184–5
  ecological 16, 155, 163–4, 172,
    179–80, 182
  human 122, 163, 182
  of housing stock 47–8, 183
  of individuals 87
  and ritual 86
  sacred 86–7, 155
  social 3, 11, 14, 16, 33–6,
    78–87, 103–4, 106, 108, 112,
    116–17, 155, 172, 179–80
  of social capital 78
Van Parijs, P. 174–7
Vanuatu
  well-being in 85
Venezuela 8, 150
voluntary organizations 74,
    172
  and contracts 114, 169
  investments by 42, 47, 93
  and volunteers 172
  and well-being 77–8

Walby, S. 205
Wales 135
Wall Street 53, 55, 72, 119, 130,
    137, 186
Washington Consensus 4, 126,
    128, 138–9, 143
  Post- 4, 127–8

welfare 3, 83–5
  economics of 32–3, 104–5
  regimes 18, 71
  to work 9, 22, 30, 66, 112,
    153, 162, 199, 209
Wicksell, K. 89, 132
Wilkinson, R. 195–6
wind power 181
women
  and education 148
  and ethic of care 109–10,
    165–6, 185
  political settlements and 175
  rights of 85, 109, 166–7
  as service workers 88, 158
  in welfare regimes 20–2, 162,
    205
World Bank 4, 8, 12, 70–1, 78,
    93, 119, 124, 126, 207
  and poverty 138–9, 143–50
World Trade Organization
    (WTO) 8, 12, 70, 86, 119,
    138–9, 145, 148–9, 204
  and GATS 145, 148, 204
Wright, E. O 174–5

Yorkshire 40
Yugoslavia 9

Zimbabwe
  care staff from 22
  inflation in 31